Samuel Copland, C. M. Smith

The Reign of Terror

Or, the diary of a volunteer of the year of the french republic

Samuel Copland, C. M. Smith

The Reign of Terror
Or, the diary of a volunteer of the year of the french republic

ISBN/EAN: 9783337121662

Printed in Europe, USA, Canada, Australia, Japan

Cover: Foto ©ninafisch / pixelio.de

More available books at **www.hansebooks.com**

"THE REIGN OF TERROR,"

OR THE

DIARY OF A VOLUNTEER

OF THE YEAR 2

OF THE

FRENCH REPUBLIC.

TRANSLATED FROM THE FRENCH

BY

SAMUEL COPLAND.

AND EDITED BY C. M. SMITH, AUTHOR OF THE "WORKING-MAN'S WAY IN THE WORLD;" "CURIOSITIES OF LONDON LIFE, &c."

LONDON: W. & F. G. CASH, 5, BISHOPSGATE,
EDINBURGH: JOHN MENZIES.
DUBLIN: JAMES M'GLASHAN.

CONTENTS.

CHAPTER I.

My Birth and Parentage.—My Republican views,—And those of the Counsellor.—A Compromise.— Going to be married.—" Many a slip 'twixt the cup and the lip."—The Requisition.—Parting from Home.—An awkward squad.—Arrival at Moulins.—Am drilled at Lyons.—Defence of the Clergy.—A forcible ejectment—A Dominican turned soldier.—My friend Anselme.—A suspicious person. —A discovery.—We are false to our principles.—Chevrieres.— Unaccountable mysteries.—A phantom supper.—A night adventure.—More mysteries.—A phantom breakfast.—The baker and the assignats. -The Revolutionary Committee and their Appetites. —Arrival at Vienne.—Wanted a billet.—A complaisant mayor.   1

CHAPTER II.

Arrive at Rousillon.—Free quarters.—Am quartered on a nobleman. —Cavalier reception.—Flunkey valour.—True nobility.—The domestic home of an aristocrat in revolutionary times.—I live in clover.—Confidences of my host.—Arrive at Valence.—The one-eyed tailor and the guillotine.— The registrar of Montmerlian.— His great peril.—Anselme saves him.—His gratitude.—Arrive at Orange.—A prosperous butcher.—The old Royalist.—Military orgies.—Throwing off the mask.—I am made Sergeant and then Adjutant.—Scene in a cabaret.—A double duel.—M. Marcotte of Avignon.—Pistache Carotte.   43

CHAPTER III.

A would-be Don Juan.—A civic fête..—The feast of reason.—A mortal squeeze.—An auto da fe.—Saving a relic.—Character and doings of Pistache.—Constituents of the revolutionary committee.—The house of detention at Avignon.—Pistache out-witted and out-bullied.—Escape of his victim.—Great news.—General hypocrisy. —Departure from Avignon,—A conspirator.—Arrival at Fayence,   79

CHAPTER IV.

A chase.—Arrive at Grasse.—Verdier the perfumer.—An unpleasant surprise.—A marriage feast.—M. Edmond.—His history.—Gerard. —A committee extraordinary.—Charity of demagogues.—A rival in trade.—Agatha Lautier.—Her history, trial, condemnation, and execution.—The advocate of Marseilles.—Horrible spectacle at the scaffold.

CHAPTER V.

Edmond and Gerard again.—Their hiding place.—Gerard's narrative. —The chateau of Grand-boeuf.—Its attack and gallant defence.— A revolutionary peasantry.—The chateau abandoned and burnt.— Escape and revenge of Gerard.—He enlists.—Anselme meditates a change of party.—The camp at Saorgio.—We are reviewed by the general.—I smell powder for the first time.—Queer feelings. —I come off conqueror.—Life in the camp.—A deserter.—His dinner and death.—A secret expedition.—Surprise and slaughter of the Piedmontese.—Anselme wounded.—I leave the camp on furlough.—Arrive at Messins.—Return to Grasse.—Transformation of Verdier.—Arrive at Toulon.—Massacre of a workman.— My own narrow escape. 145

CHAPTER VI.

I enter Marseilles.—The theatre in revolution.—My cousin Jouveau. —His character and present occupation.—The sweets of political life.—The illustrious N———.—The laceman. Levite.—I dine with the Representative.—Revolutionary viands.—The gilder.— Jouveau's petitioners.—He refuses to be merciful, and I leave him. —Feast of reason at Aix.—Adventure at St. Cuna.—I am taken for a great unknown.—A practical philosopher in an aristocrat.— I revisit Avignon.—Revolutions.—A company of honourable mendicants.—I visit Nismes.—Fête to the Supreme Being. 178

CHAPTER VII.

The Ex-Criminal Judge and his family.—His high principle.—His nephew Maurice.—"Open in the name of the Law."—Arrest of N———.—His imprisonment at Sauve.—Scene in the house of Detention.—A protesting prisoner.—A quarrel for horses.—Jouveau again.—I bargain with him for the release of the Ex-Criminal Judge.—I arrive at Saint Hypollite.—A sanguinary barber.—I wander among the mountains of Cevennes.—A fortunate encounter.—Supper, bed, and breakfast for nothing.—Citizen Rose, and the convent of Saint Benoit.—Arrival at Mende.—My father's friend.—Citizen Larouvrette.—Charrier.—A royalist victory and subsequent defeat.—Fate of Charrier.—A proposed excursion. 228

CHAPTER VIII.

The mountain solitudes.—A houseless republic.—Everything al-fresco—The wounded Count.—Brother Peter and the Spy.—Confession of the assassin.—The Count's story.—Laura and the ex-cartwright.—I leave the encampment.—Saint Flour.—Durand and his wife.—Poison.—Marital tenderness.—The Count's fearful revenge.—I am arrested and marched off to prison.—An awkward recontre.—A mean vengeance.—Locked up in my cell. 268

CHAPTER IX.

Bound for Paris.—Travelling accommodations, and travelling companions.—The laughing philosopher, and the weeping willow.—The Anglo-Spaniard.—Brutality of our conductors.—Arrival at Paris.—Prison accommodations at a premium.—The conciergery.—The ruffian Pampin.—His practical sympathy.—The political section.—Mons. Riouffe.—Madame D——.—Citizen Bertrand.—Camille Desmoulins, Danton. Madame Roland.—I am sent to the Abbaye.—Infernal treatment.—I attack the turnkey.—Tête à tête with the governor.—A dinner and a bottle.—Am removed to the Evêche.—Examined by the Judge.—Am sent to St. Lazare.—Anselme again.—Fall of Robespierre.—Release, and parting with Anselme.—Nantes, Tours, and the republican camp in La Vendee.—Captain Cherche-à-manger.—A terrible surprise.—Battle, and murder, and sudden death.—Again Defeated by Charrier.—I am knocked on the head. 308

CHAPTER X.

I escape the slaughter, and fall in with Cherche-à-manger.—We are captured by the Vendeans.—Death of Cherche-à-manger.—I am saved by Anselme.—Lucile.—A secret mission.—We are surprised by the Chouans; their matchless atrocities.—Bois Hardy and his troop.—Punishment of the false Chouans.—The villain Kernoc.—His mysterious escape.—We cross Bretagne.—I suspect Lucile.—Massacre of the inhabitants of Saint Laurent des Mortiers.—Coquereau.—The wood of La Henreuserie.—Francoeur.—A proof of Lucile's treason.—Midnight attack.—The chateau of Jupellière. —Arrival of M. Jacques.—We defeat the republicans.—Anselme and I overlooked.—My friend wounded by Kernoc.—M. Jacques' languishing death in a cave.—Anselme avenges himself on Kernoc. —Death of my friend.—Conclusion. 356

PREFACE.

The following volume gives a faithful illustration of the working of the French Convention during the reign of terror, and fully bears out the description given by the writers of that period, of the character of the men who composed that formidable and extraordinary body. The utility of the narrative consists in the truthfulness of its vivid details, in its importance as a beacon to warn the present and future generations of the danger of entrusting irresponsible power, whether to the hands of an individual, or of a public constituent assembly; and in proving that the *name* of Liberty may rest on the lips of a whole people, without their possessing either the enjoyment of its blessings, or even a knowledge of what it is.

A gentleman once congratulated Edmund Burke on the apparent prospect of the winding up of the Revolution. "The termination of the Revolution, to be sure! exclaimed the orator, "The Revolution over, why sir, *it is not begun.* As yet you have heard only the first music, you'll see the actors presently, but neither you nor I shall see the end of the drama."

The outburst of 1789 was the opening of the 'drama,' of which all Europe is eventually destined to become the theatre. The title of the piece was 'LIBERTY,' and the plot was admirably laid; the prologue pronounced in the Champ de Mai, was a visionary programme of what ought to and might have been, if the chief performer had not afterwards broken down. In the first exhibition of national enthusiasm, the actors were all purity and patriotism. Was the scene which followed, a tragical representation, or the second act of the drama? Whatever it was, when the king proved false, or pusillanimous, *or both*, the national convention "rose in the ascendant," took the direction, and the real tragedy began.

The weakness of Louis XVI, transferred the *semblance* of power which he previously held, to the Convention, which possessed the *reality*, and he lost both his throne and his life. What followed finds no parallel in history, and cannot be accounted for on any of those principles upon which the power of executive administration is founded. "No assembly says the Annual Register, for the year 1793, ever displayed a more astonishing mixture of shining qualities and of atrocious vices; ambitious, cruel, unprincipled, are epithets inadequate to convey an apposite idea of their enormities. They were true to their character from the very beginning; overturning without scruple or remorse, whatever stood in their way, and compassing their ruin without ever adverting to the rectitude or moral impropriety, or turpitude of the means employed; the only qualifications on which they seemed to set a substantial value, were courage and capacity, boldness and expedition. These divested of all virtuous or sentimental feelings, appear to have been the real attributes of those extraordinary, but not respectable names, that continued for three years, to keep all Europe in uncertain alarms, that made kings tremble on their thrones, that progressively overcame all their enemies, that changed the face of all Christendom in some of the most essential respects, that introduced systems which if, through the hand of power they may be repressed, will never be eradicated, *that found in short, an epoch from which may be dated events that are only beginning to unfold themselves, and the ultimate issue of which it is not within the compass of the profoundest politics to ascertain, but which will probably, if not certainly, be felt in the remotest ages to come.*"

NOTES

FROM THE

DIARY OF A VOLUNTEER.

CHAPTER I.

My Birth and Parentage. — My Republican Views—And those of the Counsellor.—A Compromise.—Going to be Married—"Many a slip 'twixt the cup and the lip."—The Requisition.—Parting from Home— An awkward Squad.—Arrival at Moulins.—Am drilled at Lyons.— Defence of the Clergy.—A forcible ejectment.—A Dominican turned Soldier.—My friend Anselme.—A Suspicious Person.—A Discovery.— We are false to our principles.—Chevrieres.—Unaccountable Mysteries.—A Phantom Supper.—A Night Adventure.—More Mysteries.— A Phantom Breakfast.—The Baker and the Assignats.—The Revolutionary Committee and their Appetites.—Arrival at Vienne.—Wanted a Billet.—A complaisant Mayor.

A soldier in camp, and not employed either in sleeping, eating, drinking, or killing, is at a loss to know how to pass away his time.

It occurred to me one day, that, whilst we have the history of all the generals, none have yet dreamt of writing that of a private soldier. I resolved to write my own.

B

I write with my sabre at my side, my knapsack serves me for a desk, and my pen is frightfully ill-made; I therefore claim some indulgence.

Whatever may be the lot reserved in future for these pages (scribbled between two halts) with which, (foolishly perhaps) I fill my knapsack, they will at least, have the merit of possessing that impress of actuality, which a work, written with a mind at rest, and more scrupulously studied, would probably want.

I was born at Lusignan, the 24th August, 1768. My father possessed a competent fortune, and exercised the profession of a Notary, and I was destined to follow the same profession.

When the storm of 89 broke out, my father, far from sharing the joy and the hopes that the prospect of a new political horison awoke in me, was, unhappily, suspected, and retired into the country.

Receiving in his retreat, only a very limited number of intimate friends, he soon passed for an aristocrat. God knows, but for my uncle the patriot, what would have been the consequences to him of this reputation This uncle had been, up to 89, an incumbrance to the family; incapable of pursuing the useful routine of business, of a restless and versatile disposition, he found out that society wanted *great reforms;* consequently he entered with enthusiasm into the revolutionary movement. In other respects, he was an excellent character, and in spite of a rather brusque manner—an essential accessory to his actual profession—he was not deficient in good nature or courtesy.

Amongst the very limited number of friends that my father received, there was an old *procureur* of the king; a great enemy of the republic, and the father of a charming and accomplished young lady.

Every day the *procureur* and myself had almost violent

discussions on political subjects. Although my most earnest desire was to become his son-in-law, I could not bring myself to make the least concession to him. The love of liberty obtained the ascendancy in my heart, even over the passion which the virtues and beauty of his daughter had inspired.

This state of things rendered me extremely unhappy, and I was at a loss to know how to act, so as to make my love square with my duty; when one morning, I received a visit from my intended father-in-law.

"My friend" said he, noticing my surprise, "I see that you did not expect me; but an explanation between us is become necessary. Do not interrupt me, I am about to speak to you as well in my own name as in that of your father."

"For a long time your parents and friends have remarked with pain, that you have entered upon a fatal course; I mean the revolutionary movement, which is driving France to ruin. But yesterday, you gave proof of it, by an enthusiastic address delivered at the club. Trust my old experience of men and things, when I say you are at this moment playing the part of a dupe."

"Sir" cried I, interrupting the old counsellor, this is, perhaps the hundredth time that we have debated this same subject and have never yet been able to agree upon it. Would it not be better to let this irritating conversation drop? You will never be able to alter my convictions, and I have no pretensions to change yours."

"The warmth which you display at my words, proves to me that you are not quite so sure of your own views, as you would persuade yourself. Are you then so much afraid of the justness of my observations that you dread to hear me? In that case, nothing remains for me but to withdraw."

"Speak Sir" cried I, "in no respect do I fear to hear you; in proof of which, I am ready to listen with the greatest attention."

"I thank you for this permission, and shall avail myself of it. In order to avoid all personality, I shall take the general question. A thousand persons, my dear Alexis, ascribe the revolution to as many different causes; as for myself, I see only one; it has taken place, because it *was* to take place. If the nobility had not shown themselves so frivolous and faint-hearted, the third estate so enterprising and encroaching, and the king so weak and indecisive, it is probable that the crisis that we yield to at this moment, would not have been accompanied by that hideous violence which has so justly alarmed the people of property; but the great social change would still have advanced, because it was necessary. From the day that royalty, with the view of augmenting its power, destroyed feudality, we may date the commencement of the revolution. Now, I tell you, that this new era, which you hail with joy, as being the aurora of liberty, will retard, perhaps for a century, by its immoralities and excesses, those salutary reforms which your youthful imagination dreams of, as immediately at hand. We are, in France, too much indoctrinated with the hierarchical principle, *ever to become true republicans.* There will be a changing or displacement of the aristocracy, that's all. To serve the ambitious therefore, who govern us to day, is, in my eyes, more than a blunder; it is a crime. As to associating in their monstrous frenzies, or taking part in their excess, I will not do you the injustice to believe you capable of it."

"But Sir" cried I, interrupting the counsellor, "I don't see that it follows, because a band of robbers have succeeded in prostrating Paris under the yoke of terror, that all France will be brought into bondage. Thank God! the provinces have not yet come into the arena; we have federalism."

"Here I stop you, for it is just this federalism that you preach—it stuns me to pronounce the word—to which you owe my visit of this morning. I acknowledge, with you, that this federalism is greatly in fashion just now; only, like all fashionable things, it will not last long. In the meantime, the departments arm themselves, revolt, make a great noise, and our little city, not wishing to be behind, is raising a company of volunteers."

"It is true, Sir; you may add that I have enrolled myself among them."

"I know this only too well; but allow me to address you, and I beseech you to answer me with frankness, one single question. Do you not seek in danger, a distraction from your unhappy love for my daughter. If I give you her hand, would you still think of setting out"?

"No Sir" replied I, with eagerness; if such a happiness awaited me, I would not set out."

"Your frankness gives me pleasure," replied he, taking my hand with a paternal air. "This happiness which seems to you impossible, or which you regard at least, as if far from you, is within your reach, and you may easily attain it. No transports," continued he, seeing the emotion caused by these words—"let me first finish what I have to say to you."

"I hear you Sir, but for goodness sake speak quickly."

"I am going to offer you the means of obtaining the hand of my daughter. Wait before you thank me, until you know my conditions."

"Whatever they may be Sir, provided you do not exact the sacrifice of my opinions, I subscribe to them before-hand."

"And it peremptorily involves that sacrifice."

"I shall refuse Sir" replied I, with firmness.

"Allow me; if I ask of you only a feigned abandonment of your opinions, will that be as painful to you?"

"Enough Sir" cried I, interrupting him. "I feel a deep attachment for your daughter, but it shall never lead me to dishonour. I cannot abjure my opinions."

" Then you refuse me "?

"Yes Sir, in the name of my regard for your daughter, I refuse to become a coward, and a hypocrite."

At this reply, which I supposed would raise an impassable barrier between the counsellor and myself, the former, to my great astonishment, smiled, and held out his hand.

"My dear Alexis" said he, in a grave tone, "your answer has decided your lot. I have never resolved that my son-in-law, should profess such-and-such opinions, but only, that he should be an honourable man. Forgive the snare that I have laid for you; my daughter is yours."

It is useless to describe, first my stupefaction, and then my transports. The reader will have no difficulty in imagining them.

My father and his friend agreed that my marriage should take place in three months, but I urged that the ceremony should take place without delay; my father, however, was inflexible.

Alas! three days after, the sound of the drum threw all our little city into a tumult, and the law passed by the convention, was officially published, which ordered that all unmarried young men between the ages of 18 and 25 years should hold themselves in readiness to march at the first requisition.

The next day, I received the order to join the meeting of my comrades, to nominate our officers, and form ourselves into companies. Judge of my despair! I immediately ran to the house of my future father-in-law.

"My dear Alexis" said he to me, "your father and I have done very wrong in opposing your wishes. Now that the mischief is irreparable, nothing remains for us but to bear it with courage."

"Well" cried I, "then I will serve as a volunteer, and hope for a speedy end to the war."

"Very well nephew" said my uncle the patriot, who chanced to be present, "I like to see in you, these republican sentiments. As to the rest leave it to me. I will find out a way, if the military life does not agree with your disposition, to free you from the service a few months hence. In the meantime I will send you with letters of recommendation to the most eminent patriots of the cities in which you will be garrisoned. I only fear one thing, that your new way of life will appear so desirable to you, that you will not be able to decide upon returning to us."

My setting out being resolved on, my excellent parents had nothing to do but to concert measures to render my route less disagreeable to me.

A week after, at four o'clock in the morning, everybody in the house was on foot, that day being fixed for the departure of the volunteers.

At eight o'clock, when the drums began to beat, my mother and sisters broke out into lamentations. My father, wishing to soften the violence of their grief, proposed that they should accompany me to the square, where I was to unite myself to my companions, I will not say in glory, but in misfortune. He hoped that the presence of the crowd would induce them to make a strong effort to conceal their sorrow.

It was a sad spectacle that awaited us upon the square. On all sides we saw nothing but tears, heard nothing but sobs, from mothers, daughters, desolate relatives. Never have I assisted at a similar scene of despair.

At last the signal was given for our departure. For the last time, I embraced my family, and my betrothed, and then entered the ranks. The blue column put itself in motion, and rapidly traversed the city. Soon after, we disappeared upon the grand route, under a cloud of dust.

I was for many days so absorbed in grief, that I was completely insensible to the objects presented to my view; I followed my comrades mechanically, without any consciousness either of the distance, or the places through which we passed; and it would greatly puzzle me to be obliged to tell what cities we entered, in pursuing the route to Nevers.

By degrees, however, for sorrow is transient, I recovered from the dejection in which I was plunged, and began to take an interest in the novel life which I was called to lead.

The first circumstance that awoke my attention, was a violent quarrel, which I witnessed, between two of my comrades. The origin of this scuffle, for the two combatants exchanged blows with unparallelled vigour, was a foolish dispute about some chesnuts.

"Our comrades would have done well to save us this scandal" said I, to a young volunteer, a spectator, like myself of the fray. If we wear the uniform, we should recollect that we have a sword at our sides, and not fight like a couple of street porters."

"But comrade" replied the volunteer, "you must see that a duel is impossible between these two friends."

"Why how is that?"

"Just because the military hierarchy is opposed to it. A drummer has no right to cross swords with a lieutenant."

"What! is it then our drummer and lieutenant who make all this row."

"Just so; and the drummer began it."

"This is strange discipline! after all, I dont well see how an exchange of sabre-passes can be more injurious to discipline than one of fisty-cuffs."

"There you are right; but the two champions have never handled arms in their lives, whilst they are accustomed to boxing; that is some little excuse for them."

At the termination of this scandalous row, which was wound up by glasses of brandy drunk by the combatants; I learned something of the officers who commanded us, and the following is the account I obtained. Our captain, whose age (over forty) exempted him from the conscription, was an advocate who never had a brief. Despairing of the future, and desirous of making up for the past, he entered amongst the volunteers, and spoke so fluently on the day of election, that they were compelled to make him a captain, in order to silence him.

The profession of our lieutenant, was a joiner. Residing near the barracks, he managed to retain, with the proper intonation, the words of command of certain manœuvres He consequently offered himself as a complete tactician; was believed on his own word, and promoted unanimously to the rank of lieutenant.

As to our sub-lieutenant, he was a young simpleton, 18 years old, who had just quitted the paternal roof. The grotesque manner in which he wore his spectacles, greatly amused the volunteers, who made themselves merry during the march at the expense of his excessive simplicity. He owed his epaulet to his father's character, who, although the revolution had deprived him of his rank, as a magistrate, was beloved and esteemed.

You may conceive, with such officers, what must be the discipline of our detachment. In general, when we passed through the towns, the peasants hastened—and I acknowledge that they were right—to shut their doors.

At Moulins, we entertained the inhabitants with a remarkable spectacle, for we turned out to do the exercise, which proved a pell-mell impossible to describe; the ridiculous bordering upon the sublime.

"Captain" said I, the evening of the same day, to our commander-in-chief, "I am afraid that when we find ourselves in front of the enemy, we shall cut a sorry figure."

"Citizen" replied he with dignity, "be cautious! your proposition is seditious; know that democrats can never be conquered."

The day after our deplorable warlike essay, there fortunately arrived in the city a representative of the people, followed by a battalion from Le Cote d'Or. This functionary, charged with the organization of the troops, embodied us, without entering into any explanation, with the men of his battalion.

Our captain, furious at the loss of his epaulet, took leave of us in an abrupt and disagreeable address, and returned home.

As to myself, thanks to the privilege of youth, of forgetting the past, and enjoying the present, I felt quite proud of being incorporated amongst the grenadiers of a regular corps, and began to think that the military life was not quite so bad a thing as I had imagined. I displayed my good-will and zeal with so much frankness, that it was noticed by my comrades; and a few days after they nominated me a corporal. I had then under my orders, my two former officers, the lieutenant and sub-lieutenant, the joiner-tactician, and the judge's son.

It was in this manner that, by a decree of two lines, twenty thousand officers, and more than a hundred thousand sub-officers, became common soldiers. Such an operation, however necessary, could only be performed in an army of young militiamen, in the year 2 of the republic, and by the committee of public safety.

On arriving at Lyons, I was billetted at the house of a tobacco and stamped paper merchant, who received me so well that I renounced my first resolution of going to an hotel.

I employed the week that I remained at Lyons, in taking private lessons in exercise, from an old soldier. These lessons taught me to carry my musket, and relieved me from the awkwardness of a conscript. But it was not without satisfaction that I left the second city of France; for Lyons then presented the most melancholy aspect that one can possibly imagine. On all sides we saw nothing but ruins and revelry, formidable moustachios, placards, and muskets; a deathlike silence, interrupted only by the sound of the drum, hovered over the unhappy city.

The first halt that we made after leaving Lyons, was, at a village named Saint-Priest. Overcome by the heat, I hastened, as soon as we had broken rank, to enter a *Cabaret*. Many of my comrades had already seated themselves at table, and were holding an animated discussion.

"Yes citizens, I repeat that all the misfortunes of France have been produced by the immorality of her clergy" cried a grenadier in a furious tone. "The republic has committed a grand error in permitting the forsworn scullcaps to remain in France. We ought to have cut their throats without pity."

"Hold! you are going too far, citizen" said an old soldier, sipping his wine.

"Too far do you say comrade," rejoined the grenadier with a furious look. "Well, for my part, I do not think it is far enough yet. We should burn them with a slow fire."

"Positively citizen, I think you are enraged against the churchmen."

"That's the word! Scullcaps, Vergers, and Sacristans, are all rabble and thieves! but am I to understand comrade, that you dare to take their part?"

"Why not"? answered the soldier with a perfect indifference; "there are honest men in all classes of society."

"Honest Priests!"

"Certainly! I have even known many who were very virtuous."

"Will you hold your tongue, miserable stipendary!" cried

the grenadier in a menacing tone. "If you add another word I will plunge my sabre into your throat."

"I will not hold my tongue, because it amuses me to contradict a simpleton; and I care nothing for your rusty sabre" replied the defender of the clergy, with the same *sang-froid* that he had hitherto displayed.

"Then rascal, here's at you" cried the grenadier, who, drawing his sabre, sprung towards his opponent.

Seeing that nobody appeared disposed to interrupt this assassin, I went to throw myself between the two adversaries, when the soldier, first avoiding adroitly by a leap on one side, the blow which threatened him, threw himself afterwards with such impetuosity upon the grenadier, that before the latter had time to use his sabre, he had seized him in his arms.

"Holloa! citizens, stand away from the door, if you please, said he, in a voice which displayed no emotion. "Here's a comrade whose fury chokes him, he wants a little fresh air."

Immediately, and with a super-human strength, which I should never have believed was possessed by any human being, the soldier flung the grenadier out of the Cabaret to a distance of several paces.

"Now, which is settled?" said he, returning to his place which he occupied at the table. "Comrades," he continued, "pray do not take offence at what I have done. Forgive me there, for having for a moment departed from my habitual mildness of character. But I am not fond of Hectors; and to say the truth, the conduct of that grenadier deserved a slight lesson."

These explanations were received with great favour by the company; not a voice was raised in favour of the vanquished.

"Citizen" said the Hercules to me, pushing his glass towards me, "I noticed the movement that you made to come to my assistance; pray accept the expression of my thanks."

"You certainly had no want of my assistance," answered I smiling, but since you recur to this event, may I ask you why you have undertaken what, in fact, has given me great pleasure—the defence of the clergy?"

He looked at me for a moment, and then said, lowering his voice, "I have defended the clergy from a remnant of habit. You see in me, *an old Dominican!* Considering the transformations which are now occurring," he added, "you need not be surprised to see an old monk encumbered with a musket and cartridge box; for we are engaged every day in such strange exhibitions, that extravagant and unforeseen things are the only ones which we ought now to expect. In other respects, my history has nothing in it very extraordinary."

"Nevertheless, I confess I shall be delighted if you will relate it to me."

"Willingly,—a few words will suffice. In 1790, the convent of the Dominicans at Clermont Ferrant, the capital of the province of Auvergne, in which I was chief brother, wished to revive the ancient privilege of begging, with which that order had formerly been invested, and I was appointed to go into the country on that mission. No one had a doubt respecting the success of my circuit, and each of the brothers rejoiced beforehand, in the small profits it might procure us; profits so much the more agreeable, that we had to render no account of these to the district. But alas! We did not take into account the perfidy of our neighbours the Capuchins; who having been made acquainted with the design of our fraternity, hastened to take the field before us, with their mendicants. These wretches did not confine their knavery to this movement. They ordered their emissaries industriously to spread a report amongst the peasantry in the country, that Saint Dominic having become too rich, had fallen into disgrace in heaven, and had completely lost his influence as a mediator.

The result of this manœuvre was just what might be expected, that is to say, my wallet remained desperately empty. The devil, at this juncture, brought me face to face with one of these mendicant capuchins. I must do myself the justice to say, that I shewed extreme courtesy towards my rival, but the poor wretch, intoxicated by his success, could not preserve a decent behaviour towards me; he began first to joke me about the discredit of Saint Dominic, pretended to pity me afterwards, for the fatigue of carrying my money bags, and at last wound up by falling into the greatest coarseness. What more shall I tell you? the natural consequences followed; with one blow of my fist, I felled my rival at my feet. I am to this day ignorant whether I had the misfortune to kill him out of hand. However this may be, I took flight and regained my convent, where my brethren received me with transport and assured me that my conduct did me great honour. Unfortunately, justice did not entertain the same opinion, and one night whilst I slept the sleep of the just, the officers of the marshalsea surrounded our convent. I escaped by an outlet known only to myself, and to avoid detection, enlisted as a private soldier. This, citizen, is my history."

This recital diverted me, and gave me the idea of making a comrade of the ex-dominican, who, in other respects, seemed to me a good fellow enough.

"Faith!" said I, "now that we know one another, if you like we will become friends. The isolation in which I find myself, lies heavy upon me, and I shall not be sorry to have a companion."

"With pleasure, citizen," answered he, offering me his hand; "let it be so! my name is Anselme. Between ourselves now, it is for life or death."

"Are you contented with your fate Anselme?" asked I.

"Faith, I dont complain. I like a life of excitement an

adventure, and reasonable privations do not frighten me."

"Now, are you a patriot?"

"I a patriot!" cried Anselme with an indignant air, "Never! I am a thorough-going republican."

"But is not that the same thing?"

"By the Lord—no. The patriot so-called, is commonly either a poltroon or a speculator. Either a man whose whole object is the design of appropriating to himself the property of other people, or one, who afraid of losing his head, hastens to proclaim himself a patriot, to escape the guillotine. He too, who wishes to revenge himself on an enemy, or to get rid of a rival, the proud covetous of honour, the imbecile who follows the stream, all are patriots, and yet there is not a republican amongst them."

It was decided between Anselme and me, that we would request the commandant of our battalion to put us both in the same company, and that as far as could be done, we should be billeted in such a manner as to be as much as possible together. While we were talking, the drums beat the recall, and obliged us to abandon the table, and we proceeded into the High-street of Saint Priest. It was a communication that our commander had to make to us. It related to the dispatch of a detachment into the mountains of Forez, chiefly in the village of Chevrières, with orders to arrest those who had not submitted to the conscription law. The commander asked for fifty men to volunteer for this patriotic mission, with the promise of having their names inscribed in the bulletin.

Anselme was the first to present himself, and I immediately followed his example.

"What's the reason comrade" said I to him, when, half-an-hour later our little detachment was completed, "that you wished to make a part of this expeditionary column? If I am not mistaken, our mission has nothing very agreeable in it.

To persecute, pursue, and arrest poor wretches who prefer tilling the ground and supporting their families, to going out to fight, without knowing why or wherefore, at the frontier, is a pastime which affords me very little pleasure."

"I offered myself," answered Anselme, "first because I prefer forming part of a small detachment to following a column."

"For what reason?"

"Because the columns starve the country through which they pass, and the troops half die of hunger; whilst those in a small detachment are fed, made much of, and lodged by the peasants, who, for good reasons, endeavour to insinuate themselves into the good graces of the soldiers."

"I understand. Your zeal is entirely a matter of eating and drinking."

"And of humanity also; for I am happy when I can render a service to my species. Now, in the mission with which we are charged, it is twenty to one that I shall find an opportunity of being useful to some poor devil."

We returned to the Cabaret, and were again seated at table, and conversing about our approaching expedition, when we noticed an individual who wore the costume of a mountaineer, and who, his head supported with his hands upon the table, seemed in a deep sleep. He appeared to awake suddenly, and addressing himself to us in a most decided tone;

"Are you not speaking of Forcz, citizen soldiers?" said he.

"Yes, we did speak of it" replied I, much surprised at this question; " but what does it signify to you?"

"Oh nothing citizen soldier, only as I am from the country, I thought you might not be sorry to obtain some information. That is all."

"It appears friend that you slept very lightly!" said Anselme, looking steadily at the mountaineer.

" I was not asleep citizen soldier. I was thinking just then, of a law-suit which torments me, and on account of which, I am returning to Lyons," answered the peasant."

" And what is the information you have to impart to us ?"

" Nay citizens, it is for you to question me. Do you interrogate me, and I will do my best to satisfy you. If I am deficient in perspicacity, I am at least blunt and free."

"Perspicacity, bluntness," repeated Anselme slowly, glancing a stealthy look at me, by way of warning. " These expressions, friend, do not smell of the mountains."

" I do not understand you," said the peasant, smiling with a stupid look.

At this reply, I examined the stranger attentively. From the affected assurance of his countenance, his feigned simplicity, his awkward and nervous gestures, I was convinced that he was under a disguise, and playing a part.

I then rapidly recalled the freedom we had used in conversation, and I felt that if that man was a government spy, the affair might become a very serious one for us ; and I resolved at once to clear up my suspicions.

" What is your profession friend ?" I demanded.

" I am a labourer," he replied.

" Oh, will you tell me what work you do ; for you have the appearance of a good liver, and I suspect you are more frequently at a well-served table than at the plough-tail."

" You deceive yourself, citizen, I am but a poor labouring lad, who sells the sweat of his body for a vile stipend."

" Truly! well then, frankly, by the smoothness and whiteness of your hands, one would not doubt that you are a ploughman," answered I, looking him steadily in the face. Then, turning to Anselme, I continued, " it has struck four o'clock, and I hear our comrades, who have reached the rendezvous; I dont know, but I have an idea we are to have some fun ; let's go and receive them."

c 3

Anselm understood me, and taking his musket, took his stand before the door. Rising immediately from the bench on which I was seated, I placed myself before the window of the Cabaret, which looked directly upon the street. That door and window were the only outlets from the room.

"Since you will no longer converse, I wish you good evening citizens" said the stranger, directing his steps towards the door.

"Sorry to detain you my amiable guest!" cried Anselme, turning towards him rapidly; "but your conversation is so agreeable that I wish my comrades also to enjoy it. Ah! pray remain quiet, and put down those pistols, the stocks of which I see lying across the flaps of your pockets; otherwise! you know the old proverb—it is better to kill than to be killed."

"Fear nothing sir," said the peasant, "I shall not resist; I have managed my part awkwardly, and have lost you see; raise your musket, I am an honest man, who have never contested a gambling debt. My head is at your service."

There was an accent of resignation and dignity, so perfectly natural in the manner with which the stranger pronounced these words, that in spite of my suspicions, I felt moved.

"Citizen," answered I, "we are soldiers and not informers. Our business is to fight the enemies of the republic on the frontier, to die in defending it, but never to furnish victims for the executioners. If we have used the appearance of compulsion in your case, it is because we have taken you for a spy. The fear which you displayed, on supposing that we were going to give you up, leaves us no longer any suspicion in this respect, and we will not detain you any further; you are at liberty to retire."

The stranger listened in silence; and soon tears trickled from his eyes. "Ah! gentlemen" cried he at last, fervently grasping the hand of each of us, "if all republicans acted as you have done, I should not now be disguised in a peasant's dress, and compelled to wander in the mountains. You would reckon one man more in your ranks, and one who could cheerfully present his breast to the balls of the foreigner! but alas! thanks, gentlemen, thanks! may I one day have it in my power to reward your generosity, and who knows? you are going into the mountains of Forez; the hour is perhaps not so distant, when I shall be permitted to pay this debt of gratitude! farewell."

After the departure of the pretended peasant, Anselme and I, for a moment remained silent. At last my comrade broke into a fit of laughter.

" What is the cause of your gaiety ?" asked I.

" I laugh" replied he, to think of the caprices which human destinies often present. You and I have scarcely known each other a couple of hours, and behold! we are now bound to each other by a fast friendship, and deserve the guillotine together. The fact is, it is a thousand to one that we have saved an aristocrat. Do you repent of what you have done?"

" Far from it; I am ready, on the contrary, to do so again. Only I dont think it would be very prudent to relate this adventure to the first comer."

" Oh, as to me fear nothing. People who have belonged to the church know how to keep a secret."

The day after this conversation, our detachment marched at dawn. Although the distance we had to travel, was not very great, the roads were so abominably bad, that we were three whole days in reaching the village of Chevrières, the central point of our operations. It stood in a wild, rugged, and picturesque situation, at the base of immense rocks of fantastic and whimsical forms, far from all other dwellings, and embosomed in a green mantle of immense forests.

About a league before arriving at Chevrières, we met an old

man, who, with a sickle on his shoulder, was going to his work. Our captain called him. "Show us," said he, "for thanks to all these cursed by-ways, scarcely traceable, and crossing each other in all directions, we dont know which way to turn,— show us the best road?"

"Yes citizen," replied the old man, with a strong mountain accent, and disposing himself to pursue his way; but our commander stopped him and continued his queries.

"You are from Chevrières, are you not? Well I give you to understand that your village is very badly reported in the papers of the republic. They say that it serves for a refuge for all the deserters from the requisition; that it is a true nest of conspirators against the republic; come, answer me frankly, and dont attempt to impose upon me, or it may cost you dear. Are these charges well-founded?"

"No, they are villainous lies, my good officer," cried the old man, in a patois difficult to understand; "all the young men of Chevrieres are set out for the army, and are, at this moment shedding their blood for the defence of the republic. The young girls are in great trouble, and the old men, like myself, are obliged, for want of the vigorous arms of their children, to do the work in the fields That however, is nothing; the enthusiasm we feel for the republic, sustains our courage, and prevents us from complaining."

"Did not you notice" said I to Anselme, when the old man was dismissed, "the cunning look with which that old fellow answered the questions of our captain? I dont know whether it is merely an imaginary idea, but it appears to me that there prevails in these latitudes a strange and unnatural silence.— Stop! what noise is that?"

"It is the sound of a trumpet which reverberates in the distance, with the echoes of the mountains."

"No Anselme, you deceive yourself" cried I, after stopping

a moment, to listen more attentively. "Echo has no share in those repetitions; dont you perceive that the sound is not reproduced in a perfectly identical manner?"

"What inference do you draw from that?"

"These variations prove that these invisible musicians are numerous, and disseminated over the summits of the mountains which surround us."

"You are right—those trumpet sounds proceed from hidden spies, who warn the deserters of our approach, in order that they may gain their caverns, which, in critical times, serve them for a refuge! what do you think of this explanation?"

"I think it probable that you have hit upon the truth."

"Chevrières, when we entered it, presented the aspect of neglect and solitude; the doors and windows of the huts were closed, and the sounds of our drum did not bring out one of those inquisitive people, who in the country usually run together, like a flock of sheep, at the sight of a detachment of military.

"Citizens" said our captain, alluding to this extraordinary silence,—" this reception gives me a bad opinion of the citizenship of these Forezians. However, I promise to make them pay dear for this want of respect. I have the list of the deserters, and the description of their relatives. I am going to billet you at the houses of these last, and I command you in the name of the republic, not to spare them. Drink their wine, eat, and even waste their provisions; make love to their daughters; in a word, make your stay so painful to them, that they will be compelled, in order to get rid of your presence, to deliver up the deserters, whom it is our business to arrest."

This recommendation was received by our detachment, with an enthusiasm which proved to me, alas! that the cruel orders of the commander would be only too well observed: I imparted my fears, in a low voice, to Anselme.

"What can I do in such a case?" answered he. "I am a soldier of the republic, and not a Don Quixote to redress wrongs. Let our comrades amuse themselves as they please, I shall offer no opposition to them."

"But you and I Anselme?"

"Ah well, my dear friend, we will remain what we are, honest lads, and molest the villagers as little as possible. But I dont intend to be starved."

The ranks being broke, and each of us being furnished with a billet, we proceeded towards the houses designed for us, and which were pointed out to us by some children whom we found squatted behind the garden hedges or in the angles of the doorways.

Upon entering the cabin where we were to lodge, we found a poor old woman, quite crooked and almost blind, who was spinning at her wheel.

"We are sent, mother, to keep garrison at your house," said Anselme mildly, "but fear nothing, we will not interfere with you"

"My poor house is at your service, my good soldiers," answered the old woman without leaving off spinning,—"it is all that I can offer you."

"I hope, however," said Anselme, "that you will think of providing us a dinner."

"I am afraid," she answered,—"your fare with me will be but little to your taste. If you like milk and fruit, you shall be served to your satisfaction. It is all I have."

"A cup of milk and some figs!" cried Anselme, with a comic despair, which made me almost split with laughter; "how the deuce do you suppose that we can live on such rations? let us see; you must do better than that, or I shall be angry."

"You may make yourself angry, if that will amuse you, my good soldiers," answered our hostess,—"but of what use will it be to be angry with me?"

"Take care old lady; rather than allow ourselves to die of cold and hunger, we will kill your whole poultry yard, sack your garden, and burn your moveables!" cried my comrade in a stentorian voice, and indicating to me, by a jerk of his head that I must not take it as serious.

"I have neither poultry-yard, nor garden, my good soldier! as to burning my moveables,—look round you,—what do you see? a broken chair, a spinning wheel, and a little straw,—that's all that I possess in the world."

"Well then we will kill you" cried Anselme in a sharp voice.

"Kill me, my good soldier," answered the old woman in the same monotonous and resigned tone which she had preserved during the whole of the conversation. "It is a real service that you would do me. I am old and infirm, and a burthen to everybody about me. My son, who would have been able to soothe my last days, the same that you accuse of disobedience, has been dead these many years, and has left me alone in the world. Ought I not to wish to go and join him in heaven?"

"An old sorceress," said Anselme to me humourously—"I am afraid there is nothing to be got out of her."

"Nay Anselme, if that unhappy creature has nothing,"—

"The truth is, she does not appear to revel in wealth. But you see, the night is approaching, and we are still fasting. Suppose we go out and forage.".

"Let's try first to procure ourselves a dinner by paying for it, and if we cannot do that—why then we must plunder."

I went out with Anselme in order to go through the village, but after rummaging all the houses, and exploring the environs, we could not procure ourselves the least portion of food. Our comrades were in a similar position with ourselves, whilst on all sides we were saluted with oaths and imprecations. As to the scanty inhabitants,—they did not number a score,—whom we met in the village, they were all alike infirm and aged, and appeared so near second childishness that the most exasperated men of our detachment did not dream of venting on them their ill humour. At last, night came, and despairing of success, Anselme and I returned to our hut, to accept the milk and figs that our old hostess had offered us. Unfortunately when we arrived, we found the old lady gone.

"Anselme" said I,—"the proverb declares that 'he who sleeps, also dines!' For want of something better, let's go to bed."

"That appears to be the only alternative left us, and is far preferable to racking our brains for nothing,—let's go to bed."

We then retired into the closet, at the end of the cabin, having previously barricaded the outer door which opened to the street. We threw ourselves, dressed as we were, upon a bunch of straw, which represented our bed, and were already dropping asleep, when we seemed to hear some one walking in the narrow passage.

"Who's there"? cried I, seizing my musket.

"A friend, and by chance," answered a voice which seemed familiar to me.

We sprang at one bound upon our feet, and greatly confounded, that after having barricaded the door, any one should be able to enter the dwelling. We advanced with fixed bayonets.

Almost at the same moment a ray from a dark lantern lightened our chamber, and we perceived, with an astonishment which I cannot describe, the pretended peasant, whom four days before, we had met in the cabaret of Saint Priest.

"It appears to me, gentlemen," said he, smiling,—"that I am destined to die by your hands; for twice only has chance brought us together, and each time your muskets have been levelled against me."

"How have you been able to get in here?" demanded I.

"In a very simple manner—by the door."

"It was securely barricaded," cried I, "and—but look, that's strange! The bars have not been taken away, it is still closed."

"'Tis true enough," said Anselme, "are you a magician, citizen?"

"I am nothing more than a man whom you have treated generously, and who comes in his turn, to do you a slight service," replied the pretended peasant. "I certainly do not mean that I have thereby acquitted myself of you by so small a matter; my intention is only to pay you the interest of the gratitude that I owe you. I have opportunely brought you a supper."

"A supper!" cried Anselme with joy,—"Faith, that's not to be refused; I am dying of hunger."

The mysterious stranger then placed upon the ricketty table, a tolerably heavy basket, from which he drew a cold fowl, two bottles of wine, bread and fruit.

"It now remains, gentlemen," said he, "before taking leave of you, probably for ever, for I dont think we shall ever see each other again, to reiterate to you my expressions of gratitude, and to give you my advice. Take care, during your stay at Chevrières, never to venture alone in the environs of the village."

"Why so? Are we then in an enemy's country?" I asked.

"If you had taken the trouble to reflect a moment, and to recal to your mind what is the commission with which you are charged, you would not have addressed that question to me" answered he.

"The fact is" said Anselme, "the citizen is right! We have not been sent here precisely to promote the welfare of the peasantry, and I can well conceive that the inhabitants of Chevrières are not over fond of us. I freely confess that I shall not be sorry to leave this village."

Oh, as to that, fear nothing. You will not remain here
D

long," said our mysterious and unknown friend, smiling in a very significant manner. " Now adieu !"

"Allow me citizen," cried Anselme, seizing the stranger by the arm; " why do you think it is probable that we shall not remain many days at Chevrières. ? "Because the commander of your detachment will undoubtedly not be pleased here. Observe his countenance to-morrow, you will then see in it the traces of wakefulness, caused by his reflections during the night. But time flies, and I must be ten leagues from Chevrières before dawn. Again, thanks, and adieu."

The unknown then gave us both a warm shake of the hand, and I went towards the door in order to open it for him, when he all at once extinguished his lamp, and disappeared, leaving us in darkness.

On again procuring a light, we examined with the greatest care, the ground and the walls: our musket stocks, wherever we struck, produced only a dead and blunt sound, proving clearly that no secret outlet existed in the hut.

" Truly," cried Anselme, "we are frightened out of our senses. I think it will be best not to perplex ourselves any longer about this mystery. Let's sup, that will divert us from it."

As I had been fasting from the morning, I accepted the invitation, and we sat down to table.

I must do this justice to our eccentric friend, of whom be it said, by the bye (for I do not think it right to hold out false hopes to the reader) he will not again appear in our history;—I must do him this justice of acknowledging that his fowl was cooked to a nicety, his two bottles of wine, of the best quality, and his fruit of the choicest.

This repast being finished, Anselme again betook himself to his bundle of straw, and prepared to sleep. For my part,

"I am sorry for it, but you must not pass here!"

"Why not, soldier? I dont know of any existing law which forbids a citizen from going to his work at any hour he pleases."

"It is not a question of law, you must follow me this instant to my captain."

"Walk on, and I'll follow you" answered the stranger, in a tone of raillery.

"Listen" said I, "I am neither an informer nor a savage, but a soldier. Now, as certain circumstances lead me to think that the detachment of which I form a part, is exposed at this moment to danger, I arrest you provisionally, to enable me to clear up my suspicions."

"That's another thing, citizen, and I have nothing to say against it. Do your duty; but do you know where your captain lodges?"

"Well, I confess I do not."

"Then it is I who must conduct you to your officer" said the unknown, interrupting me,—"this will be the easier for me, because he lodges at my house."

The labourer then walked before me and stopping, after going a few paces, before that large and handsome house, of which I have already spoken—

"Here it is"—said he, "let us enter."

He passed first, and calling aloud for a servant, desired him to bring a light. At the same moment a mountaineer presented himself with a lamp.

"Light us John," said my prisoner, "we are going to the captain."

John passed through three or four rooms, and stopping before a closed door, "must I knock?" asked he, addressing his master.

"Yes John, but knock softly; it is possible the captain is not yet awake."

I was going to speak, when I was interrupted by the voice of the captain, who, in a tone of alarm, demanded what we wanted.

"It is one of your soldiers, who wants to speak to you," answered the labourer.

A moment after, the captain, with a lamp in one hand and his sword in the other, cautiously opened the door of his chamber, and recognizing my uniform,

"What do you want with me at this hour?" said he roughly. I noticed that our commander looked extremely pale, and that his countenance betrayed inquietude and agitation. As for the labourer, an ironical smile, full of contempt, raised the upper lip of a handsome and well defined mouth, and imparted to his physiognomy, which was in other respects, noble, an air of hauteur, singular for a man in his situation of life.

"I wish to have a private conversation with you" replied I.

"Then citizen, do me the pleasure to retire," said the officer addressing the latter, in a tone of politeness quite unusual to him.

The mountaineer moved towards the door in obedience to this order, when I detained him.

"Pardon me, captain," cried I, "I have just arrested this man, and as I am not sufficiently acquainted with him to leave him at liberty on his parole, and it is also probable that we may want him to explain some facts to us, I wish to secure his person. If it is not disagreeable to you, we will send him to the end of the room, whilst our conversation lasts, and we will speak in a low voice."

At this proposal the mountaineer remained unmoved; but the captain, immediately, said with an indignant look, "why have you arrested this brave citizen? Who gave you the order and the power?"

"I thought I ought to take your advice, captain, respecting the circumstances.

"Well then, you are wrong. The inhabitants of Chevrières are citizens devoted to the republic, and are to be treated with respect; do you hear? For the rest, our commission is terminated. There are no defaulters in this village, and to-morrow we must be upon the march again. Now, explain yourself quickly; what communication have you to make to me?'

" None now, captain. I believed that our detachment was in danger; that they wished to draw us into a snare; but from the moment that you guarantee the perfect honesty and the good dispositions of the inhabitants of Chevrieres, it only remains for me to hold my tongue and withdraw."

"Yes I see, after all, you dont know this country so well as I do, but your proceeding proves that you are a good republican. Good night; I will not forget the zeal you have displayed on this occasion, and will take care it shall be noticed."

The embarrassment and painful hesitation with which the captain pronounced these words, astonished me much, but still less than his resolution.

To quit Chevrières in twenty-four hours, when it had been agreed that we should remain there in garrison as long as any of the defaulters remained at large, appeared an inconceivable thing, although as the reader will recollect, it had been predicted by our amphytrion, the pretended peasant.

What were the means practised with our officer, thus to make him forget his duty, it is impossible to say. I can only relate the fact; I was retiring, when, the labourer who accompanied me, requested me, as I passed the dining room, to enter for a few moments.

" It is the least you can do, citizen," said he, with a slightly satirical look, " after all the mischief you have brought on yourself, that you should restore your spirits a little. If you are so disposed, I shall be happy to drink to your speedy departure from Chevrières."

" Sir," said I, " I bear no malice, and willingly accept your invitation."

I was not sorry indeed to have the opportunity of conversing a little with this unfortunate labourer, who was compelled to rise so early in the morning, to work in the fields for want of servants ; and who notwithstanding, was the owner of a house so well furnished. He was about forty or forty-five years of age ; his countenance, bronzed by the sun, was remarkable for the regularity of its features, and still more for their marked expression of boldness and dignity.

" May I ask you citizen, what is your name ?" said I.

" My name is Jacques ; and the villagers call me,—I dont know why—' Monsieur Jacques.' "

" Probably because of the education you have received ?"

" You quite mistake my condition, I have never had an education. I read very badly, and can scarcely sign my own name in a legible manner."

" And yet, there is in you, Monsieur Jacques, a certain air of assurance and authority.—"

" But you see what I am,—a peasant."

" An inhabitant of the country,—yes—that is, indeed your position. Only, I dont exactly know how I have got the idea, I figure to myself that there is in you a double nature ; you appear to me a mystery personified."

" Come, soldier, I see you are fond of a joke," cried Monsieur Jacques. " Let us drink the parting cup, and return, you to your post of observation, I to my fields."

" A parting question Monsieur Jacques ; pray inform me what were all the armed men whom I saw come out of your house ? I confess to you that this affair puzzles me extremely."

" Faith ! what you call a mystery, is the easiest thing in the world to explain. These men represent the greatest part of the inhabitants of our village, who, fearing to be ill-treated by your detachment, have fled into the mountains. Have you finished your interrogating?"

"Faith, you are so complaisant Monsieur Jacques, that I cannot resist asking you to clear it up. Why, then, were all these men armed with scythes and muskets?"

"Ah, you noticed the scythes and muskets! Well I will not attempt to deceive you, although it would be very easy; I confess freely that these arms were destined to attack your detachment, if it had attempted to commit those excesses which unfortunately are but too common."

"Thanks for your frankness Monsieur Jacques; it teaches me at least, that there are no republicans at Chevrières."

"No, citizen, we are not, and we never will be, republicans at Chevrières, whilst the power remains in the hands of the banditti who govern France! But it is time for me to proceed on my way. Allow me to re-conduct you to your quarters."

On returning, a new astonishment was in reserve for me. On entering the hut, I perceived my comrade Anselme seated before a table, abundantly served, assailing with ardour, a magnificent pasty.

"Ah! do you see Monteil," said he with his mouth full; "you are just in time to help me."

"How have you procured this splendid repast Anselme?"

"Do I know myself? Do I care about it? We are in a country of enchantment, and faith, I confess that I begin to find all these surprises very agreeable."

"But still this table has not furnished itself."

"What do you know about it? That would not at all astonish me. All I can tell you is, that on waking just now, I perceived this rich ordinary awaiting us."

"It's very odd! After all, we must take what comes."

Faith! I would willingly consent to take a ten years' lease of a life like that which I have led since last night. I may truly say that I have not left off eating ! But, by the bye, how is it that you have come back so late ? What have you been doing ?

I then detailed to Anselme the various events of the night, but had the greatest trouble to convince him of my veracity. The resolution of our commander appeared to him a thing so very extraordinary, that he could not credit it.

Anselme had scarcely left off eating, when we heard the sound of the drum beating the muster roll.

A quarter of an hour later, the company was mustered, and our commander ordered us to commence our march. I cannot express the astonishment of our comrades at this order. As for the officer himself he looked excessively pale, and seemed much pre-occupied.

"I am very much mistaken," said Anselme to me, in a low voice, " if something very serious and mysterious has not happened to night, to have made so great an impression on our captain. Mark his troubled look, like a man condemned to death, and marching to the scaffold! I would cheerfully give a month's pay,—if they do pay us,—to know the end of this mystery!"

Up to the moment in which I write, the curiosity of Anselme has not been satisfied.

"A few days had scarcely gone by after we quitted Chevrieres, when we stopped at a town, the name of which I cannot recollect.

The roll-call of the drum being over, we received our billets for quarters. Mine as well as Anselme's, gave us a baker for our host. My companion was delighted at the destination assigned to us. In fact, bread was, at this period, a very rare commodity, and not always to be procured even for money, so that the prospect of having it at discretion, was a very satisfactory one.

Anselme, insinuated himself so quickly into the good graces of our host, that this latter gave us a two pound loaf for supper.

Fatigued with the day's march, we were about to retire to our beds, when we saw a ragged old man with a ferocious countenance enter the shop; he demanded a loaf.

"Willingly citizen," said our host to him. "Only, before I serve you, will you show me your money?"

"Do you take me for a thief or an aristocrat?" cried the buyer with indignation.

"I take you for a hungry man and nothing else. Now, as it happens every day, that people, without money, fling themselves upon my goods, and cut into them with excellent teeth, before they tell me of their poverty, I have taken the resolution of not giving my bread till I have touched the value of it."

"Oh you have nothing to fear from me citizen. Hold, here; give me the change."

The fellow drew from the pocket of his vest, a slip of paper, black and creased, which he presented with an air of triumph to our host.

"What's that?" Asked the latter.

"Parbleu! It is an assignat of twenty livres! Come, I say serve me quickly, and give me the change."

"I prefer not serving you, and returning you your assignat!" cried the baker, "what the deuce am I to do with it?"

"What care I! You are either a patriot or not; if—"

"I am a patriot; that is undeniable; but that does not prevent me from being also a baker," interrupted our host quickly. "As a patriot, I take your assignat; as a baker I return it to you."

"Take care," said the beggar in a menacing tone;" the law punishes the traitor with death, who refuses the paper of the republic."

"Parbleu! Hunger also punishes with death, the poor wretch who has no money. I prefer the first kind of death to the second."

"Is that your resolution?"

Quite so citizen; good night."

"Perhaps citizen" said Anselme to the baker, "you were not altogether prudent towards that man. For half a pound of bread you would have been quit of him."

"It is a very easy thing for a soldier to speak thus" said our host, "but if you were to be put in my place, you would soon think otherwise. Do you know that there does not pass a day that I do not receive a score such visits as that every hour! Now if I had the weakness to yield in one instance to threats, what would be the result? Why, that I could then never refuse a single rag of paper, and, before a fortnight, would be reduced to the most frightful distress. I shall continue to refuse the assignats."

Our host withdrew, and Anselme and I also had retired to the bed, when we were alarmed by violent and rapid blows upon the door.

"The brute has not deceived us; after having barked, he comes to bite!" said the baker coolly, returning to us. Here's the revolutionary committee!"

Furious blows again shook the door, which the baker hastened to open.

A dozen men in cloaks and capped with red bonnets, thrust themselves into the shop. They represented the revolutionary committee.

"Citizens what is it you want?" demanded our host without changing countenance.

"We want, *and we are going*, to guillotine you, wretch!" cried the president, "because you have refused the national money, the assignats!"

"I refuse the assignats!" cried the baker with an air of deep indignation; "Well! That does seem a little singular to me! Why, there's no one so eager and curious as myself after assignats! And I can give you a proof of it. If you will walk into my back shop, I will show you a trunk that runs over with assignats of all kinds, all shapes, all values, and all sizes. I can assure you nobody runs after assignats like me; it is absolutely a passion with me,—"

"Your lying protestations can do nothing against a fact" said one of the members of the committee. "We have already received numerous complaints on your account, and wishing to satisfy ourselves if they were well founded, we, this night, sent an emissary, who demanded a loaf, offered an assignat, and has been rejected by you."

"Ah! yes! I recollect," said the baker laughing. "I thought no more about it. The fact is, it's true. I wanted to have the money."

"Then you confess your crime?"

"My crime? Oh no, I confess a fancy, a caprice, which passed through my brain, and nothing else. As to the rest, if you will allow me a few words of explanation, you will at once see that my wish to obtain cash, arose from my patriotism. When I require silver money, which sometimes occurs, ('tis of no use to conceal it from you) it is honestly to prevent it from falling into the hands of the federalists and aristocrats, and keep it in the interior. In other respects my citizenship is well known enough, and ought to prevent you from doubting my veracity To night, I have had another idea. I have been told that they have melted the statue of our lady, in order to make pennies.—You understand; is it not so?"

No: but this talking is all useless."

"What," replied the baker briskly, "dont you understand

you who are such enlightened people, that I wished to possess some of the new pennies, in order to have the occasional pleasure of giving a fillip to what has been the body of Louis XVI? I always fancy that I could catch him in the middle of the nose."

At this vulgar sally the committee laughed heartily, and our host continued with great volubility :

" But now the history of the assignats is explained, you must be convinced citizens that it is I who have reason to complain to you of the calumnies that are circulated about me. I am obliged to refuse so many people, that I have enemies on all sides ? Would you believe it ? They have even gone so far as to say, that my bread does not contain one fifth of flour, and as I also sell wine, they have added that three persons were taken seriously ill from having drunk a glass with me. Well citizens, allow me to profit by this happy chance of your presence here to give the lie to these calumnies. You owe this to justice,—You must now taste my bread and wine, and I consent to forfeit my head if you find any reason to dislike me on account of the quality."

Whilst saying this, the baker had covered his counter with a clean white table cloth, and then placed upon it a dozen bottles of wine, a ham of appetizing aspect, and several golden-crusted loaves.

The members of the committee appeared to watch these proceedings with considerable satisfaction ; at length one of them addressing the president,—

"Citizen" said he, "I know that eating out of regular hours is injurious to the health, but certainly, we owe every thing to justice, and I think it is our duty to ascertain whether the citizen baker has been calumniated, or whether he is supplying bread that may be hurtful to the public health."

"It *is* our duty," said the president ; and all the revolutionary committee seated themselves at the counter.

E

Two hours after, the president, in a thick clammy voice, gave the signal for a retreat, and declared, as he staggered out of the shop, that the baker was a good citizen, and had been unjustly calumniated.

The next day, at an early hour, the battalion was on the road. Our last rendezvous of the day was at Vienne in Dauphiné.

We arrived very late in that city ; and as my comrade and I were harassed with fatigue, we hastened to the quarters indicated in our billet.

"I hope" said Anselme during our walk, "that we are about to be received with open arms, and enjoy a genuine hospitality."

"Are the Dauphinese then, so very hospitable ?"

"What! Dont you know the complaint of the Wandering Jew! Why everybody knows, that that indefatigable and immortal walker passed through here in 1767, and that—

"The fat and greazy citizens
Of old Vienne in Dauphinié
With more good humour than good sense
Wanted to talk with him ; but he, &c., &c."

"But look ! If I am not mistaken we are arrived at our destination."

We stopp'd before the house mentioned in our billet,— and rung the bell gently. Nothing stirred.

"I think they have not heard us," said Anselme, giving another and stronger pull at the bell handle.

" Perhaps they are not willing to receive us."

"Ah my dear friend, can you thus calumniate the inhabitants of Vienne. Don't you know that the Wandering Jew formally states, that the citizens of Vienne in Dauphiné are of a very good natured temperament?"

"In the meantime they don't hurry themselves to open the door for us."

"They certainly have not heard us ; I will ring again."

This time Anselme pulled the bell wire with such violence that the handle remained in his hand.

Five minutes passed in profound silence; no sound proceeded from the interior of the house.

"Well" said I to the old monk, "what do you think of this negative reception ? The Viennese enjoy, perhaps, in regard to character, an undeserved reputation.—"

"Impossible.—The Jew is precise in this respect! He says— 'of a good natured temperament.' The construction is very plain, and leaves nothing to wish for. Our future hosts must be asleep. I will wake them." Here he cast his eyes about him, and perceiving a stone-mark* pulled up, weighing about two hundred pounds,—

"This will do the business," said he ; "this flint will enable me to make them hear."

The old monk then flung the stone-mark against the door which trembled on its hinges, but was not broken open.

Almost at the same moment, an old woman appeared at a window of the first story, and demanded in a voice in which anger and fear were mingled in equal doses, what we wanted?

"We are furnished with a billet my amiable citizen" answered Anselme quickly.

"In that case you may go your way, for we have not a bed in the whole house to offer you" said the old woman.

"We are accustomed to sleep upon the bare ground, dear lady," answered my companion ; "so, if you will give us in exchange for the bed to which we have a right, a decent supper, the matter is easily arranged."

"We have lodged troops all this week, and our cellars as well as our store-rooms are empty, citizen. You will not find in all our house an ounce of bread. But if you wish me to

*A Boundary Stone.

point out the address of a rich proprietor, who will make it a pleasure to receive you and treat you well, I am at your command,—that's all I can do for you."

"What do you think of that, comrade?" Said Anselme. "Shall we take this address?"

"Do as you think proper."

"Then give us this address, citizen, and make haste, for I am dying of hunger."

The old woman obeyed, and then shut her window precipitately, wishing us good luck.

"Come," said Anselme with a sigh, "we shall sup late to day; but if we sup at last, it will not be quite so bad; let's push on."

My comrade then taking the stone, which he had used with so much success, put it under his arm, and signed to me to follow him.

"Are you going to carry that stone with you, Anselme," said I, "what's the use of it? Are not the citizens of Vienne of a very good natured temperament?"

"My dear friend" answered he, "I am sinking with inanition, and I am not sorry to take this precaution. As to the Viennese citizens, I dont know what to think of them. This flint is easy to carry and I shall keep it."

On reaching the new house to which the old woman had directed us, all that we obtained was a fresh address.

"If they mock us again this time, I'll hunt up the mayor of the city, and stir him to some purpose;" said Anselme furiously.

Five minutes later, a third refusal which we received, so much exasperated my companion, that he decided to accomplish his threat. We went to the house of the mayor.

"Come, Anselme, calm yourself" said I to the old monk, who walked so rapidly that I had some trouble to keep up with him. "What's the use of being angry?"

We lodged at Valence with a little one-eyed tailor. I still see the hideous rascal, with his lean and fleshless body, his false, restless, and cruel eye. "Citizens," said he abruptly, as we entered his dark shop, "are you satisfied with your commander?"

"Certainly," answered I.

"And with your captain?"

"Equally."

"Do your officers scrupulously fulfil their duties,—are they patriots?"

"What have you to do with all that?" cried Anselme.

"I have this to do with it,—that I belong to the committee of surveillance, and that if your epaulettes are not quite pure, I will denounce them."

"And, do you fancy that we would give up our officers to you?" said I.

"You would be very wrong to hesitate," answered he, "for their arrest would leave an opening for your advancement!" Here the rascal called his daughter.

"Ninette" said he to her, "dress yourself. I shall take you to night to the society. I hope citizens, that you will attend the sitting. But supper is ready, place yourselves at the table."

Our host, during the repast, did not for an instant, cease speaking.

"Do you know, citizens," said he to us, "that Valence, at this moment, overflows with fops and counter revolutionists. I have undertaken the task of furnishing three hundred acts of accusation. I know the plots of our aristocrats; let the infamous wretches tremble!"

"Out upon your butcheries," cried Anselme; "let these propositions alone, they spoil my appetite. If you so delight in shedding blood, why dont you take a musket and follow us to the siege of Toulon?"

"I shall not agree to calm myself till after supper" answered he, more and more furious.

We soon arrived at the door of the mayor's house.

"Wait, I'll ring," said I to Anselme; but he held me back by the arm.

"No" answered he, "that act of condescension is unworthy of us! A triumphant entry can alone redress us for the refusal we have met with. Let me ring!"

Seizing with both hands the stone which he had brought, my comrade took his aim, and flung it with frightful violence against the house door; then, before any person had time to come, he repeated the attack impetuously, and the door fell in with a crash.

"Ah! Ah!" Said he with an air of triumph "The breach is open. To the kitchen! Alexis, to the kitchen!"

The appearance of a man, girded with a tricoloured scarf, and with alarm depicted in his countenance, moderated the warmth of my companion.

Without giving the mayor,—for it was he,—time to speak, "Citizen," said he, "thy commissaries mock us, and I have not yet supped. I am mildness personified in general; but may I be guillotined this instant if I don't set fire to your house, if you attempt to refuse us supper and bed."

"I beg pardon, in the name of my commissaries" said the mayor, "but if you knew what a horrible position they are placed in, your warlike bowels would be moved. Since the troops have ploughed up the country, they have been so laid under contribution, that I do not exaggerate when I assure you that fully half the population find themselves reduced to an ounce and a half of bread per day for their whole support.— But don't make yourself uneasy,—I shall instantly have supper provided for you."

"That's something; but a bed?"

"Although my wife is on the eve of her confinement, she is about to rise and yield hers to you. As to my own, it is hardly necessary to add, that it is at your service."

"Is your wife near her confinement?" Interrupted Anselme; "Then she has need of repose, so do not disturb her. We are not cannibals. But have you not spoken of a certain supper?"

"It will be ready instantly! Come in."

At the sight of a substantial repast which was brought to us, the brow of my companion became quite cleared, and turning towards me,—

"Ah well" said he, "the report of the Wandering Jew is not wholly void of truth. The citizens of Vienne in Dauphiné are of a very good natured temperament."

"When one breaks open the doors of their houses?"

"In fact I must admit, that without my expedient of the big stone, we ran a great risk of going to bed fasting, with the stars for a canopy."

Our repast being finished,—and with Anselme, a repast only terminated when there remained nothing on the table but the cloth, we begged the mayor to shew us to the place where we were to pass the night, and, exhausted with fatigue, retired to rest."

CHAPTER II.

Arrive at Roussillon—Free quarters—Am quartered on a nobleman—Cavalier reception—Flunkey valour—True nobility—The domestic home of an aristocrat in revolutionary times—I live in clover—Confidences of my host—Arrive at Valence—The one-eyed tailor and the guillotine—The registrar of Montemilan—His great peril—Anselme saves him—His gratitude—Arrive at Orange—A prosperous butcher—The old royalist—Military orgies—Throwing off the mask—I am made serjeant, and then adjutant—Scene in a cabaret—A double duel—M. Marcotte of Avignon—Pistache Carotte.

The next morning we hastened to rejoin our battalion, which had formed in rank upon the square. During the whole time our march lasted, that is to say, till we reached Roussillon, which is about four leagues from Vienne, we saw only a bleak and barren country.

On the arrival of the battalion at Rousillon, our commander found orders from the superior authority, which directed him to distribute us in garrisons in the neighbouring villages and towns.

This news, which afforded to my companions the prospect of marauding and emoluments, was received by most of them, if not all, with great pleasure. As for myself, it dismayed me. I had made up my mind that I was to go and fight on the frontier, and I could not reconcile myself to the idea of being employed as an instrument of vengeance on the inhabitants. However, it was necessary to obey. At the same time I determined to exercise extreme moderation in the accomplishment of my instructions.

The next morning, I was directed to a hut about a musket shot distant from Rousillon, of which I was to take possession.—I did so; but finding, after a stay of a few days, that my presence was an unbearable tax upon the exceeding poverty of my host, I resolved to seek fresh quarters.

One morning I saw the mayor of the town passing my door and resolved to avail myself of the occasion to accomplish my project.

Accosting the municipal officer, "Citizen" said I, "I wish to speak to you; I am but a corporal, it is true, but I inform you, that my cousin-german is one of the convention.—Now, I come to the fact,—"

"Your uniform alone is enough to procure you my good offices, citizen soldier;" answered the mayor.

"What I demand is a matter of justice only; I desire that you find me another lodging; and,—understand us well,—I desire that it may be at the house of a rich man, or, at least, one in easy circumstances, that my presence may not cause him sacrifices beyond his means."

The mayor reflected for some seconds, then fixing his eyes upon me, "Are you courageous, citizen?" Asked he at last.

I answered coolly "I am a Frenchman and bear the uniform of the republic."

"Then follow me, I am going to give you new quarters."

"Very well, and at whose house?"

"At the house of the citizen Pierre, the ex-baron of I no longer know what."

"Ah, I understand you! But how is it this baron has not emigrated?"

"Why should he fly, if his conscience reproaches him in nothing" said the mayor. "Hold citizen, here's your billet. I wish you much satisfaction in the change."

It appeared to me that the municipal officer pronounced these words with a singular look; but I troubled myself little about that.

After some enquiries about my route, I at last arrived before a magnificent chateau, surrounded with an immense park, and away from all other dwellings. Such was the quarters assigned to me by my billet.

Observing that the entrance gate was not locked, I pushed it open, and entered boldly into the court-yard. As no one presented himself to receive me, I struck, with the stock of my musket, upon the pavement of the court, and began quietly to unfasten my knapsack, like a man, who knowing himself at home, feels perfectly at his ease.

Seeing that no one came to meet me, I went towards the entrance of the chateau, when a fat little man, wearing an ample periwig, appeared at the top of the steps, stared at me in silence, and deigned at last to approach me.

Thinking I had to do with the baron, I resolved to make him pay dear for his arrogance.

"Hallo! Man of the musket," said he, screwing up his mouth, "what do you want? Who sent you here?"

"I am here to take possession" answered I mildly.

"Possession! What's that?" repeated the baron, with a contemptuous air,—"some patriotic invention. We don't want that merchandise here; you may go your way."

"First, will you read this order citizen?"

"An order! Is there still a power in France?"

"There is—that of the republic."

"I don't recognise it," said the baron throwing the billet at my feet.

This last insult filled up the measure ; I burst out :

"Miserable wretch !" Said I, advancing up to him, "there still exists another power ; it is that which a bold man possesses over a coward, that which I now exercise over you ! Pick up that paper, wretch—quick—without losing a moment, lest I crush you !"

The baron decided to pick up the billet, and returned it to me.

"Present it on your knees !" I cried, in an access of wrath—and take care—your hesitation may cost you your life !"

The baron, seeing me raise my musket, fell at my feet.

"Now citizen" said I, "we are quits. If you wish to avenge your honour, I am at your service."

The only reply the baron made, was to run off, crying "An assassin ! Help ! Help !" I set off in pursuit and entered with him into the chateau. Scarcely had I cleared the flight of steps, than I found myself surrounded by five or six footmen, who were in the anti-chamber.

"If any of you touch me I will lay him dead at my feet," cried I loudly.

"Knock down that bandit !" cried the baron to the excited valets.

It was a scene of confusion impossible to describe.

At this crisis the appearance of a man of about fifty years of age, very simply dressed, and of an imposing figure, produced a dead silence.

"What is the matter ? What is going on here ? Why this tumult and these cries ?" Demanded the new comer.

"It is," replied I, "that I am fallen into an ambuscade."

"Who are you sir ? How came you here ?"

"The uniform that I bear answers that question. As to my presence in this chateau, this billet will explain it."

The stranger took the billet that I presented to him, examined it, and returning it to me with much politeness ;—

" You are perfectly correct" said he, "but this does not explain the scene of violence which has just passed. Have they failed in attention to you? Have you reason to complain of my people?"

By this question I found that I had grossly deceived myself in taking the fat little man with the wig, for the master of the chateau, and that that title belonged to the new comer.

"Yes citizen," answered I, "they wished, in fact, to insult me; but as my redress has exceeded the offence, I do not complain.—"

"Your conduct is inexcusable" cried he, addressing the domestics, who, trembling and confused, dared not lift their eyes. " The uniform of a French soldier, has a right to the respect of all ! And hospitality is one of those sacred duties which we ought always to exercise. Thank this soldier for his generosity, which prevents me from giving up the names of the offenders."

The confused domestics immediately stammered out excuses to me, but I stopped them by a motion of my hand.

" If you will follow me, I will myself conduct you to your room," said the unknown to me.

I bowed, in sign of acquiescence and thanks, and followed my guide.

Immediately after I was installed in an apartment magnificently furnished, the windows of which looked all over the park.

" You will find here all you want for your toilet," said my conductor. "For the rest, if you want anything, you will only have to ring ; the servants are at your commands."

"Truly Monsieur Le Baron," answered I, " I don't know how to thank you for your graceful complaisance. It is impossible to exercise hospitality in a more noble manner."

"I have more reason to thank you for this title of baron which, from pure courtesy and good breeding, you have just given me," said he, smiling. " But dinner will be ready in half-an-hour; I will take care to have you called when we sit down to table, for I hope you will do us the honour of sharing our humble ordinary. *Au revoir.*"

I had finished dressing, when the baron himself came to announce that dinner was about to be served up. I followed him to a magnificent gothic dining-room. Almost at the same instant the folding doors opened, and a valet announced " Monsieur Le Marquis, M. Le Chevalier, Mes Demoiselles, M. L'Abbé."

One may guess with what curiosity my attention was directed towards the new comers. The first who entered, whom the valet called "the marquis," was a stout and handsome old man, with bushy white moustachios, and a martial air. The Chevalier, a youth of sixteen or seventeen years, presented nothing remarkable in his person; he wore a court dress of the latest fashion. The two young ladies, who entered after the Chevalier, might be thirteen or fourteen years old. The Abbé was a fat stubby man, with a ruddy insignificant face, the type of his fraternity.

The baron, before sitting down to table, presented me to the guests. Scarcely were we seated, when a swarm of valets invaded the dining room, and set about serving us.

"After dinner, when the Abbé had returned thanks, my host proposed to take me with him a tour of the park; I accepted his offer.

Our conversation touched in nothing upon the events of the day. He incidentally informed me, that he had served thirty years in the cavalry regiment of Royal-Champagne, and that he retained an agreeable recollection of his military career.

I felt a strong desire to interrogate him, but politeness restrained the expression of my curiosity. The day passed in a very agreeable manner, the old commander read to us from Brantomes lives of illustrious men.

At ten o'clock, after having had prayers in common, we separated. My host wished me a good night, and accompanied me to the door of my room, preceded by a footman carrying a lighted candélabra.

During the three or four first days after my arrival at the chateau, no incident worth recording happened to break the monotony of the calm and happy life I led.

The fourth day,—it was Sunday,—my host asked me, after breakfast, if it would be agreeable to me to attend mass.

My curiosity led me to accept the offer, and I proceeded half-an-hour later to the chapel, which I found filled with the peasantry of the neighbourhood.

My host and his family were seated on the ancient seignorial bench; they gave them incense, and *offered them with great ceremony*, the holy wafer. All this was so opposed to the new habits of France, that for a moment, I doubted the reality of what I saw. I asked myself if I was not dreaming?

During the week which I still remained at the chateau, my hosts continued their attentions. It was impossible to extend the duty of hospitality further than they did.

At the end of that week, I received an order to rejoin the corps immediately.

I hastened to communicate this news to my host, and to thank him for the kindness I had met with at the chateau. He wished me a good journey, and, resolving to conduct me to Rousillon, ordered his carriage.

" Truly, my dear sir," said he, when we found ourselves alone and side by side in his coach, I cannot too much praise you for the discretion you have displayed. During the fifteen days that you have lived amongst us, you must have exercise.: great strength of mind to repress your curiosity. Ask me now for any explanations you wish for, and I am ready to answer you "

F

"Then, will you explain to me, how it happens that in a general revolution, when the least return to the past, is a thing considered and punished as a crime, you have not effected the slightest change in your mode of life; that you keep your servants in livery, your Abbé in Cassock; that you bear your title, and celebrate mass in public in the chapel of your chateau? These things are inexplicable to me."

"They are, however, very easily explained. The extreme freedom of action which I enjoy at this moment, is the fruit of my past life. I have always been kind to everybody, and above all to my vassals. Here's the fact in a few words. You know that every one of us possesses certain tastes and fancies. For myself, I have a fancy for pleasure and gaiety; nothing gives me so much pleasure as the sound of laughter, or the sight of a cheerful countenance. I have therefore, found gratification in the exercise of kindness. Thus, if one of my peasants was in difficulties, I helped him out of it; if he married, I gave him a portion, and placed the resources of the chateau at his service on his wedding-day."

"When 89 arrived, 1 was, *at first* on the point of emigrating; but my peasants came in a body and entreated me with so much earnestness not to abandon them, that I had not the courage to repulse their prayers, and remained. Only I took care to make certain conditions."

"My friends, said I to them, you are attached to me, and I to you. I will remain with you on one condition. Let us agree, that for us the revolution does not exist; that we will continue out of the reach of it, and live in peace as heretofore; is that a bargain?"

"My freedom was entirely successful; my peasants swore that they would never give me reason to complain of them, and that, as they could not hope to become more happy than they were, they would in no respect involve themselves in the tempest."

"Friends, said I to them, you are right; for, suppose you were to burn my chateau, and destroy my estate, what would be the result to yourselves? Why, inasmuch as my means have always been at your service, you would destroy your own chateau, your property, your riches, and would commit not only a crime, but a gross folly in respect to your own interests."
"Such, continued my host is the language I used to my peasants, and they comprehended it. In short, to conclude these explanations, I must confess that I have been rewarded for my good sense, by a season of unspeakable happiness."

"Having now nothing to fear from my peasants, I had still to dread the new revolutionary authorities. I make no hesitation in avowing that I made use of indirect corrupt means with them; I bribed them in short, and made it their interest not to molest me, or suffer me to be molested."

"I thank you much, sir, for these explanations; but there is still one question which I much wish to put to you. I cannot understand how you should have ventured at once to confide in a person of whom you knew neither the family nor the antecedents!—In short, may I not be a traitor?"

"If you think that I do not know you, you are in error. Do you suppose that an old cavalry captain does not know mankind? Recall to yourself your entry into the chateau. Insult roused you to indignation and violence. Now, a hasty man is rarely a traitor. From the moment that I saw you pursue my steward with so much fury, I knew that you would not betray me."

As my host finished speaking, we arrived at Rousillon, where I rejoined my comrade Anselme.

From Rousillon we took the route by Valence, where our battalion arrived in a very bad condition. The privations to which our men had to submit, alternating with the excess in which they indulged when occasion offered, produced much sickness.

The tailor remained silent for a few minutes, but we had soon to submit anew to his frightful proposals. His wife, seeing the disgust that this conversation caused us, attempted to calm the sanguinary enthusiasm of her husband, and the daughter joined in. "Come father, do pray calm yourself," said she, taking the frightful little monster by the arm. "It is almost the hour for the sitting." And she led him away.

"Ah gentlemen," said the tailor's wife, when they were gone, "I beg of you not to put my husband into a passion. If you knew what he is capable of,—Do you know that scarcely two months ago, that wretch,—my husband,—caused one of my cousins, the friend of my childhood, to be guillotined."

"And you remain with the monster!" cried Anselme.

"I must do so, alas! for Ninette's sake."

"Ah, your lot must be frightful my poor woman," said I in a tone of interest.

"So much the more frightful sir" answered she, "that at the bottom, my husband is not cruel; it is the fear of being guillotined himself, that has made him what he is. Knowing his own weakness of character, he feels secure only in making his superiors tremble! May God preserve him from the remorse of having sent me to the scaffold!—"

"How can you entertain so monstrous an idea!"

"Alas, I know only too well what I say; but" added she changing her tone, "you must be fatigued, if you will follow me I will shew you to your room."

It was with real pleasure that, at day-break the next morning, I found myself on the march with my battalion, upon the road to Montélimar.

On arriving at Montélimar, we were billetted at the house of the registrar, who treated us handsomely, and regaled us with an excellent supper.

"Truly, my dear Alexis," said Anselme, after sitting two

hours at table "this registrar is endowed with excellent qualities. Really, I should be happy to have it in my power to show my gratitude."

In expressing this wish, Anselme little suspected that chance would so soon call on him to realize it. We were in a deep sleep, when a tumult in the house awoke us. We leaped out of bed.—It was evident that something serious was the matter.

Having hastily dressed, we descended to the hall on the ground floor. The first thing we perceived was our brave host the ex-registrar, who, seated upon a sofa, between his wife and two young children, was bathed in tears.

"What has happened my dear sir" I abruptly asked.

"Alas" replied he, with a deep sigh, "you see in me, a man who has not long to live! I shall soon be guillotined. But let me relate the circumstances, that you may judge—

"I had connected myself, on a certain occasion, with the president of the district, thinking that it would contribute to my security. Now it happened, that one day this unhappy man was pursued as a federalist, and begged me to keep for him a bundle of papers of great importance, which, if found upon him, would at once conduct him to the scaffold. I took the papers, and locked them in a great dark closet, which I used as a dressing room. It is now nearly four months since, and I thought no more about it, when, this morning, a member of the revolutionary committee has summoned my servant in the name of the law, to open the doors to him; and he has put the seals upon the door of the fatal closet, and informed me that the committee will come to day in a body, to prosecute the search. You see my friends," said the unfortunate registrar "that as soon as the member of the committee was gone, my first care was to ascertain if it would not be possible to get into the closet without breaking the seals. Alas, I see no possible means of getting in, in order to withdraw the papers, which will take me straight to the scaffold. Now, having told you my position, have I not reason for weeping?"

"Well," said Anselme, "I must try to find some way of getting you out of the scrape."

He then began to reflect seriously, during which our unfortunate host fixed his eyes on him with an inexpressible mixture of hope and despair.

"Friends" cried Anselme abruptly, "I have found what I was looking for. Tell me, is the closet which contains the fatal papers a large one?"

"About half as large as this hall."

"In that case, you are saved; up, at once, and follow me."

There was so much authority in the manner of speaking of the old Dominican, and the danger was so imminent, that we at once obeyed. Arrived before the door of the fatal closet, Anselme tore off the seal of wax, bearing the emblems of the republic.

"Rash man" cried I—"

"Silence" said he sternly. "My dear host, take away the papers of the ex-president, and get them out of sight. You, madam, place a bed at once in the closet,—quick—quick—make haste! There now, 'tis done; good! Crumple the curtains, and tumble coverlet, as if the bed had been used; that's it, perfectly!—Alexis go and fetch our muskets, they are in our room. Remember! *We slept last night in this closet*—it was madame who arranged this, without the knowledge of her husband.—You understand? Go, run off all of you and leave the rest to us."

Scarcely were the host and his wife gone, than Anselme began to raise a hubbub, worthy of a Huron warrior, and to launch terrible blows against the pannels of the door.

"Here's the member of the committee coming up," said a voice from the next room.

Seizing our muskets by the barrel, we precipitated ourselves violently against the door. It fell in fragments, and we found ourselves in the presence of the member of the revolutionary committee, who, blinded by the dust, and stunned with the noise, fell back hastily before us.

"Really citizens" said he, on recovering from his surprise, "you would have done well to wait till we came to liberate you. I am here to remove the seals."

"Ah, is it you citizen sealer?" cried Anselme, "How dare you imprison the defenders of the country? I dont know what withholds me from breaking your head, you miserable traitor!"

The member of the committee was so much frightened, that he remained for some moments without speaking a word. At length he stammered forth an apology, and cursorily examining the closet, where of course he found nothing—took his departure.

"Well, my dear sir" said Anselme to our host, as soon as the officer had left us, "what do you think of this farce?"

I will not repeat the endless benedictions heaped upon us by our host. Before taking a final leave of him, we advised him to see the member of the committee again, and to tell him that we had left him with great coolness, and he could plainly see that we were angry with him, for the disagreeable and involuntary trouble he had caused us.

Our host thanked us cordially for this advice, and promised to follow it; he wished us all kinds of happiness, and swore that his gratitude to us would remain as long as he lived.

The next morning, it was scarcely light when the drums beat. We hastened to rise and join the battalion. The ranks were just formed, and we were about to march, when I was accosted by an old woman, whom I recollected as the servant of our host of the previous evening.

"Citizen" said she to me, "my mistress, fearing that you

may want provisions on your route, has sent you these two jars of preserves."

Thinking that it would be a want of courtesy on my part, to refuse this insignificant present, I fastened the jars to my knapsack, and begged the servant to present my thanks to her mistress.

"What the deuce are you carrying there?" Demanded Anselme at the first halt we made.

"They are preserves."

"Indeed! Are you so very fond of sweets, then?"

"Not at all. It is the registrar whom you saved yesterday, that has sent this present, which I shall not be at all sorry to get rid of."

"That will be a very easy matter; give them to me, I adore delicacies."

"With the greatest pleasure; hold, here they are."

I then untied the jars and handed them at once to Anselme.

"Gooseberries and apricots!" Said he, casting a glance upon the covers. "They are just what I have a predilection for. Faith, as we dont know who lives or who dies, it will perhaps be prudent to begin upon the gooseberries at once."

Pronouncing these words, my companion, quickly opened the jar, when all at once, uttering an exclamation of surprise,—
"Ah parbleu" said he, "here's something that pleases me much more."

Upon uncovering the jar, Anselme had found fifty louis' wrapped in an assignat of fifty livres, and surrounded with a bundle of cotton. His name was written upon a small piece of paper, fixed upon it with a pin.

"Ah! But that is not all" resumed he, "here's another packet.—Ah! That has got your address. Will you allow me to open it?"

This second packet contained twenty-five louis', and these

words traced with a pencil on a sheet of paper:—" Citizen nothing is lost in my house! I send you, by my servant, the money which you have forgotten in your chamber. Long live the republic!"

"Well" said Anselme, "what do you think of this excellent present? For my part I am quite melted in thinking of the feastings that await us. Truly, we may well say, that a good action never fails to bring its own reward!"

I shall not describe day by day the halts that we made after leaving Montélimar. Such a detail of the names of the villages and towns would possess no interest with the reader. I shall come at once to Orange, where, once more, chance, which had so often favoured me in my billetings did not abandon me. They sent me to the house of a butcher.

My first feeling, upon crossing the threshhold, was one of pity for the fate of the unfortunate persons who were obliged, by their profession, to live in such an atmosphere. But scarcely had I entered the interior of the house, than my pity at once evaporated. Judge of my astonishment when, on entering the back shop, I found myself surrounded with furniture of the richest quality, worthy of the dwelling of a grand-seignior.

"Well," thought I, "this butcher must be some duke or marquis, who, in order to avoid the guillotine, has opened a butcher's shop." I began to examine the luxurious ornaments which surrounded me, when the door opened, and the master of the house entered. He was an awkward fellow, but wore an embroidered satin waistcoat, and a red velvet cap with gold flowers.

"Citizens" said he to us, "if you are gentlemen, you shall want for nothing; I will cram you with food. If you breed any riots, I warn you that I have credit enough with the committee to have you denounced, and I shall not fail to do so."

"Citizen" said Anselme, "there is some good in your discourse, but the bad predominates. That you should propose to regale us in the first instance, is very praiseworthy of you; but it appears to me ridiculous, that you should, without any cause, threaten us by virtue of your credit with the committee. If it amuses us to get tipsy in your house, we shall not lay any constraint upon ourselves. If you make any to-do about it, I shall pitch you, with all the respect due to a host, into the street. I have spoken."

As the athletic appearance of Anselme perfectly justified this language, the butcher lowered his tone.

"Citizen" answered he with a coaxing look, "you have misunderstood me. Amuse yourselves as much as you please; only respect my family."

In about an hour, one of the butcher's boys came to the attic where they lodged us, to tell us that supper was ready.

On entering the back shop, we found a table sumptuously furnished. Nothing was wanting. Six covers were set on; four for our host, and his family, and two for Anselme and me.

The butcher's wife, her daughters, and husband, were richly clothed. She wore a mantelet trimmed with ermine. As to the lace on the two girls, I easily recognised by their length and design, that they had been torn from some church linen.

This discovery led me to examine the furniture, of which I had only taken a passing view. I found that it was composed of unmatched pieces, and all the luxury of the house was evidently nothing more than the spoils of victims, and the products of pillage.

I remarked that the large chimney piece, before which we were seated, was composed of the finest marble, and by the light of the flame, I perceived upon the hearth a latin inscription which attracted all my attention. It was an epitaph engraven upon a tomb-stone! This wretched butcher had plundered even the dead for his personal benefit!

I took the tongs and clearing the ashes and coals which partly covered this inscription succeeded in deciphering it, and found that this marble had been placed upon the tomb of a young and noble lady, 19 years of age, of the name of Glandered, who died in 1541.

Such are the vicissitudes of human life! Who could have foretold to the noble relatives of this young lady, that in two centuries and a half after her death, the marble on which they had engraven the expression of their grief, would be torn from their daughter's tomb, to serve as an ornament for a butcher's hearth.

After quitting Orange, and before we arrived at Avignon, the battalion halted at a small town, the name of which has escaped me. As the houses the town contained were but few in number, the authorities billetted four men upon each of the householders.

In company with Anselme and two other comrades, I had therefore, to ring at the gate of a pretty country-house, at which we were billetted. A servant about fifty years of age and very neatly dressed, came to open the gate.

"Citizens" said she, "I have a favour to ask of you. It is, that you will respect the repose of my master, who is old and paralytic. He is a soldier like yourselves, having served his country forty years. He has already directed me to place all that he possesses at your service."

"But, my good citizen," said one of my comrades, "I doubt whether our uniform will please your master. The colours of to day, are not the same as they were then."

"Oh, my master is a good patriot" said she.

As soon as we arrived, we were conducted into the hall, in which sat the old veteran, stretched out in a large arm chair.

"You are welcome citizens," said he, attempting to force a

smile; "I have directed my servant to provide everything you need. I wish you to want for nothing. Perpetué," added the old chevalier of Saint Louis, "these citizens must be fatigued; conduct them to their rooms that they may rest themselves till supper is ready."

"Faith," said Anselme when we were alone, "this old gentleman pleases me much; only I rather mistrust his zeal for the republic; but it is all the same to me, provided he carries out the gastronomic programme he has placed before us. You know, that, in regard to opinions, I am extremely tolerant."

When the hour of supper arrived, Perpetué came to inform us, that her master was waiting for us, and we hastened to follow her. We found the table furnished with numerous dishes, and bottles of wine of all qualities. One may conceive the reception given to this repast, by six soldiers, generally in want of the necessaries of life, and frequently half famished. When the conversation began, our host, though old and infirm, displayed the greatest enthusiasm and ardour for the republic. He scarcely pronounced two words, without interlarding his speech with the words "liberty and equality." If we could believe him, the republic was about to absorb the whole of Europe, and the day of kings was gone by for ever.

I cannot describe the painful impression I experienced, at hearing the old man declare himself in this manner. I knew that he could neither think, nor desire what he said, and that fear alone made him speak thus. I felt ashamed for our epoch, that a man in the decline of life, having already one foot in the grave, should think, in order to save the few days that remained to him on earth, that he must belie his opinions, in the presence of French soldiers. Were we therefore, descended so low, that, under our uniform, they feared to find an informer, or an assassin! As to my comrades, excited by their abuse of the generous wines that loaded the table, they exhibited

G

a mirth as foolish, as it was uproarious ; and, regardless of the age of our host, they sung,—or, more properly, roared out, bacchanalian, patriotic, and some few looser songs.

From time to time, the involuntary contraction of the brows of our host, and the look of anguish that Perpetué exchanged with him, fully revealed how much these two beings suffered from our presence.

"Come citizen, talk to us," cried one of my comrades, addressing the servant,—"are you dumb? I dont understand it."

"Sir,—citizen, I am employed in serving you, and cannot mix in the conversation," said Perpetué.

" In *serving us!*" replied the soldier, "what aristocratic phrase is that ? Remember, old lady, that there are neither masters, nor mistresses, nor servants now—only citizens. You do not *serve* us ; you *help* us, which is a very different thing."

"Yes, citizen that's what I meant to say; I made a mistake—"

" Well, well, now that we have no further need of your help, come and sit down at table with us, and drink a glass. Come, make haste !"

"What ! I sit down to table!" exclaimed the poor Perpetué, casting a side-long look of affright at her master.

"Certainly, at table !" resumed our companion ; "and why not? Ah, I see what it is, coquette; you want me to offer you my arm,—"

"Come, come, Perpetué, why do you make him entreat thus ?" said the old chevalier to her, mildly. "Come sit by me ; I will help you in my turn."

"But sir—but citizen, you can't mean it," cried she, still more embarrassed. "What I ! No, it's impossible. I never shall dare,—"

"Now, look at the little aristocrat," said the soldier. " Are we to believe, my friends, that her master, as she calls him, is

I resolved to keep watch, and the closet where we were, being inconveniently hot, I took up my position upon the threshhold of the outer door. It might have been about half-an-hour that I had thus breathed the fresh air, when I thought I perceived through the shades of night, at a hundred paces from me, some moving shadows. I took my musket, and advanced softly upon tip toe, in the direction in which I had discovered the figures, and gained a bushy hedge, in which I squatted myself, in spite of the brambles and thorns which tore my clothes and scratched my hands. Judge of my astonishment, when I saw, coming out of a very large and handsome house, the most remarkable one in Chevrières, a hundred men, all armed with scythes and muskets. Yet, in the morning when we arrived in the village, there was scarcely found, as I have already stated, twenty inhabitants, including old folks and children! How then could one house produce so considerable a troop of people? I was lost in conjecture. However, my discoveries ended here; for these men, having exchanged a few words amongst themselves, in a voice so low that it was impossible for me to catch a single syllable, separated instantly, and went off in different directions.

After waiting another hour, during which no remarkable event occurred, I determined to abandon my post of observation, and regain my cabin. I succeeded, after some trouble in emerging from the hedge, when I found myself face to face with a man whom the darkness prevented me from seeing distinctly.

"Who's there?" cried I, levelling my musket.

"A Frenchman and a friend," answered the stranger in a calm and sonorous voice.

"What are you doing out at this time of night?" I demanded.

"I am a poor labourer, who having no servant to help me in my work, am obliged to set out for the field at four o'clock," answered he.

not that partizan of equality and fraternity, that he pretends to be ? Otherwise, why does she make so many excuses ?"

"My master is as patriotic and republican as anybody," cried the unhappy Perpetué, sobbing. "You see, he has prayed me to come and sit down at his side. If I have refused, it is because I am not hungry. But now, in short—I'm going,—"

In fact, the poor creature took an arm chair, and installed herself, without further delay, by the side of her master.

The soldier, who was the author of this scene, which I have related, just as it occurred, was not a brutal man ; but he was obstinate, and uneducated, and entertained a complacent opinion of his power of pleasing. Delighted with his triumph, and already greatly excited by drink, he began to jest, and emptied bottle after bottle, in honour of the handsome aristocrat Perpetué, as he called the good old creature. Till at last, yielding to intoxication, and almost to delirium, he broke a bottle in two, and raising the improvised cup, with a trembling hand,—"My friends," said he, "take off your caps, and imitate me. I drink to the guillotine ! Death to the nobility ! The scaffold for ever !"

At this infamous toast, I saw the old chevalier change colour ; then, with an incredible effort, he raised himself, in spite of his paralysis, to his full height.

"Gentlemen," said he, in a calm, and strongly-accented voice,—"I drink to the past glory of France ! To her freedom from the cowardly and cruel tigers who now oppress her ! To the memory of her noblesse, murdered on the scaffold ! To the triumph of royalty ! To the downfall of the butchers."

With these words, he emptied his glass at a single draught, and then fell heavily into his arm chair.

Surprised beyond expression, at this unexpected scene, we remained profoundly silent, and the old soldier availed himself of it, to continue.

"Gentlemen," said he, "for ever, cursed be this day, which has witnessed my dishonour. I am seventy years old, and have passed forty-five under the flag of France, and never before, have I violated my conscience. Has, then, the fear of death, when I may possibly have only a few hours to live, made me descend, even to a lie, and led me to deny my king, and my former life? Yes, gentlemen, remember my words, in order to report them to the purveyors of the guillotine. I hate the republic, with all the strength of my heart and soul. I feel a disgust, approaching to madness, for those men, covered with gore and filth, who, under the pretext of governing France, rob her of her blood, her treasure, and her honour. I have witnessed, with tears of rage, the fall of that royalty which had placed us at the head of Europe, made us great as we were, and which has fallen, only, by its excess of clemency. Long live the king!"

Overcome by this extraordinary effort of anger, he inclined his head on one side, and lost all consciousness. Perpetué flew to his assistance, and, weeping, lavished upon him the most anxious and affectionate attention. I was much affected, and even Anselme, whose looks met mine, had a softened expression of countenance. As for our companions, the one who had produced this scene, by proposing the health of the guillotine, was in a deep sleep; the other, a big Strasburgher, stupid when fasting, and completely senseless after indulging in eating and drinking, lit his pipe, with a *sang-froid* that proved, that what had passed, had but little interest with him. I then rose, and motioning Anselme, drew him into an embrasure of the window.

"My friend," said I, "it is quite necessary to make our two comrades dead drunk, to prevent their recollecting anything of this, to-morrow; or, if a confused recollection of to night passes through their brain, they may attribute it to a dream.

We must not allow them to denounce this poor old man. What he has done is nothing,— so I may reckon on you to make our two companions completely drunk."

"I have never shrunk from a good action," answered Anselme gravely : "besides, it has been my intention, from our first arrival here, to pass the night in drinking."

I then assisted Perpetué to carry the paralytic to his bed, and embraced the moment, when we found ourselves alone, to remove her fears as to his fate. The poor woman was so much moved, that she took my hand and wept, without being able to utter a word of thanks.

The next morning, when our battalion was on the point of setting out, the lawyer of the commune came to ask the soldiers, if they had any complaints to make of the hosts, who had lodged them, during the night. I do not know whether any of them availed themselves of this enquiry. All that I could say, was, that my two comrades slept in a cart, that they were dead drunk, and that, it was impossible for them to utter a syllable, so religiously had Anselme kept his promise.

Avignon, where we soon arrived, proved to me, the theatre of an event, that was most strongly impressed on my memory.

The following was the order of the day, which the morning after the arrival of our battalion, in that city, was posted over the fragments of a bill of sale, of a domain.

"Liberty, unity, fraternity, equality, indivisibility, or death!!

"The sans-culottes of the battalion, are informed, that they will proceed to day, at three o'clock in the afternoon, to the nomination of five corporals, one serjeant, an adjutant, a sub-officer, and two sub-lieutenants,"

" Done at the rendezvous, at Avignon, in the year 2 of the French republic, one indivisible, and imperishable."

Signed, Grand Jean, commandant.

When I read the order of the day, I felt a secret presentiment, that, before the end of it, I might probably be advanced. My presentiment was fully realized. At half-past two, the drums beat, and at half-past three, I was nominated serjeant, and, precisely at four, they proclaimed me adjutant.

I was complimenting Anselme, who, had just been nominated corporal, and he, in return, was offering me his congratulations on my epaulet, when the master-tailor of the battalion accosted me with a profound bow, and asked if I would accompany him to the rendezvous. I did so, and in an hour after my nomination, I was equipped in a complete uniform.

Seeing myself so well rigged out, I could not resist the inclination to shew myself, and I entered a café. I found there, a numerous company, among whom, reigned a profound silence. To see the uneasy countenances of the guests, one would have thought, that they were on the eve of some important event; and, scarcely was the door opened, when, immediately, the whole attention, of those present, was, spontaneously and anxiously directed to the new comer.

"What is passing now?" I asked of a stranger.

"I dont know, citizen," answered he. "Possibly, it may be, the public papers that are expected."

"But, does the reading the public papers, put a stop to all conversation, at Avignon?"

"Ah! Nay, citizen, it is that—you understand,—when we dont know—"

"When we dont know what?" repeated I.

"Well, citizen, the events that have taken place at Paris, we dare not say too much about them—you see, there are people, who, having committed themselves, in Avignon, before they had learned the tenor of the public papers, have lost their heads on the scaffold. So folks are cautious, before they venture on a conversation, which events, may construe into a crime."

This explanation had scarcely been given, when the public papers arrived. One of the guests took and broke them open, mounted a chair, and commenced reading.

Scarcely had he cast his eyes upon the Journal, when he began to wave his hand in the air, shouting, "long live the mountain!" The silence which reigned, became still more intense; for that gesture and cry, must announce some important event. The audience scarcely breathed. In short, a little after, we learned the condemnation to death of the "twenty-one."

At the announcement of this triumph of the mountain, which clearly explained the position of affairs, the guests of the café, broke out into loud applause. It was but one cry of rage, against the federalists, whom they loaded with imprecations. In a word, fear transformed the guests of this café, into true cannibals.

Greatly disgusted with this spectacle, I soon rose, and, having paid my reckoning, went towards the door, shrugging my shoulders, with an air of contempt, which was observed by all the company. Not one of the guests dared to notice my gesture, or even to demand an explanation of it; and it was not till I had crossed the threshhold of the door, that a spontaneous cry against me, was raised throughout the café.

"Down with the moderate!· The coward runs away! To the lamp-post with the federalist!"

These vociferations made the blood rush to my heart. Letting go the door, which I held half open, I slowly turned towards my accusers, and, in a calm, firm voice, "citizens," said I, "I was going, because your proposals disgusted me, and not because I feared your presence. Since you appear to doubt my courage, I shall remain ten minutes longer at this table. If any one of you desire that I should cut off his ears, he will find me quite ready to accommodate him. I am waiting."

Upon hearing my impertinent challenge, a profound silence succeeded the clamour, and no one took up my glove.

While sitting in silence, I overheard one of my table companions say to another, "faith, my dear Fontaine, I am anxious to go away, only I am afraid that my doing so, may be interpreted by Scevola, as a mark of sympathy with the federalists."

"I want to go myself, Michaud," replied his companion, "and I am kept here by the same fear; for having refused to give Scevola credit yesterday, he has a spite against me."

"Suppose we avail ourselves of the departure of this officer, and thus escape?"

"You are right; that's a good idea."

This short, but expressive dialogue, confirmed my views, and proved to me that I was right, in attributing the ferocity of my neighbours to fear. Wishing to help them out of their difficulty, I rose from the table, and went again towards the door. They hastened to follow me, but their manœuvre did not answer their expectations. Scarcely had they got half across the café, than Scevola quitted his seat, and, taking Michand by the ear,

"Halt there, citizen," said he, in a sharp tone, "we want your voice, to celebrate the triumph of the mountain. You must remain here."

"But citizen," said Michand, turning pale, "I cannot thus lose my time, my business suffers."

"What do you say? Lose time? What means this want of respect, for us and the mountain? Remain here, I say, or beware."

"But citizen, I am free," cried Michand, "my time is my own."

"And this blow too! Nobody will doubt the propriety of it," said Scevola, who suiting the action to the word, struck the unhappy Michand a violent blow on the face, with his hand.

At this outrageous insult, Michand's face became crimsoned: and, turning to his aggressor,

"Scevola," said he, in a voice of reproach, "it is not reasonable, that, because I refused to give you credit for two ells of cloth, you should strike me thus."

"*You* refuse me credit, wretch!" Resumed Scevola, furious at this exposure, "you lie! If I struck you, it is because it amuses me. If I repeat it, it is for the same reason, and a second blow, more violent than the first, was struck upon the cheek of the merchant. The guests of the café, burst into frantic "bravo's," and cried, "long live Scevola!"

I was so indignant at this second outrage, that I was on the point of taking part with Michand, but he did not give me time, for, addressing Scevola, he said—

"Scevola, you are a scoundrel, I challenge you to fight."

"Fight! With you!" cried Scevola, laughing;" hear that, citizens! Michand wants to measure swords with me. Who will be his second?"

"Scevola," said Michand, "I see nothing to laugh at, in my proposition. I know very well that you are a duellist; but, do you accept my challenge?"

"Parbleu! Did I ever refuse a challenge, simpleton? Come, who are your seconds? Choose them carefully, for I warn you that, after I have done with you, they will have to take their turn."

"Citizens, who will accompany me?" asked Michand; but nobody answered him—the reputation of the terrible Scevola, was too menacing.

"If you will do me the honour to accept my assistance, I will do my best, to take care of your interest, citizen;" said I, breaking the silence.

"Ah sir, you are very good, and I thank you," cried the unhappy man, clasping my hand with fervour.

"Fear nothing, citizen," said I; "I have seen many man-killers, who kill nobody; they are bullies, who build their courage on the terror, with which they inspire their opponents before fighting; but, once sword in hand, and all that theatrical intrepidity evaporates, as by enchantment."

"Is that intended for me, citizen?" said Scevola.

"Precisely,"—said I, looking steadily in his eyes.

"Good!" said he; "we will resume this conversation afterwards."

" I hope so; let us set out."

The combat being determined on, it was resolved, at the request of Michand, who wished to get it over as soon as possible, that it should take place immediately, we therefore made an appointment to meet in half an hour, at one of the city gates. I went to our quarters to see if I could find Anselme, and to procure swords. Michand accompanied me. Anselme was gone out, and they could give me no clue where to follow him. As we had no time to lose, I took swords, and proceeded followed by the two merchants, towards the city gate, where we were to meet our opponent.

Scevola, attended by two knaves of his own cast, was already on the ground.

"You are alone, citizen," said he; "I dont see your second."

"And I here?" exclaimed Fontaine, advancing with a resolute look, which surprised me. Do you reckon me for nobody?"

"You!" answered Scevola, shrugging his shoulders; "a dealer in cotton and needles! You dont know what a duel is! But it matters little. The point for me is, first, to kill this beggarly coward, Michand, and afterwards, give a lesson to some one that I know,"

"If, citizen, Michand will consent to it, some one that you know, will be happy to take his place," said I to the hector.

"Not at all," answered he, "I am for doing things in the regular way. Michand is put first to open the dance."

So saying, Scevola threw his cloak behind him, and, showing his naked breast, "I dont like waiting," said he.

"Farewell, Fontaine," murmured the poor draper, mournfully, shaking hands with his friend. "It's all over."

The combatants being placed at the proper distance, I gave the signal, and they crossed swords. "I have no fear," said Michand, in an under tone,—"and yet, I feel as if I was going to swoon."

"Come, courage !" said I, briskly, "we are looking at you."

From the manner in which the unfortunate man held his sword, and the correct way in which Scevola fell into his guard, the issue of the combat could not be doubtful, and I made up in my mind to stop it, the first blood that was drawn. Scevola, with a beaming countenance, laid down the law.

"Michand," said he, "I will not touch you, without your knowing which is the pass that kills you. I will choose, in consequence of our former friendship, the most easy stroke to be parried. What we call, one, two—"

"What am I to do, citizen?" said Michand to me.

"Parry tierce and quart—that is to the left or right, or, vice versa, according as he attacks you, whether or without— arms—parry and thrust, as soon as you have met the sword of your opponent," said I to him.

"Parbleu," cried Scevola, breaking into a laugh, "this is a curious duel. I like your conversing with your second, and asking his advice. It is quite novel! It does not matter; what I have said, I will do. Attention, to the pass! Brave Michand. One—two—"

The hector thrust in, executing the announced motion, and the unfortunate Michand, uttering a piercing cry, fell to the ground, for the sword had gone through his body. I immediately flew to his assistance, and, raising him in my arms, tried to staunch the blood, which flowed from his wound.

As the combat had taken place behind one of the city gates, and the distance from them to the draper's shop, was not very great, I resolved, with the help of his friend, the mercer, to convey him, at once, to his house. The latter, as soon as the draper had received the fatal wound, appeared changed into a statue. Stiff, motionless, his eyes wide open, and his brows knit, his whole person presented the appearance of perfect abstraction.

"Fontaine," murmured Michand, in a feeble voice," wont you come to my help?"

At these words of his friend, he seemed to wake, as if, out of a dream.

"Did you call me, Michand?" cried he, pressing his hand before his eyes. "Be quiet,—the moment is come—you shall see."

"Fontaine then, slowly approached Scevola, who, since his triumph, had not ceased to jest, in an indecent manner, with his seconds, but the latter did not reply to him. He wiped his sword, although it presented no traces of blood.

Standing close to him, the mercer looked him in the face, with a ferocity, strangely in contrast with his habitual physiognomy, which, was rather void of energy. Then, in a voice, which foretold a storm,

"Citizen," demanded he. "is it to your skill, or, the chance of arms, that we must attribute your triumph?"

"Parbleu," said Scevola, "do you think then, you beggarly fop, that I have been a master at arms ten years for nothing?"

"So then, before fighting with Michand, you were sure of having the advantage of him?"

"Certainly, but take care; you begin to annoy me with your questions."

" Then, if you had that conviction, it is not a duel that you have fought. It is nothing more or less than—"

"That will do—assassination! What next?"

"That next!" And two smart blows, dealt by the mercer, with all his might, fell on the cheeks of the duellist. "Now take your sword, cowardly assassin! I thirst for your blood, and I cannot wait."

"Thus speaking, he seized the sword of poor Michand, and Scevola put himself on his guard. I at once perceived, by the paleness of his countenance, and the indecision of his movements, that he was no longer master of his actions.

Scarcely were the combatants face to face, when Fontaine, with an impetuosity which betrayed both his inexperience in arms, and his fury, blindly threw himself upon his enemy.

A few seconds later, the ex-master at arms, extended at full length on the ground—ejected torrents of blood from his mouth, in consequence of an inward wound, and was dead in a few minutes.

This second duel, so unexpected, took place so rapidly, that we had not time to interfere between the combatants. Never shall I forget the look of profound astonishment and stupefaction, reflected in the countenance of the pacific mercer, when he saw his adversary fall. His triumph appeared a thing so little, either possible or probable, that he could not believe the evidence of his eyes.

"What!" cried he at last, waving his bloody sword, "is it not more difficult than that, to be brave and kill a man! Ah, God of heaven! If I had known it sooner, what humiliations, what cowardice, anguish, and quaking I should have avoided!— Now, that I know what my anger is worth, woe to him who tries to frighten me! Ah! You knaves," continued he, intoxicated at the idea of his triumph, "you chuckled at seeing

Scevola sacrifice my poor Michand ; dare to laugh again, and I will slash your faces with my sword."

During the few minutes which had passed since he was wounded, the condition of the unfortunate Michand had grown so much worse, that when Fontaine came to find us, we gave up the idea of taking him home in our arms. I therefore went away, and entering the first house I came to, borrowed a mattress, and, assisted by some spectators, who had followed me, we laid him on it, and Fontaine and I proceeded to his house. I will not describe the anguish of the draper's wife on seeing the bloody body of her husband. After having received the thanks of Fontaine, who assured me that, in future, he would not suffer himself to be intimidated by the Scevolas, who so much abounded at that period in the cafés, and other places of public resort, and that he knew how to silence them. I returned to the rendezvous.

There I heard news, which the previous evening would have delighted me, but which now, after my appointment as adjutant, greatly displeased me. The representatives had stopped our battalion in its march upon Toulon, and decided that we should remain at Avignon, until the arrival of the recruits, who were expected to replace us in that garrison.

The soldiers, therefore, were lodged in barrack, and I, in company with Anselme, was billetted at the house of a man named Marcotte.

M. Marcotte was a stout man, of forty-five or fifty years of age. He received us with great urbanity, and invited us to dine with him the same day. We found at table fifteen guests, and the conversation at once turned upon the political events of the day.

All at once the door of the dining-room opened violently, and the same servant who had received us when we arrived, flung herself, out of breath, in the midst of us, exclaiming in a low voice,

"Gentlemen, here's your cousin coming up stairs."

At this announcement, which I could not understand, the conversation suddenly ceased as by enchantment, and a dead silence succeeded.

"Come, converse gentlemen, converse," said our host; "otherwise we shall awaken the suspicions of my cousin. Let us take the first subject that comes. Let's talk about the theatre."

Scarcely had Marcotte spoken, when the door opened a second time, and a new guest entered. I concluded that this must be the cousin announced, and I examined him with attention.

"Ah! Good day, cousin," cried our host, shaking him warmly by the hand, "what a long time it is since I saw you, nearly three days! It is not right to neglect thus, one's family and friends."

"What would you have, cousin? the business of the republic before all! My situation, as member of the committee of surveillance, allows me not a moment of repose."

"It appears that the infamous conspirators are at work?"

"Always! But woe to them, we watch them."

"So much the better: clap them in prison! They will only get what they deserve!" replied our host, affecting great gaiety, "faith, you come just in time;. we have been talking for an hour about women and actresses—that is just in your line, invincible Don Juan!"

This compliment seemed to greatly flatter the new comer, who began to smile with a foppish and mock-modest air; the more ridiculous, because in his person, he was the most perfect type of ugliness that one could imagine. With the leave of the reader, I shall devote a few lines to his portrait.

This cousin of our host might be about five feet, or five feet two, at the utmost in height. His meagre body was surmounted with an enormous head, covered with a thick mat of hair, of a reddish cast; his countenance presented an expression of low wickedness, which accorded perfectly with his unquiet eye, which was never fixed upon any object. It was impossible, on seeing him, even for the first time, to be deceived as to his character. I judged that his moral features were in complete harmony with his physical conformation.

The sequel proved to me, that my opinion was far from being erroneous; except that, whatever disagreeable and unfavourable impression this man had produced in me, I did not expect to discover in him the amazing depravity he afterwards displayed. This cousin of Marcotte's presented one of those monstrous types, which, too frequently, for the honour of humanity, were produced by the storm of 93.

Since the triumph of the revolution, this man had exchanged his christian names of Eugene Edward, for those of Pistache Carotte, which were derived from the new republican calendar. Scarcely was he seated at table, when he engrossed the whole conversation, and no one was heard to speak but himself.

He began by railing at the federalists then sung the praises of the mountain, and concluded by giving a rapid and scandalous sketch of the principal families of the city. 1 remarked, that not one woman found favour in his eyes; he reviled them all.

"What you are saying is not generous, cousin," cried our host, affecting to smile; "for, in fact, with all these women whom you accuse, the crime of most of them consists actually, in not being insensible to your merits. Really, you are a mischievous fellow!"

I saw by his leering look, that this reproach very agreeably flattered the little monster's self love.

"Faith," answered he, with the greatest impudence, "I find that the virtue and reputation of the women are not such sacred things, but that they can after a good dinner, offer them to their friends, by way of dessert.

"Take care, cousin; in thus following the example which your predecessors, Richelieu and Lauzan, have bequeathed to you, you will end by passing for an aristocrat."

"Oh, as to that, there is no danger. My patriotism is too well appreciated, for them to think of placing me in the list of all these court fops.

"What!" said I, in a low voice to Anselme, "can it be possible, that this hideous monster, has ever been able to attract the attention and affections of any woman? Our's is a melancholy and singular epoch, in which we cannot discriminate between beauty and deformity, vice and virtue.—"

"This Pistache," answered Anselme, in the same tone, "seems a knave, full of perversity, and cunning. I have not been a monk ten years of my life without knowing a little of hypocrisy and impudence; take my advice, and if he offers you his friendship, do not refuse it. You will find him a curious subject to analyze, and may, besides, turn the intimacy to the advantage of the unfortunate."

"You may be right," said I,—"leading a wandering life, I have no reason to fear the continuance of a disgraceful connexion. I will accept the confidence of Pistache, if it is offered."

My resolution, once formed, I frequently addressed myself to my future friend. This condescension on my part, seemed to flatter him, so much the more, as he had seen me observe an obstinate silence towards the other guests.

"Citizen," said he, when we quitted the table, "I hope, if your battalion remains some time in garrison in this city, that we shall often see each other. Come and dine with me, I will take you to see the house of confinement, which is just now placed under my inspection. There is some business in hand, you shall see!"

"What do you mean, by 'business in hand. ?"

"Oh, that's too long to explain ; we will talk of that at a future time. Fear nothing, you will not lose by waiting."

Citizen Pistache, after having clasped my hand, prepared to depart, when, changing his mind all at once :

" By the bye, citizen," said he, " I forgot that my time tomorrow will be occupied with a patriotic féte, which we are to give in the city; we will put off, if you please, our meeting till the following day."

" I am at your command. But what is this féte, which is to take place to-morrow ? I have not heard it spoken of."

" I easily believe you," replied my friend Pistache, laughing heartily,—" for that féte is just a surprise, which we are preparing in the city. Oh ! Dont trouble yourself ! It will open with such brilliancy, that you will not want twenty-four hours notice to induce you to take part in it. There will be pleasure for everybody."

CHAPTER III.

A would-be Don Juan.—A civic féte.—The feast of reason.—A mortal squeeze.—An auto da fe.—Saving a relic.—Character and doings of Pistache.—Constituents of the revolutionary committee.—The house of detention at Avignon.—Pistache out-witted, and out-bullied.—Escape of his victim.—Great news.—General Hypocrisy.—Departure from Avignon.—A conspirator.—Arrival at Fayence.

After the departure of cousin Pistache, there was not one voice raised in his favour: the strife was, who should most blacken his character.

" My dear adjutant," said Marcotte, drawing me aside, " I have a favour to ask of you."

" Speak, I am at your command."

" I have noticed during dinner, that my cousin Pistache, seduced, probably, by the brilliancy of your epaulet, and proud of forming an alliance with an officer of the republic, has loaded you with civilities, and I have no doubt, that he will finish by making a league with you! Now, as my relative is very curious and inquisitive, he will pester you with questions about my domestic affairs, and he might, if your answers implied any deficiency in regard to my patriotism, injure me considerably. Do me, therefore, the favour to answer, that you have never before met with a more pure and genuine patriot than I! That every night, I regret that the day has not witnessed the fall of more heads; and that I foam with rage at the nobles who emigrate, and priests who refuse the oath."

" But," said I, interrupting my host, " you wish then to pass for a monster, in the eyes of your cousin ?"

" You dont yet know my cousin. The infamies which I ask you to attribute to me, constitute virtues in his eyes! If he takes me for the villain that I make myself, I am a saved man! If not, I shall be in great danger!"

" What! Do you think your cousin capable of denouncing you?"

" He! If he were to meet with some scoundrel, who would give him false information respecting me, and whom he could subpœna to give evidence against me, I am certain that he would not let the opportunity escape of destroying me."

" The citizen Pistache is then a true Brutus!"

"Alas! My dear sir, he only obeys the envy and hatred of which his heart is full; the patriotism, of which he makes a parade, is only a tool in his hands; in private, he ridicules the republic, and would to-morrow, if royalty triumphed, become *a reactionary as ardent*, as he is to day, a fiery patriot! may I reckon upon your goodness to misrepresent me to him ?"

" I will do so! But how did this hatred originate, that your cousin shows towards society? Had he any reason before the revolution to complain of it ?"

" You have just put your finger upon the wound. The ambition of my cousin has always been, to pass for a seducer. Now you may easily imagine, how many checks and humiliations he experienced, and seeing that his ridiculous pretensions were repulsed, with the disdain they deserved, he ended by professing a shameful cynicism, which soon laid him under the ban of society. Not willing to have the appearance of yielding to this universal reprobation, he collected around him, all the men of vile character in Avignon, and thanks to his fortune, which he dissipated with a kind of furious rage, he has at last become the hero of this unclean circle. This senseless prodigality very soon reduced him to distress, and he found himself utterly abandoned. His resources exhausted, he probably contemplated suicide, when the revolution broke out. Judge what must have been his joy! He immediately set about taking his revenge upon that society, which had driven him from its precincts. It is unnecessary to add that he became a furious patriot. Organizing insurrections, directing pillage, haranguing the multitude, he soon acquired that prodigious popularity, which he now enjoys, and abuses. From that period to the present, Pistache, although ruined, has found means to lead a sumptuous life. As to the resources he has at his disposal, I neither know, nor desire to know, what they are!"

" Do you know, that after the portrait you have given of your cousin, it will be difficult for me to connect myself with him."

"You will do wrong to repulse his advances," said Marcotte, quickly. " The most respectable people in the city are happy when Pistache will even permit them to touch his hand."

The day after this conversation with my host, I was leaning upon the window-sill, observing with sadness, the dull and silent aspect which the city of Avignon presented, when, all at once, I thought I heard the lugubrious sound of the Tocsin.

I was not deceived! Soon, furious cries became mingled with the brazen sounds, and I saw a multitude, which seemed in a delirium, covering the recently deserted streets.

I was immediately about to abandon my post, to render myself at the quarter, when a singular spectacle nailed me to my window. In the midst of the crowd, which thus howled, elevated upon a table, upon which also were several sans-culottes, was a kind of hideous dwarf, raised upon the shoulders of his companions, who, kicking, yelling, and gesticulating like a maniac, seemed to direct the movement. Enthusiastic acclamations followed his words.

This man was citizen Carotte Pistache, my new friend!

"Ah!" said he, as he passed before the window where I stood, and saluted me,—"you see I did not deceive you yesterday, in promising you a fine fête the next day! Come with us; it is the ex-good-God of the ex-scullcaps who pays all the expense! We are going to have a jolly row!"

Puzzled, and surprised at the appearance of this popular avalanche, I put on my uniform, and hastened to the quarter, where I might be wanted. I found the troops assembled in the barracks, without any orders to take arms.

The adjutant-major, whom I met, came up to me laughing, "Well, colleague," said he, "what do you think of the fête?"

"What fête?"

"The *feast of reason,* which the sovereign people are celebrating; they are now plundering the churches."

"Ah! Is that what you call the 'feast of reason'?"

"Exchange it, if you will, for the triumphs of philosophy over prejudices! It amounts to the same thing. Will you accompany me?"

"Thank you, I have some matters to finish. I will rejoin you by and by."

I was about returning home, when I perceived Anselme, who was turning the corner of the street. Seeing me, he ran towards me.

"You know, Alexis, that I am a good republican," said he, hastily,—"well, upon my honour, I regret that all these wearers of cloaks have not one head, that I might have the satisfaction of crushing it at one blow of my fist! I cannot express the rage I feel, in seeing all these ferocious brutes destroy, with savage howlings, those sacred objects, which from our earliest infancy, we are habituated to respect and venerate! I cannot express the pleasure it would give me, to be able to knock some of them down!—Come along with me!"

"Where will you go?"

"To seek a quarrel with some one, to calm my nerves."

After five minutes walking, we were stopped by a compact crowd, which encumbered the steps of a church they were then pillaging. Anselme did not think of retracing his steps. Placing himself before me, he set to work with his elbows and shoulders, with such energy that the crowd immediately opened before us, and cleared us a passage. We soon penetrated into the sacred enclosure.

Never shall I forget the hideous and vile spectacle which presented itself to my view. Picture to yourself demons in rags, and overcome with drink, who, with blasphemy on their lips, and intoxication in their eyes, rushed with sacrilegious fury against the altar, tearing, and treading under foot, with hoarse cries of triumph, the sacred ornaments that decorated it, and braying in chorus, the dismal "*Ca ira*," that song of assassins, which has accompanied the agony of so many victims! Other *sans-culottes*, armed with hatchets, and mounted on ladders, loosened, and threw down upon the ground the statues of the saints, placed about the church. Some of them also amused themselves by breaking the painted glass of the gothic windows. It was a noise, a tumult, a confusion, without a name, and too hideous for description.

"This is what they call the feast of reason!" said Anselme.

We were going to withdraw, when a sans-culotte, whose costume, or to speak more properly, *absence* of costume, certainly justified the title, stopped before us, brandishing a crucifix, and preventing us from passing, compelled us to hear one of those strange speeches, rendered so common in those days, by the most profound ignorance, united to the most unbridled impudence.

"Long live liberty, the guillotine, and fraternity," said he at the end of his harangue, addressing himself particularly to Anselme. "Let us embrace, citizen."

On saying this, the sans-culotte wanted to throw his arms round the neck of my companion, to give him the fraternal embrace; but Anselme repulsed him with a gentleness and moderation which astonished me,

"I have listened to you, citizen, without interruption," said he, quietly, "because it might be that you had something serious or sensible to demand of me, or to teach me. You have, therefore, no reason to complain. As to embracing you, not perceiving what use it will be, either to you or me, and as you are frightfully dirty, you will allow me to decline it, and to continue my walk."

"You are an aristocrat?" cried the sans-culotte furiously.

"Not the least in the world! But there is no necessity, that I know of, to soil oneself by contact with a wine-bottle, picked out of the mud!"

"Is it thus that you treat the people? Take care! If you refuse to fraternize with me. I will have you hanged up at the lamp-post."

"There is no answering that fraternal argument," said Anselme, with an air of submission that I could not understand. "Let us embrace, since you require it."

My comrade then extended his arms to the sans-culotte, who, delighted at having compelled a soldier to obey him, threw himself into them, crying, "liberty for ever."

"Take care then, you stifle me," murmured the sans-culotte, after a hug of some seconds, his countenance turning quite crimson.

"Every one has his own way of embracing," answered Anselme, "for my part, I make conscience of all that I do."

Although not a muscle moved in the physiognomy of Anselme, I saw at once, by the flashing of his countenance, that he was under the influence of intense anger; "Now then, comrade," said I, striking him gently on the arm,—"leave that drunkard, and come with me, I long to be out of this tumult."

Anselme made no reply. I saw by his fixed and burning eye, that he no longer even knew me, his fury having absorbed all his faculties.

Then passed a scene, which, were I to live a hundred years, would not be erased from my memory, although it lasted only five or six seconds. Anselme, his eyebrows contracted, his nostrils extended, and his upper lip raised, recovered from his immobility of position. By a gesture, slow, but indicative of terrible force, he clasped the body of the sans-culotte against his breast, then raising it in the air, he all at once opened his arms, and let him fall a motionless corpse upon the ground! As for myself, it appeared to me, when he gave him that fatal hug, that I heard the sound of breaking bones. I cannot express the agitation I felt.

"Come, my dear friend, let us set out," said Anselme to me, in the most peaceable tone,—"my nerves are now much better."

As at least three-fourths of the people who had desecrated the church, were in a state of complete intoxication, and involved in an indescribable hubbub, from the altar to the portal, no one paid the least attention to the fall of the sans-culotte, and we withdrew without being molested.

Two hours after, a new scene of disorder threw the whole city into alarm. Those who had pillaged the church, having brought the product of their devastation upon the grand square of Avignon, had constructed of them an immense pile, to which it was intended at night to set fire. When it was dark the auto-da-fé commenced.

Anselme, who, since his episode of embracing, was become more calm, looked on unmoved; once only he seemed to lose his presence of mind, on seeing a statue of Saint Dominic thrown into the flames.

We were retiring, when the noise, arising from a dispute, which took place near us, attracted our attention.

"Let's go, and see what's the matter," said Anselme.

It was a young girl, poorly clad, but possessing great beauty, who, pale as a corpse, and so much agitated that she could not speak, was exposed to the threats of some viragoes. A man with a decent exterior, although wearing a rusty cloak, was taking her part, with more zeal than success, when we arrived.

"There! Silence Mothers!" cried Anselme, in a tone which overpowered the noise of the dispute, as much as the roar of a cannon would do the smart crack of a musket. "Silence! And explain to us mildly! Why are you so exasperated against this young woman? What have you to charge her with?"

"What has she done?" exclaimed one of the scolds.—"She has abstracted one of these church toys, upon which, the good patriots are now executing justice!"

"Is that true, citizen?" asked Anselme of the young girl.

"Yes citizen," replied she, in a voice scarcely intelligible,—"it is true!"

"Is it a thing of any value?"

"Here it is," said the poor child, shewing us a small relic.

"Why, that is not worth twopence! cried Anselme, turning towards the old woman. "What harm is there in the citizen's taking away this trifle?"

"We don't pretend that that action is a crime," replied the

old woman ! "Let the citizen tell us what motive has induced her to act as she has done ; then, let her trample this relic under her feet, and we will leave her at quiet."

"I have taken up this relic, to preserve it from the outrages of the crowd," answered the girl, raising her voice; "as to committing the sacrilege that they demand, I should prefer death."

There was so much dignity in the tone of this reply, that I felt quite moved.

"Come!" cried Anselme, "here's too much time lost about this trifle ; the dancing is begun, who will give me her hand?" So saying, he took the two harpies who seemed the most bitter against the young girl ; and, whirling them round with an irresistible force, waltzed them off.

"My dear young lady," said I to the girl who had so resolutely saved the relic, at the risk of her life,—"will you allow me to escort you to the door of your house ; for, in such a night as this, it will be imprudent for you to cross the city alone."

"I thank you sir," answered she, blushing ; "I have a companion with me."

She then pointed out to me the man with the rusty cloak, whom we had seen taking her part, and who, upon her making a sign to him, came up and offered her his arm.

Seeing that the child did not require my services, I was going away, when all at once, her companion uttered an exclamation of terror, and letting fall her arm, which he already held, he seemed to wish to take flight.

Looking forward to ascertain what might be the cause of so sudden an alarm, I perceived the hero of the fête, my friend Pistache Carotte, coming round to our side. At the same moment, the young girl and her guardian commenced a rapid flight.

"Ah the beauty! Is it me you are thus flying from? cried Pistache, at that instant, attempting to pursue the fugitives.

"Stop citizen," said I, seizing him forcibly by the arm, "I wont let you see that young girl."

"You will not," repeated Pistache, in a half-pleasant, half-serious tone, "Do you know that you express yourself with a remarkable authority?"

"An authority imparted by jealousy. If you offend me, so much the worse for you. I despise your anger. I repeat that I will not allow you to see that young girl, and you shall not see her."

"Ah then, it is a suspected person who conceals herself."

"No. On the contrary, it is I who conceals her! Oh, you may well assume your innocent looks, citizen Pistache, I know you too well, not to have reason to be jealous.

Upon hearing this declaration, Carotte Pistache smiled with a ridiculous expression of simplicity. "Fear nothing," said he, in a patronizing tone,—"the list of my victims is sufficiently well filled up, that I do not require you to add another name—it would be a grain of sand in the desert."

He put his arm within mine, and invited me to his house. It was easy for me to perceive that he was under the influence of liquor, and I rejoiced at this discovery, which promised a greater freedom on his part.

The apartment occupied by Pistache, was situated in one of the oldest houses, of one of the least frequented streets of Avignon. "Truly citizen," said I, after having mounted the dark, narrow, and tortuous staircase, which conducted to his den,—"I am astonished that one of the elect of the people can lodge in such a paltry room."

"Don't you see, that my profession, being that of a patriot, I should be lost to morrow, if I were drawn in to follow the example of those whom I oppose. It is essential for the people to believe, that, in defending their rights I defend my own;

that in revenging them, I revenge myself also, in a word, that our interests are identical. From hence alone, springs the confidence I enjoy. This dark and dilapidated lodging, the miserable and comfortless appearance of which alarms you, serves to conceal my private life and personal inclinations, as the ragged mantle of Diogenes served to hide his pride. But make yourself easy. In spite of these cracked walls, these dark and narrow windows, my lodgings are not so destitute of all resources as they appear to be. Saying this, citizen Pistache pushed a spring hid in the wall; a door opened immediately, and I beheld the most wanton boudoir one can imagine, and worthy in every respect, of the most luxuriant ci-devant. An alabaster lamp, suspended from the ceiling, threw over a rich velvet furniture, disposed with perfect taste, a soft and quiet light, which gave a stamp of elegance to this mysterious *retiro*.

" You see," said citizen Pistache, "that I am not so miserable, and so much to be pitied, as you would believe. Let us drink to the health of my amours!"

The member of the revolutionary committee then drew from a magnificent sideboard, a decanter, and placing two glasses of the purest crystal before us, he filled them with a delicious liqueur.

"To the health of my amours!" repeated he, in a hoarse voice, which betrayed a recent debauch. "You were afraid to night," he continued, "that I was going to deprive you of your conquest. Ah! My poor friend, how little you know of me! That woman whom you withdrew from my notice, was some young and pretty grisette, was she not?"

"You have guessed right."

"Well! My dear adjutant, know, for your future government, that a girl of the people, were she endowed with the most fabulous beauty that ever existed on the earth, would obtain from me neither look nor smile! You appear surprised! Now, if you knew the history of my youth,—in fact, why should you not, I will relate it to you?"

"You will afford me a great pleasure."

"When I was young, do you see, my greatest defect was vanity, and the love of unbridled luxury. You will readily conceive that, with such inclinations, I attempted to introduce myself into high society, to form liasons with the handsome and proud dames, whose elegant immoralities were no mystery to anybody. Well! Would you believe it? These women treated me with an insulting indifference. They ridiculed my vows, and my prayers, and made sport of my passion. These insults, instead of for ever destroying my hopes, rendered these women more handsome in my estimation, and my love for them,—a love full of fury and spite,—increased even to madness. I resolved on vengeance."

"You will readily comprehend with what joy I hailed the first symptoms that announced the revolution; with what feverish ardour I threw myself into the first struggle, and with what fury I fought. At last, victory has come, and I now take my revenge upon the past. The people think me a great man, and cite me as a model of patriotism! I don't befool them badly! What I most delight in, is to see those proud women, with whom I was formerly a ridiculous and presumptuous clown, now tremble on their knees before me, and ask mercy! You cannot have an idea of the fierce luxury I enjoy in humbling those haughty dames. Making them pass through all the alternations of hope and despair, I incessantly hold over their heads, a cleaver and a smile. Let us drink again to my new amours."

The frightful monster filled our glasses a second time; and dissimulating the deep horror with which he inspired me, I drank with him the toast that he had proposed.

"But citizen," said I,—"how is it that these incarcerated

aristocrats,—for I think you have spoken of those ladies,—can have recourse to you, and implore your protection? I should conceive that, by your position, you can do much harm, but not repair that which is done? You have certainly the power to send a head to the scaffold, but not of depriving it of a victim!"

"Am I not a member of the revolutionary committee?"

"Certainly; but you are not *the* revolutionary committee. You represent only one voice."

"You do not know the composition of this committee. Shall I tell it you?"

"Faith, that would give me great pleasure."

"Well then! Listen to me. You shall see that I can act according to my caprice. But stop,—to give you an idea of my power, there is a young *ci-devant*, the daughter of the Ex-Marquis de R——, known by all Avignon for her beauty, and hypocrisy, or virtue,—for it is the same thing,—who is considered haughty and proud to an excess. It is now near a week since I had her father incarcerated; will you bet a hundred livres with me that, to-morrow night, the superb Amelie will not be at supper tete-à-tete with me? Say, will you?"

"Let us leave this aristocrat, who possesses no interest with me," replied I,—" and return to the revolutionary committee, of which you make a part."

"Our revolutionary committee," resumed Pistache, "reckons nine members, including myself. Four of these are absolutely fit for nothing, but to say yes or no; and to do this, they wait for the example of their colleagues. I can make them cry as I please, 'Long live the tricolor flag,' or, 'Long live the Fleur-de lis!' 'Long live the republic,' or, 'Long live absolute monarchy!' These four votes are at my service, and insure the fulfilment of all my wishes. As to the rest, one of them would be, perhaps a great republican, if he was not influenced by a rapacious avarice; he may detest the aristocrats, but I am sure that no person appreciates their gold better than he. We know before hand, the price he sets upon an enlargement, an arrest, a permission to visit, or speak to a prisoner, or to take off the seal."

"But if that is known, how can he both indulge this avarice and retain his place, and the confidence of the people?"

"He pursues the aristocrats to the uttermost, arrests, incarcerates, and guillotines with unparallelled zeal, and that suffices to keep up his popularity. Let me recapitulate; here are the four imbeciles whom I lead at will, the miser whom I know how to govern by his interest, and then myself; that makes six votes out of nine, at my disposal. You see then, in fact, that I am the sole and only master of the city, and that, when I cry, 'Long live the revolution!' It is absolutely as if I cried 'Long live Pistache Carotte Marcotte!'"

"Truly citizen, it is impossible to applaud your arrangements too highly. Now, allow me to take my leave of you, for it is late, and you have need of repose."

"Farewell! I expect you to-morrow without fail. Do you promise me to come?"

"Certainly I do."

I then hastened down the staircase into the street, and was glad to breathe the pure night air.

The next day I was on duty at the head quarters, when the great patriot Pistache Carotte enquired for me.

"My dear friend," said he, with some embarrassment, "I am come to take you to dine with me. The revolutionary committee have invited you to a grand banquet, at which they will meet to day. You cannot refuse. I have spoken to your commander, and he has given you leave till to-morrow. Come along!"

As soon as we were away from the quarters, citizen Pistache reverted to the conversation of the previous evening. I judged by his ambiguous questions, that he reproached himself with his own imprudence. I pretended not to perceive his fears, and took care, by my replies, to calm his uneasiness.

"I must now take my turn at the house of confinement," said he; "Come with me, I will not detain you long."

The house of detention at Avignon had formerly been a convent of Cordeliers. It contained, closely stowed together, about two hundred prisoners.

"Do you see that statue of Saint Francis there, over the gate?" said Pistache,—"it was I who had his head cut off. I consider that symbol excellent and significant. The sight of it recalls to the incarcerated, the lot that awaits them."

We then entered a vaulted vestibule, terminated by an iron grating.

My companion was then announced from within. I amused myself in examining the prison. I found myself alone, in the middle of an immense corridor. Seeing the pretty little blonde head of a child, who was squatted in an obscure angle; I smiled kindly at him, and beckoned him with a friendly sign of my hand. The child, after hesitating a few seconds, approached me; his fear subsiding, he began to play with the scabbard of my sabre.

"Ah my friends, you may come out—the soldier is not wicked!" cried he.

On this appeal, a dozen young children of both sexes, who had kept squatted in the recess of the windows, appeared suddenly, and surrounded me with childish curiosity.

"How did you come here, my little friends," asked I.

"It was because our parents were not wise," answered the eldest amongst them.—"They have put them in prison, and they allow us to come and play here in this corridor during the day."

"My mamma is very good," cried a little girl,—"you won't kill her, citizen soldier, with your sabre?"

"No my child, fear nothing," answered I, with emotion,—"we will do no harm to your dear mamma."

"Oh how good you are!" cried the poor child, throwing herself upon my neck.

The sight of these unfortunate children made me sick. I hastened to leave them, and again descended into the street. I was walking backwards and forwards before the prison, when a mild and trembling voice addressed me, and broke in upon my sad reflections. "In the name of heaven, sir, procure me the means of seeing my father!"

I started, and raising my eyes, I saw before me, with her hands clasped, and her eyes filled with tears, the most delightful person the imagination could picture. "Ah! Is it you citizen?" cried I, with astonishment at recognizing the young girl who, the evening before, had been insulted by the crowd on account of the relic, and was saved by Anselme.

"You sir!" cried she on her part.—"Ah it is God who has sent you! You may render me the greatest service,—forgive me," said she, immediately stopping,—"I forgot that you are the friend of citizen Pistache."

"It is a great honour undoubtedly mademoiselle, to pass for a bandit. Fear nothing; true, I know citizen Pistache, but I do not hold with his opinions. Believe me, that if it is in my power to be of any service to you or yours, I will not let the opportunity escape."

"Ah sir! If you knew all! The life of my father, and consequently my own, depend on the will of citizen Pistache."

"And why not address citizen Pistache himself, citizen?" said a rough voice at our side.

I turned round and saw Pistache who fixed an ardent gaze on the young girl.

"Ah!" said he, laughing maliciously,—"I did not know that you had such noble acquaintances. Is this the grisette, about whom, you showed yourself so jealous last night?"

"To day is the first time I have had the honour of seeing mademoiselle; I do not even know her name."

"Then allow me to introduce to you," said Pistache, affecting to assume the air of a man of the world,—" Mademoiselle R— the daughter of the Marquis of R— one of the present residents of the house of detention."

"Mademoiselle," said I, bowing to the lovely and timorous creature, "lay aside your fears! The citizen member of the revolutionary committee is much more compassionate than he would have you suppose, and will do himself a pleasure in protecting you in your misfortunes."

"In fact," cried Pistache, "the citizen knows, that for a long time I have expected her visit. She has only to fix the day and the hour that is agreeable to her, and she may depend on finding me at home. However, I recommend dispatch, for to-morrow the revolutionary committee will bring the affair of the marquis to a termination."

"Ah! Citizen," cried the young girl with heartfelt emphasis,—" my poor father is innocent."

"A ci-devant is never innocent!" said Pistache coarsely, interrupting her. "As to your father,—I doubt whether he will escape with his head!"

At these fearful words, the young girl became pale as a corpse. "What am I to do? What will become of me, citizen?" cried she, in a supplicating voice, and raising her eyes, filled with tears, the expression of which would have disarmed a tiger.

"You must not lose so much time as you have done," answered he sharply,—"but call upon me immediately. I am too busy to talk with you now. I shall be at home to night from eight to ten o'clock. See that you are punctual."

Twenty times, while the villain spoke, was I upon the point of rushing upon him and treating him as he deserved. The thought alone, that this violence could only aggravate the position of the Marquis of R—— retained me. As to his devoted child, she bore the insult with heroic resignation, and betrayed only by a deep blush, the poignant emotion she felt.

"You don't answer me," said Pistache, taking me by the arm, and preparing to go,—" Must I expect you to-morrow?" The young girl started; then giving me a singular look, she answered Pistache, to my astonishment, in a calm voice,— "To night, at eight o'clock at your house!"

"I knew it well!" murmured the member of the revolutionary committee, with a sneer. "Ah! These ex-great ladies are all alike; they all have their price."

Ten minutes after, Pistache Carotte presented me to his colleagues, as being one of the most distinguished and efficient officers of the army, and one of the purest of patriots. They received me with marked distinction.

In the absence of cheerfulness, the dinner went off with animation; we talked only of politics. The siege of Toulon, the army of Italy, and that of the north, the convention, Robespierre, Danton, the Jacobins, Chaumette Hebert, and the revolutionary tribunal, were all subjects of our conversation.

At the hour of the sitting the party then rose, and I was about to withdraw, when Pistache, seizing me by the arm, said, "I arrest you as a deserter! I shall not let you thus go in quest of the pretty aristocrat! I am not such a fool! You must go with me to the sitting!"

"But I have not the honour of being your colleague, and cannot intrude myself into the hall of your conferences."

"Undoubtedly you can; we always deliberate in public."

Not wishing to awaken his suspicions, I followed him without further entreaty.

Whilst the committee were discharging their duties, I employed myself in turning over the leaves of a large register placed before me; it was the journal of the criminal processes. I noticed that the form adopted by this tribunal, was as expeditious as it was simple, and admirably calculated to furnish a rapid succession of victims to the guillotine.

Two things struck me in looking over the register,—the first, that at the morning sittings, the same facts were more severely judged than they were at the sittings after dinner; the second, that whenever they had not material evidence, whatever might be the offence, the accused were simply sent to the house of detention; but that, as soon as they had obtained written proofs, they were turned over to the committee of public safety.

Taking advantage of the excitement occasioned by a very serious denunciation brought before the committee, I managed to make my escape, without being perceived by Pistache, and concealed myself in an obscure cabaret. My intention was, to remain perdu till evening, and then to waylay the daughter of the Marquis of R—— as she was proceeding to her rendezvous, to apprize her of the peril she incurred, and to offer her my disinterested services.

I was absorbed in my own reflections, when a light knock at the door of the room I occupied, recalled me to the reality, and stopped my dreaming.

My first thought was, that Pistache had discovered my temporary retreat, and was come to sound my intentions. I resolved to treat him with the contempt he deserved.

"Come in," cried I, at a second knock. The door opened softly, and a shadow seemed to glide towards me.

"Who are you?" I resumed, rising quickly.

K

"The daughter of the Marquis of R——," answered a trembling voice, which I at once recognised as that of the young Amelie. She fell, rather than seated herself, in the chair I offered, and immediately began speaking: "I cannot yet understand how I have been able to muster courage enough to take the step I have done," said she, in a confused voice, and casting down her eyes.—"The imminent danger to which my father is exposed has alone impelled me."

"Forgive me, mademoiselle, but how have you discovered that I was sheltered here?"

"I have followed you all the day," she replied. "I am aware sir, that my presence here is a serious imprudence; but alas! the times of disaster and overthrow in which we live are my apology. I will not abuse your patience. A few words will suffice to explain myself. This morning I intended to repel, with all the indignation and horror it deserved, the proposition of Pistache, when, from the feeling of pity I thought I read in your eyes, I was led to hope that heaven had sent in you, a protector for my poor father and myself. Perhaps, thought I, this young man who seems to pity me, has a sister, and will, for her sake, grant me his protection."

"You have not deceived yourself mademoiselle," cried I with warmth;—"I am devoted to your service. Tell me, what must I do?"

"Accompany me to the house of citizen Pistache, and swear to me upon your honour, that you will answer for that of my family."

"I swear to you in the name of my sisters, mademoiselle," cried I, with enthusiasm.—"It is now striking eight o'clock, let us set off."

During the long walk to the house of Pistache, mademoiselle R—— related to me her history, which was very simple. Her father, the Marquis of R——, confiding in his innocence, had not thought of emigrating. But soon, from the abominable excesses which pervaded all France, he found that he had deceived himself, and his resolution was altered; but it was then too late; the highways were watched, the most severe orders issued, and it was impossible for him to escape. In short, within a month from that period, his house was invested by a horde of savages, who, after having pillaged every thing, brought the marquis himself a prisoner. His daughter, who by good fortune was staying at the house of a sick old aunt, remained at liberty.

" To relate to you now sir," said the young lady, "the proceedings I have adopted, the humiliations, incessantly recurring, to which I have had to submit, would be beyond my power. Had it not been for the encouragements held out to me by an old priest, an ancient friend of my family, whom I had the good fortune to meet with, and who, although proscribed like my father, forgot his own danger, to assist me in my solicitations, I feel that I should not have had the courage to support existence much longer! My intention was, to present myself at a public sitting of the revolutionary committee, and cry—' Vive le roi!' for the purpose of being incarcerated."

" Forgive me mademoiselle," said I then,—"for a question which must be painful to you: but tell me what has been up to this period, your knowledge of Pistache?"

" Citizen Pistache," replied she, after a momentary silence, "was not unknown to me before the revolution."

" What! Was he received into the house of the marquis your father?"

" Never received in any respect," answered she, with a dignity which charmed me;—"it is true, that he came many times to the chateau on business. Here is involved a confession that is painful to me to make, but I will not hide anything from you. The last time that he set his foot in the chateau,

I went into my father's library whilst he was there. The sight of him caused in me a movement of disgust, which I had not the presence of mind to conceal, and which he undoubtedly remarked. Judge what must be my confusion, when the following day I received a letter from the miserable wretch!"

" A threatening letter undoubtedly ?"

"Alas! No sir, a love letter! He had observed the disagreeable impression his appearance had made on me, he said, but he was willing to wait, and hoped everything from the future! He finished by adding, that the times were stormy, and that the support of a devoted heart and a valiant arm was not a thing to be despised during the tempest."

" What did the marquis your father say to it ?"

" He never knew of that letter. When a daughter receives such undeserved insults, she should know how to hide them from her father! For myself,—this insult appeared so gratuitous, so destitute of common sense, that I soon lost the recollection of it."

" Ah! I understand the rest! The revolution arrived."

"Alas! Yes sir, and M. Marcotte, become citizen Pistache-Carotte, the most influential member of the revolutionary committee, was not slow to avenge himself for the contempt that I had shown him, by causing my poor father to be incarcerated."

"Fear nothing mademoiselle," cried I with warmth, " a being so vile as citizen Pistache, can never be courageous! If he rejects my requests, I will have recourse to force! I have determined to liberate your father, and he shall be free !"

" Ah! Sir," answered the young lady with a softened voice, "may God reward you for your generosity. I accept your aid!"

We had now arrived before the dwelling of Pistache. A dim ray of light, glancing through the interstices of the casement, apprised us that the wretch already awaited his victim.

We ascended the stairs, and I knocked gently and mysteriously at the door of the formidable member of the revolutionary committee.

"Who's there?" cried the voice of citizen Pistache.

"It is I, the citizen Amelie," answered mademoiselle R—— immediately. A key grated in the lock, and the door opened.

" Enter citizen," said Pistache, "only try another time to display a little more punctuality,—a little more of the respect due to a member of the revolutionary committee!"

Pistache, while speaking thus, stood before the door, in order to make mademoiselle R—— submit to the humiliation of remaining standing before him ; he then withdrew to leave her a free passage. Profiting by this movement, I came out of the dark corner where I had hidden myself, and softly pushing mademoiselle R——before me, I entered at once into the apartment. At the sight of me, Pistache appeared struck with astonishment, but his stupefaction soon gave way to wrath.

" What do you here, brigand!" cried he, advancing fiercely towards me. Be off without delay, or beware of my vengeance."

Instead of replying, I sharply shut the door, and double locked it ; then putting the key in my pocket, I crossed my arms and looked sternly at him. He turned pale.

" Ah! Ah!"—resumed he, affecting to laugh in a blustering manner,—"I see you are in a jesting humour this evening—you want to mystify me—go, there's enough of that ; I have to talk with the citizen respecting a matter which concerns the safety of the republic! Do me the pleasure to leave us alone as quickly as possible."

"My sweet and excellent friend," answered I quietly,—" I am ready to comply with your wish—on two conditions."

"Explain yourself quickly," answered he, assuming a serious air ; what do you want?"

" Two very simple things. First, that mademoiselle R.——

retires as she has come, that is, with me,—secondly—that you sign an order for the liberation of her father."

"Really, you are exceedingly modest! It is impossible to find a more disinterested person than yourself!"

"Most delectable Pistache, my time is precious, and in spite of the charms of your conversation, I can't consecrate more than five minutes longer to you. Do me the pleasure to answer me categorically; do you accept my ultimatum, yes or no?"

"Ah, miserable serpent! cried Pistache, grinding his teeth, "do you dare to beard the lion in his den? I will soon fetch those who will punish your temerity."

"Citizen Pistache," said I, looking him in the face,—"I warn you, that if you attempt to leave this room, I will kill you like a mad dog, as you are!"

"This is then an ambush, an assassination!" cried he, casting on me a look of fear.

"Call it what you choose,—but the only part that remains for you, is, first to sign the order of enlargement that I require, and to leave me afterwards to depart in peace!"

"Sign that order! Never! I would rather cut my hand off!"

"Between the sacrifice of your hand, and that of your life, there's a wide difference."

"What do you mean by that?" cried he, whilst a nervous trembling seized his whole frame. "Would you assassinate me?"

"We *kill* venomous reptiles, not *assassinate* them."

"Then your intention, if I refuse to obey you, is to kill me."

"Yes citizen, that is my intention."

"Sir, I entreat you," cried mademoiselle R—— now, for the first time taking up the conversation; but I interrupted her, without giving her time to continue.

"Mademoiselle," said I, your intervention at this moment

can have no effect upon my resolution; will you be good enough to leave me alone an instant with my honourable friend. Our conversation has arrived at a point, at which the presence of a female is no longer possible. Wait for me on the stairs : I will rejoin you immediately."

Saying this, I grasped the hilt of my sabre, and opening the door, made a determined sign with my head to mademoiselle R—— to go out. She obeyed.

"Never shall I forget the deep and hideous expression of terror, reflected on the countenance of citizen Pistache, when we found ourselves alone, and face to face. Yet, after a few seconds, having reflected, he appeared more at ease.

"Citizen," said he,—"I think, that in order to finish this scene, which threatens to become ridiculous, we must endeavour to be a little more reasonable. What service will my death be of to you, what benefit will you derive from it? Nothing whatever! My being dead would not prevent the ex-ci-devant Marquis R—— from remaining in prison, or being judged and executed. Now I will take another view of the case. Having discussed the utility and opportunity of my death, let us see what will be the consequences of it. First, if I do not deceive myself, it will produce amongst the patriots, a vehement desire of vengeance! Before four and twenty hours you will be identified as the author of the crime. Eight and forty hours after, your head will roll on the scaffold ! What answer do you make to that ?"

"A very simple one, my dear Pistache. First, if you were no longer in this world, the Marquis de R——, whom I have resolved to save, would possess one enemy less. There will be then a chance, by putting in play all the influence we possess, of withdrawing this unfortunate ci-devant from his difficulties ! Thus you see, your death presents a view eminently propitious to my project. Now I pass to that perspective of the scaffold which you hold out to myself. Well, my dear friend, allow me to differ from you, in the view you take of it. Not only would they not pursue me, but they would, on the contrary, applaud my deed."

"Are you a fool? What answer would you make to the revolutionary committee, when it interrogated you?"

"The committee would not interrogate me, for this simple reason, that I should go to it before it called me. Now hear the little speech that I would make to it!—"

"Go on, I confess I feel interested."

"Citizens," I should say to them, "yesterday I thought I possessed in a friend, a good patriot; but that patriot was only a traitor, sold to the foreigner! Groan with indignation, and redouble your vigilance, on learning the name of this infamous wretch! It is citizen Pistache-Carotte your colleague! Last night, the wretch, excited by drink, unveiled his projects, and finished by offering to let me share with him, at the price of my honour, the gold of England. You may guess what must have been my reply, an energetic and contemptuous refusal, and the promise that I would expose his unjustifiable conduct, and denounce to you this crime of high treason. The monster, discovering how greatly he had deceived himself in respect to me, threw himself upon me, armed with a poignard, to put the seal of death upon my mouth. In the contest that took place, I had the misfortune to kill the wretch; I say misfortune, because I regret that for the sake of example to other traitors, his head has not fallen on the scaffold! Such, my dear Pistache, will be the discourse that I shall hold to the revolutionary committee."

"And you fancy that they will give heed to such a calumny, destitute of all proof."

"I am certain of it, and for this reason. I will reveal to your old colleagues, the existence of that luxurious boudoir, which you had the imprudence to show me last night! The people will then surround your house; and, at the sight of these carefully-concealed riches which you keep for yourself, whilst, in public, you affect poverty, the cry of rage and opprobrium which will rise against your memory, will be such, that they will very probably bear me in triumph, whilst they will drag your corpse in the kennel. But time passes, my dear friend, and I am in haste. I will grant you yet five minutes of reflection! These five minutes gone by, either you shall give me the order of eularged for the marquis, or you shall die. I will not add another word; make your choice!"

"Adjutant," replied Pistache, "I never thought you so decided, as you have shown yourself this evening! You have gained your point, and it only remains for me to act."

He seated himself immediately before his escritoire, and wrote two lines upon a paper bearing the heading of the revolutionary committee, which he handed to me.

"There!" said he, "are you satisfied?"

I took the paper, which being drawn up according to the ordinary forms, was an order for enlargement.

"Very well, my dear Pistache," answered I,—"I am satisfied." I was about to withdraw, when the sans-culotte detained me.

"My dear friend," said he,—"what I esteem above all things in a man, is energy and courage. You have this night displayed a vigour, that raises you for ever in my estimation. Do you wish that we continue friends? I swear to you, for my part, that I make this offer with all my heart, and without any after-thought of taking revenge."

As I had nothing to gain by making a mortal enemy of the dangerous and powerful sans-culotte, I assured him, that our discussion had in no respect changed the sentiments I entertained towards him, and, in appearance at least, I cordially clasped the hand that he offered me.

I cannot express the joy I felt in bearing to the poor child, who awaited me on the stairs, the order for the liberation of her father. But if the reader asks me, what course I would have pursued, if the citizen Pistache had refused to accede to my demand, I answer,—" Faith I know nothing about it !"

It would be impossible to paint the feelings of mademoiselle R——, on receiving at my hands the document that had saved her father's life. Her emotion was so great, that she remained nearly a minute without the power of pronouncing a word. Having received her thanks, I bade her farewell.

Returning to my lodgings, I passed a very agitated night., I feared that Pistache, no longer subject to my compulsion might revoke the order of liberation which I had violently forced from him.

Scarcely was it day, than I dressed in haste, and presented myself at the house of citizen Pistache, whom I found still in bed.

" Ah! Ah!" cried he, on seeing me,—"it appears my dear friend, that you still doubt your triumph, and do not think it complete. Set your mind at ease ! Far from harbouring resentment, I am very grateful for your conduct to me last night! It has taught me that I must never trust any person for the future. However, in order to make an end at once of that subject, I will remind you, that I reckon upon the promise you made me, not to reveal to anybody in the world, the existence of my boudoir."

" It is a promise that I will keep ! At the same time, allow me to ask you one question. How is it that amongst so many persons, who have had access to this mysterious boudoir, not one has yet denounced you ?"

"How innocent you are grown again to day," replied Pistache shrugging his shoulders, " Don't you understand that my boudoir has always served as an antechamber to the scaffold !

Now, I don't know a more discreet confidant than the guillotine!"

"Thus then, mademoiselle R——," said I, "would"—

"Parbleu, if she had remained here last night, she would have been guillotined to-morrow with her father," answered Pistache coolly, without giving me time to finish the question.—

"Why, how pale you look—child, you will never be anything but a gloomy and sorrowful revolutionist! Farewell—I am off to the sitting."

I returned home, and after breakfast I proceeded to the quarters, in company with Anselme, when, all at once, I heard the drums beat, and the trumpets sound, and numerous discharges of musketry resounded throughout the city: soon the population, who seemed seized with madness, filled the streets, uttering cries of joy.

"What does all that mean?" said I to my companion.

"Faith, I don't know; let's mingle with the groups, and ask one of those fools who are anticking themselves out of breath."

"What has taken place citizen?" enquired I of a middle aged man, who danced, clapping his hands, and crying at the top of his voice,—" Vive la republic! Vive la Montague!"

"What!" replied he, with an indignant air,—"are you then ignorant of the great news! Toulon has fallen into the hands of our army. The English have fled, and we triumph!"

"Are you very certain of the perfect authenticity of this news?"

"Am I certain!" replied he. "Can we then, possibly doubt the triumph of the republic?"

"Nay, it is because this triumph has made us wait so long."

"There, let me alone," cried my informer.—" You hinder me, by your questions, from giving way to my joy, and will make me pass for a suspected person."

On arriving at the public square, we found the municipality surrounded by an immense multitude, each of whom kept expressing his joy. One might have called them a nation of madmen.

Amongst the citizens whose enthusiasm rose to the most extravagant pitch, I observed my host M. Marcotte. On perceiving me, he blushed, at first, to the whites of his eyes, but soon assuming his part, he threw himself into my arms with all the appearance of drunken madness, and clasping me to his heart;—

"Ah my dear citizen," said he in a stentorian voice, so as to make himself heard at fifty paces distance,—"I sink under the weight of my joy! I fear I shall die of happiness! Vive la Montagne, à bas les Anglais!"

Not to mortify our timorous host too much by my presence, I left him almost immediately, but for a long time afterwards I heard his voice, above the clamour of the crowd; he evidently wished to make himself remarkable.

I must confess that the triumph of our arms, caused in me a great degree of vexation, when I reflected that it prevented me from the baptism of fire; for since I wore the epaulette, I felt a warlike ardour, and a desire to distinguish myself, which I had not previously believed myself capable of. The perspective of dragging sadly, from garrison to garrison, across France, adding at every step, to the disasters of the country, gave me but little pleasure. I should greatly have preferred finding myself, with a musket in my hand, face to face with the foreigner on the frontier.

It was not without regret, that when the day of departure arrived, I quitted Avignon; not that my stay in that city offered anything very agreeable; far from it. But the hospitality of the brave Marcotte was so hearty, his house so well managed, and his daughter Clotilda so charming, that I could not avoid manifesting feelings of deep regret.

We passed through several towns between the 16th and 24th of Nivose, on which latter day we arrived at Draguignan, where I was so seriously indisposed during the night, as not to be able to march with the battalion the next morning. I remained in bed until towards noon. The few hours of repose completely restored me, and I again mounted my horse at two o'clock. The cold was intense, and after having ridden about four leagues, I stopped at a little inn to warm myself and take a glass of hot wine.

" Ah officer," cried the innkeeper on seeing me enter, "you should have been here half-an-hour sooner; I would willingly have given an assignat of 100 livres to have had you at my side.—Look what a condition they have left me in!"

In fact, I remarked that the cloak of the speaker was stained with blood, a bandage covered his head, and he had lost two of his teeth.

" What has happened?" I asked; "You appear to have been beaten by some drunken fellow."

" Oh no citizen, the wretch was perfectly sober."

" Then perhaps he refused to pay the expense of his entertainment?"

" On the contrary, he wanted to pay me in gold."

" Well then, if this person was neither a drunkard nor a thief, why have you come to blows with him? Perhaps he insulted you?"

" Citizen," answered the innkeeper, "the man that massacred me thus was a conspirator."

" A conspirator! How do you know that?"

" Parbleu, that was not very difficult to see I saw him draw several louis d'or from his pocket, and he gave me one to pay me. Ah! said I to myself, here's a ci-devant who is about to emigrate; he won't come over me that way! I therefore took the piece of gold, and under the pretext of going to get

L

change, I ran to give notice to the committee of surveillance of the presence of this subject in my inn. 'Well,' said the president, I'll call my men; do you return as quick as possible, and detain this ci-devant, if he seems inclined to leave.' I therefore made all haste, and in five minutes reached my house."

" Well, have you got me the change?" said the ci-devant, looking me sternly in the face.

At this demand, I turned pale, for in my hurry I had quite forgotten to get the louis changed. The wretch looked at me in a curious manner, and then all at once advancing towards me;

" Friend, said he, "I despise and detest the traitor and the spy. Why have you sold me? When are they coming to arrest me? Come,—tell the truth, or you are a dead man"— and he put a pistol to my breast. Then, as I did not answer, he stunned me with a blow from the stock, and instantly took to flight."

" And the committee of surveillance?" Demanded I.

"I am now waiting its arrival."

" Well citizen; in this affair, it is my opinion you have only had what you deserve."

I quickly paid my reckoning, and remounting my horse, proceeded on my route. A little before reaching Fayence I perceived Anselme waiting for me, quietly camped in the snow, in the middle of the road; and together we rejoined the battalion.

CHAPTER IV.

A chase.—Arrive at Grasse.—Verdier the perfumer.—An unpleasant surprise.—A marriage feast.—M. Edmond—His history.—Gerard.—A committee extraordinary.—Charity of Demagogues.—A rival in trade.—Agatha Lautier; her history; trial, condemnation, and execution.—The Advocate of Marseilles.'—Horrible spectacle at the scaffold.

At Fayence we were billetted at a house whose proprietor lay dead. We were however, well treated, and in return conducted ourselves with decorum.

We resumed our route early in the morning, and had been marching for half an hour, when several musket shots were discharged near us; we then perceived a troop of ragamuffins in pursuit of a young man, who was flying before three. He ran with a rapidity almost fabulous; clearing, with the lightness of a stag, the fences that lay in his way, and it was plain that if a ball did not reach him, he would escape. He soon disappeared from view.

"Why have you thus tracked that young man, citizen?" Demanded I of one of the pursuers.

"Ah! the wretch," replied he, "He is a federalist, a conspirator with the foreigner, who has sworn to burn the city."

It was near four o'clock when we arrived at Grasse. Our entry was far from triumphant, for our battalion were, for the most part, in such a state of sickness and rags, that we resembled mendicants rather than soldiers. The next day, when we ought to have got on our route, none of the men came to the call, and the commandant found himself constrained to put off our departure to the day following.

Borne down by privations, exasperated by the misery that they had endured, our men fell into a state of revolt, and declared that as they were volunteers they would refuse to go forward. Our commander having no means of compelling their obedience, had recourse to the district directory, who, after a very summary enquiry, declared that the battalion was in such a condition that it could not continue its route, and that we might remain at Grasse till the representatives should give an order for the dispatch of the equipments we were so absolutely in want of.

I was lodged with a perfumer, a bachelor, between thirty and forty, whose name was Verdier; he was a generous man, and of a tolerably cheerful character.

A week had passed since the battalion had rested at Grasse when one morning I took my firelock and loading it with shot, I went over the country with the intention of killing some birds. In the afternoon I began to think of returning to the city, when I perceived some fine ruins on a hill at a short distance. A labourer informed me that they had formerly been a house of knights-templars, and I resolved to visit them. Arriving at the foot of the massive walls, I seated myself upon a stone, and fell into a reverie, which so absorbed me that I soon forgot the dinner hour which had passed, as well as the distance I had to walk to reach Grasse. I was aroused by a rough and imperious voice behind me, and the reader may judge of my surprise, on perceiving two men masked. My astonishment yielded to fear, when I saw that the eldest of the two had taken my firelock from my side.

" What right have you with my arms?" cried I, in an imperious tone, in order to intimidate him.

At this question, the masked man turned to his companion, and burst into a laugh. "What do you think of that question Edmond?" said he.—" I must confess it amuses me."

"I doubt whether you will succeed in amusing yourself at my expense, citizens" said I.

" Ah! Ah! You are uneasy," cried the stranger.

" The officer has reason to be so," said the young man.

" You are wrong my friend, a French epaulet ought always to be respected."

" You know our agreement; I have a right to interrogate this officer."

" True, you have," answered the young man.

" And also, if I please, of blowing out his brains, in case his replies are not satisfactory."

The young man made an affirmative sign of the head, and kept silence.

" Now that you are warned," continued the mask addressing himself to me, "I am going to interrogate you."

" Answer citizen, I conjure you!" said the young man, in a mild and supplicating voice.

The elder mask shrugged his shoulders, and turning to me said,

" What are your political opinions?"

" I am, and always shall be, a republican."

" That's no answer. Are you a federalist or a mountaineer?"

" Neither; the federalists seek the ruin of France, and the mountaineers her dishonour."

" That's what many sensible people think!" cried the young man —" Come my friend, I think you have no fault to find with this officer. The sun is below the horizon—let us go."

" You easily satisfy yourself Edmond! This answer does

not at all content me—and I will purge the land of a murderous sans-culotte, and shoot this man!"

"You should first have warned me that you are thieves and assassins," cried I; for then I should have avoided the shame of parleying with you. I now ask but one favour, that you will allow me to write a few words to my family; and that you promise me that you will forward the letter to citizen Verdier, at whose house I lodge at Grasse — "

"Do you lodge with Verdier!" cried the young man with surprise; "then you have nothing to fear. Gerard," continued he, addressing his companion,—"do me the pleasure to leave this officer alone?"

"You will allow me, Edmond," said he, "to keep the firelock that I have taken from him."

"That's only fair! Let us set out."—With that the two men disappeared in the ruins.

Puzzled and confused at this adventure, I immediately returned to the city, where I did not arrive till night.

On my return, I related the circumstances of my mishap to Verdier, and told him the effect produced by the mention of his name.

He appeared so embarrassed and confused, and his cheeks were so suddenly covered with a deep blush, that I could not avoid remarking the change.

"My friend," said he, after a moment's silence, "I will not conceal from you, that one of the two men who have stopped you is, if I am not deceived, one of the best friends I have. Be good enough not to speak to any one of your adventure. May I reckon upon your silence?"

"If you swear to me upon your honour, that these men are neither thieves nor assassins, then I will hold my tongue."

"Then I swear,—I hope soon to be able to give you the key to this enigma. At present, it is a secret that does not belong to me."

Shortly after this conversation, Verdier proposed to me to accompany him to a village about two leagues from Grasse. whither he was going to assist at the wedding of one of his cousins. There being nothing to prevent me, I accepted the invitation.

The house at which we stopped, was the best in the village. The entrance of Verdier into the hall, which contained a numerous company, was triumphant, and showed how much my host was esteemed. I also was received with great cordiality.

The repast was just served, when the door of the diningroom opened, and a new comer, clothed in the dress of a hunter, and covered with an ample mantle, presented himself and saluted the bride. The appearance of this personage produced upon the guests a deep impression. Pale, silent, their eyes cast down, all those who so lately made the vaults of the hall resound with gaiety, seemed now stupified. One only amongst them uttered an exclamation of joy—this was my host Verdier.

The entry of the stranger had been so sudden, that I had not observed him; but when he took his place at table by the side of Verdier, I examined him with the most sedulous attention. In his countenance shone a noble boldness and intrepidity. Never could falsehood have tarnished his lips.

" What my friends," said he; casting a look slowly around him,—"has terror reduced you to that degree of abasement that you are afraid to acknowledge me."

These words brought the blush of shame upon the foreheads of the more generous, and many, to expiate their weakness, hastened to shake hands with the young man.

" My dear Edmond," said the bride, addressing him,—"it is not the fear of being compromised by your presence which affects the cheerfulness of our friends, but that of your imprudence, which makes you expose yourself so lightly.'

"I have perhaps, in fact been wrong in quitting my lurking-place," answered he. "But what would you have my good Sidonia! The life that I lead is so sad and frightful, that I could not resist the desire of being present at your feast!"

Scarcely had he spoken when, for the first time his eyes met mine. Hidden behind a large bouquet of flowers, which stood at the end of the table where I was seated, I had remained till then, out of his view. On perceiving me he could not overcome a momentary surprise, but taking his determination;

"Citizen," said he, saluting me with a friendly motion of his head,—" Chance offers you your revenge. One word from you and I am lost."

These enigmatical words produced a great sensation amongst the guests, and all looks were centred in me.

"Citizen," answered I, affecting great astonishment,—"I do not understand you. It is probable that you are deceived by some resemblance, for never till to day have I had the pleasure of meeting you."

When the repast was ended, "my dear friend," said Verdier to me in a low voice,—"come with me I beg of you. I have a great favour to ask of you."

I followed my host without speaking a word, to a small chamber, where we found Edmond. Verdier shut the door upon us, and then turning quickly towards me;

" My dear friend," said he,—"I thank you for your discretion; we are alone here, and nobody can hear us. I well know that you have recognised my cousin as one of the men you met masked in the ruins."

" Since you speak so frankly, my dear Verdier, I do not hesitate to say that five minutes after the arrival of your cousin I had recognised him. Let me add that although I am completely ignorant of the causes that have occasioned Monsieur to be outlawed, I feel persuaded that they are honourable to him."

" Thanks sir, for your good opinion," cried Edmond, "on my soul and conscience, I believe I deserve it! For the rest, if you wish to know my simple history, I am quite ready to relate it to you."

"If the recital is not too painful to you to make, I shall be delighted."

"Why should it be painful?" I have nothing to reproach myself for! This is it then in a few words,—"

"I claim the right of speaking," cried Verdier, interrupting his cousin; "Edmond, although I would not impugn his veracity, never fails, when he speaks of himself, to suppress his merits. I therefore ask to take his place in the office of narrator,"

" Granted!" said I smiling.

Verdier, without loss of time, began as follows :

" Edmond, from his tenderest childhood exhibited a warlike disposition, quite at variance with the ideas that his father, my uncle, entertained of his future course, for he had intended him for the priesthood, but relinquished that design from observing the boy's military disposition."

" Sent to Grasse to commence his studies, Edmond, from a turbulent and undisciplined boy, became at once remarkably studious, and his progress was such, that at the age of seventeen, he was the first student of.the university of Aix, where he graduated; and he was nominated advocate with great applause."

" During his stay at the university, he acquired an extraordinary influence over his fellow students. Prodigal of his friendship, the unfortunate and the persecuted were sure of finding in him protection and succour."

" At last came the revolution. You may conjecture with what enthusiasm my cousin received the generous ideas, and utopian projects of the innovators. The abolition of privileges, the affranchisement of the people, that touching and universal fraternity which they held out as an affair so easy of accomplishment, found in him the most fervent and devoted champion of our whole province.

"Edmond organized the national guard of Grasse, and became administrator and president of the district. He was intoxicated with patriotism and good intentions, and believed in the fraternity of the whole world."

"Alas! this beautiful dream lasted but a short time; designing men, seeing the success of the revolution, usurped its power, and trampled on the generous dupes whom they had put in the foreground in the hour of danger; and in a moment perverted the benefits derived from it."

"Edmond was deprived of his post of president of the district,—he was calumniated and repudiated as an aristocrat. The elegant habits of my cousin gave a certain appearance of truth to this charge; and the indignation which he publicly expressed at the excesses of the revolution, finished by alienating from him the mind of the masses."

"In short, things arrived at such a pitch, that Edmond was compelled one night to fly for his life."

" Since that period the life of Edmond has been one uninterrupted series of privations and dangers. Some days ago an innkeeper denounced him to the revolutionary committee; the next day he was pursued by the national guards of our city, who fired several musket shots at him!—"

"What!" cried I, interrupting Verdier, "was it your cousin who beat with his pistol stock the face of the master of the hotel between Draguignan and Fayence! Faith, I can but compliment him upon it, for that beggar well deserved the correction. As to the last pursuit of which you speak, did it not take place the same day of our arrival at Grasse?"

"Yes, exactly! But how came you to know that?"

"Parbleu! by the excellent reason, that I was myself a witness of that event. One of the national guards whom I interrogated, told me that the man whom they chased with such fury, was a traitor, sold to the foreigners."

Verdier was about to continue, when violent blows were struck upon the window sill. Edmond drew from his pockets a brace of double barrelled pistols. A few seconds passed, full of anxiety for Verdier and myself.

Soon fresh blows resounded, struck with more violence. "What shall we do?" said my host in a low voice; "if we open that window, it will give entrance to the enemy. If we answer, it will betray our presence!"

"The straight line is my favourite course, my friends," said Edmond. "They knock, let us open."

Before we had time to oppose his movement, the young outlaw darted towards the window, and hastily taking off the bars, opened the shutters. Then, with a bold front, sparkling eyes, and assured look, holding a pistol in each hand, he placed himself before the window.

What was my astonishment, when a single man wearing a ragged dress, and with his face covered with a black mask, presented himself to our notice. "Ah! Is it you Gerard," said Edmond. "Faith, you knocked so violently, that I thought there were at least twenty soldiers! What is the object of your visit at so late an hour?"

The new comer sprung into the room.—"You ask," said he, "what has procured you the honour of my visit at this hour. It is the interest I feel in your safety. You have been seen coming here, and must withdraw immediately—Come, follow me, let us set out!"

"My dear Gerard," replied Edmond,—I thank you from the bottom of my heart, for this proof of devotion. But I will no longer let the barking of these mad dogs trouble me in my occupations and pleasures. I have been tracked enough, I have fled often enough. Now Gerard, you know my intentions, and you know that when I once form a resolution, nothing will make me change it. Thanks once more and adieu."

" Do you fancy then," cried Gerard, "that I will abandon you thus ? We have agreed upon a defensive alliance. They are coming to attack you and I shall remain."

"That's very good sir," cried I, advancing from behind one of the shutters where I had remained hidden since the arrival of Gerard. "Edmond, I flatter myself, will change his resolution when he understands that his obstinacy may involve your death."

Gerard, on seeing me appear, threw himself backward, and drawing a pistol from the pocket of his cloak ;

"Treason !" cried he,—" we are lost !"

"Where do you see a traitor, and in what respect are you lost?" answered I, astonished at his attitude and words.

"I comprehend Gerard's error," said Edmond, laughing till the tears came,—"Your uniform of an officer of the republic, and above all, your countenance which he has not had time to forget, explains his surprise. He undoubtedly supposes that the manner in which he acted towards you yesterday, when after being taken by surprise, and robbed of your musket, he wanted to shoot you, lies yet at your heart, and that you will take your revenge for it. Be assured Gerard," continued Edmond,—"the citizen has forgiven both of us our insult, on account of our misfortunes."

"I cannot fear Monsieur," said Gerard, uncocking his pistol, "still I am resolved not to fall alive, like a fool, into the hands of the citizens sans culottes."

"You are undoubtedly sir, an emigrant noble?" demanded I of Edmond's friend.

"I, noble !" replied he, accompanying his words with bursts

of laughter. "Oh no! Before the revolution I held the office of steward."

"A steward!" repeated I with astonishment.

"Yes citizen, a steward! But that does not prevent me from being pursued now as an aristocrat."

"Truly you greatly astonish me. I should like much to know your history."

"It is not long. I passed the first half of my life as a soldier in a regiment; the second half, as a steward behind a door. However, if I relate to you the events that have occurred to me during the last week that I filled that modest office, I assure you, however little you may love the smell of powder, you would listen to me without interruption, and with great pleasure."

"I am passionately fond of the smell of powder; relate it."

"I thank you; but that would require too much time; for I still hope that Edmond is not going to persist in remaining here to await the arrival of the gendarmes—"

"May the deuce take me away if I budge!" cried Edmond.

"Mr. Edmond," said I,—"forgive me if I insist upon you following the advice of your friend Gerard. I must observe to you that, at this moment, it does not merely concern yourself, but also madame your sister! Think then, what a sad remembrance of her wedding will remain, if you fall into the hands of your enemies!"

"I thank you sir for your words, they bring me to reason. For my sister's sake, I will endeavour to withdraw myself once more by flight, and save my head from the executioner."

"In three days from this time," said I to Gerard, "I shall be found, towards four o'clock in the afternoon, at the foot of the old chateau of the templars, and at the same place where I had the honour of making your acquaintance. Then, I shall be much obliged, if you will not forget to bring me back my
M

musket!—Now gentlemen, adieu! Set off, and may God protect you?"

An hour after they had departed, I set out with Verdier on my return to Grasse, where we arrived towards midnight.

The next morning I went to find Anselme, and to relate to him the adventure of the previous evening, and ask his co-operation in the accomplishment of a scheme of Verdier for saving his cousin, which he had communicated to me during our return to Grasse.

This scheme was ingenious enough, and was as follows. He proposed that a letter should be so contrived as to fall into the hands of the revolutionary committee, and which should show that Edmond had gone abroad.

The only difficulty,—and it was no great one,—was to get the letter into the hands of the revolutionary committee; and it was to manage this, that I went to consult Anselme, who found means to accomplish it satisfactorily.

"You have saved the life of my cousin," said Verdier to me, throwing himself upon my neck,—"I have just learned that the committee will hold an extraordinary public sitting this evening."

"Well, my dear friend, we will attend it then, if you are disposed to do so."

"I ask nothing better."

At a quarter before eight we set off to attend the meeting of the popular society. We arrived at the very moment when the sitting was commencing. A great ferment reigned amongst the members. On all sides they were discussing the reason of this extraordinary sitting. The most ridiculous suppositions were circulated. They related to the discovery of a Saint Bartholomew of the patriots, contrived by the aristocrats of two English regiments, which, hidden in the neighbourhood, were to take Touritte and make it a fortress. The traitor

Edmond was pointed out as the chief of these criminal enterprises.

When the two branch candlesticks were placed upon the table of the secretaries, and lighted, the president put on a cap of red wool. He then proposed the hymn, and the public sang with great enthusiasm the couplet of '*Amour sacré pour la patrie.*'

This preliminary accomplished, the president called for it again, and then announced that the sitting was opened.

Scarcely was this done, than a stout man with broad shoulders and a plain face, ornamented with enormous moustachios, rose, took off his fox skin cap, and said,.

"President, I demand the word."

"The society grants it to you," said the president.

"Citizens," said the stout man, addressing the assembly, "they say that this rascal Verdier, is at our doors with two regiments of English satellites; that a great number of foreigners have arrived, who affect to call themselves Frenchmen. Citizens! the country is in danger! To arms, citizens! Let the drums beat the generale, let cannons be pointed against the house of seclusion, let—"

"Citizens!" cried the president,—"I pray the assembly to grant me the word. (*Applause.*) Citizens! Why this tumult, this agitation? They pretend that great dangers threaten us; is it in confusion that we are to look for our safety? Woe be to him who sleeps in a false security, but a thousand times woe to the impious man who, without cause, would influence the anger of the people! That sacred fire should not burn for the amusement of simpletons; like the powder of our batallions, it should burn and sparkle only when employed in tho extermination of the enemies of freedom." *(Applause.)* "Who dares to deny that Verdier is a traitor, capable of every crime? *(Applause.)* Nobody! But it does not follow that he is dangerous. No; Verdier, far from marching upon Grasse with two English regiments, flies the land of freemen; he is gone abroad. Behold a letter written by him to his family, which has been intercepted by a brave sans-culotte, and brought to us this very morning."

At this stage of his discourse, the president, unfolding the letter, read it to the assembly.

The sitting was about to be raised, when a member of the society, advancing with a savage look, pronounced the following words, which the reader may well believe, produced in me a very painful emotion;

"What are we to do then, brave sans-culottes, with the accomplices of the traitor Edmond Verdier? I demand that his family be put under arrest, and the seals placed upon their papers, furniture, and effects! Above all, let his cousin the perfumer, that corrupter of the good taste of the people, be pursued to the utmost."

"I support the motion!" cried another voice.

"Parbleu! I rather think," cried my host,—"you are both perfumers like myself; only as I sell the best articles, and you the worst,—I sell a great deal, and you sell nothing. Now if you could get rid of me as a competitor, it would really be a capital thing for your business! I demand that the assembly pass to the order of the day upon that question of lavender water and pomatum, which is too much below its dignity."

"The order of the day!" shouted out the crowd, and Verdier was saved. It was near one o'clock in the morning when the business terminated.

"This is a bad night for me," said Verdier when we went out.

"Why so, my dear friend? Have they not, on the contrary, voted the order of the day, over the accusation brought against you?"

"Yes; but the member who demanded that measure has been nominated a member of the committee, and because his trade had failed, he thought it necessary to dive deeply into politics. Now, I know that man, and that he will return to the charge. It appears to me as if my head was half off my shoulders already."

The day after the sitting of the popular society, of which I have endeavoured to give the reader a scrupulously exact report, I was conversing with my host before the door of his warehouse, when we saw passing, a poor woman with a pale countenance, haggard eyes, and whose air of deep sadness attracted my attention.

Verdier called to her.

"What's the matter now, Martine?" asked he in a kindly tone.

"Ah! my good M. Verdier," answered she wildly,—"this is the last time that you will see me! In a few minutes I shall no longer be in this world!"

"You are foolish, Martine! What are you talking about?"

"Alas! it is the truth. This morning the committee of surveillance made a descent upon my house, where they found a little wheat, that I had saved by carefulness and privations. My poor husband having taken the responsibility of it upon himself, has been arrested and thrown into prison!"

"At present I am left with my two unfortunate children, who have eaten nothing since yesterday, and are dying of hunger!"

"And what do you mean to do?"

"Suffocate them, and then cut my own throat," answered Martine wildly. "Innocent creatures! Why should I suffer them to die thus by inches? Is it not better for them to escape from all the sufferings that await them, and that will be wholly terminated by death?"

At this horrible confession, Verdier, rousing himself from the reflections in which he had been plunged, addressed Martine;

"So much the worse for you if you abuse my confidence;" said he,—"follow me."

When he got into his shop, Verdier turned to me, and pointing to the street door :

"Will you, my dear friend," said he,—"although an officer, mount guard a moment? If by chance, any commissary of the society of surveillance should present himself, cough three times running. to warn me of their visit."

"Willingly; you may depend upon me."

The perfumer went off, and returning directly, put a parcel into the hands of Martine. "Here, my good neighbour," he said "is your wheat! Do not betray me, and go back to your children. No thanks! When you have consumed this wheat, if you are still destitute, come to me again, I have provisions in store!"

"Ah! my good M. Verdier, may God—"

"No thanks," interrupted my host,—"do not betray me, that's all I ask of you."

"My dear friend," said I to my host, when the unfortunate mother was gone,—"what you have done is very good, but are you not afraid, that in listening thus to the dictates of your heart, you will probably involve yourself in misery, in your turn? Such is the scarcity that now prevails, wheat is more precious than gold, and your conduct is too generous!"

"Not so much enthusiasm, my dear friend," answered he smiling,—"and don't make so much of so small a matter! You may have remarked that bird-cage set in the wall of the back shop; it conceals the door of a closet, which holds sixty quintals of grain! It is a reserve, known to no one in the world but myself, and you now, excepted, which will serve to feed my family when it shall be reduced to the last extremity. For the rest, nothing is more easy than to supply myself with grain!"

Verdier had scarcely finished pronouncing these words, when tumultuous cries, proceeding from the street, drew us anew to the warehouse door. We saw a numerous assemblage, who came towards us; then soon alas! in the midst of this agitated mass, we distinguished the unfortunate Martine, who, pushed and tossed about on all sides, had her clothes half torn off, and her hair dishevelled. We learned from one of the spectators of this scene, that the poor woman having let fall one of the corners of the cloth which contained the wheat that she carried, the grain was scattered on the ground; in an instant a person threw himself upon her, calling her a monopolist, and had her arrested.

The unfortunate woman in passing before us, threw upon us a glance full of entreaty, and raising her voice as if she were addressing the crowd;

"Citizens! I conjure you," she said,—"let me return to my children who are waiting for me; what is to become of those innocent creatures thus abandoned?"

Verdier answered this indirect appeal by a look of intelligence; and the poor Martine, seeing that she was understood, and that her children had found a protector, went away without adding a word, or offering the least resistance.

"Come my friend," said Verdier a little after, and taking his hat,—"I am the involuntary cause, it is true, but still I am the cause of the misfortune of that poor woman, and I ought, as far as I can, to repair it."

Half an hour after, the children of Martine, entrusted to an old woman who knew my host, found themselves beyond the reach of cold and hunger.

The good perfumer and I returned to the house, when, in

crossing the square, we were attacked by a man whose repulsively ugly countenance and impudent address, certainly spoke little in his favour.

"I have no doubt about your opinions Verdier!" cried he, raising his voice so as to attract the attention of the passers-by,—"you are the worthy relation of your cousin! Like him, an aristocrat, a pensioner of the foreigner, an emissary of the ci-devant Princes of the house of Bourbon! Yes, I have proofs in hand of your treasons! Tremble!"

The crowd, on hearing these formal accusations repeated with a loud voice, immediately gathered round Verdier.

"And by what proofs do you support these accusations?" Demanded my host of his furious enemy.

"By a proof which you cannot deny, because it still exists! Yesterday, I sent to purchase of you a pot of pomatum, in order to discover the fraudulent method you employ in the manufacture; now, the label, which I have carefully preserved, bears three fleur-de-lis, surrounded by these words: Pommade-à-la-royale!"

At this revelation, a cry of indignation broke from the crowd; when my host, without losing anything of his sang-froid, turned the laugh upon his assailant by his answer.

"Ah well, yes! I agree," said he,—"that you may find upon my pots some old labels; but you know, citizens, that from time to time, we comb the heads of the royalists well; is it not therefore right to give them also a little pomatum?"

Scarcely were these words pronounced, than a universal burst of laughter shook the crowd, who immediately dispersed.

"Now that we are alone my dear brother," said Verdier, addressing his accuser,—"let's talk reasonably. What do you want? That I should give up a trade in which I succeed better than you? That I should free you from my dangerous competition? That is the true motive of your hostility to me, is it not? Will you engage to cease all hostility against me, and no longer to pursue me, if I promise that before the end of a month, I will shut my shop, and cease to be a perfumer? I speak to you now with sincerity, and play with your cards on the table; answer me and act with the same frankness."

"It is certain that if you act thus," answered Verdier's brother member, in a considerably softened tone,—"you will acquire such claims to my good will, that unless I am a monster of ingratitude, it would be impossible for me to injure you. I have no objection to take your stock off your hands."

"Well then, it is agreed," said Verdier,—a month hence, my stock shall be yours."

"Truly my friend, I begin to think that I have judged you wrongfully," cried the new member of the committee of the popular society, clasping the hand of my host! "What would you have? The fault lies in the bad reputation of your cousin Edmond, which has been reflected upon all his family."

Verdier, after having answered these amicable advances, with an appearance of sincere cordiality, took leave of the member. For myself, I felt indignant beyond expression. "I hope my dear friend," said I,—"that you will not keep to this bargain, which cannot be serious."

"I beg your pardon there," answered he,—"this bargain is the most serious thing in the world, since the non-execution of it would involve the loss of my head! I have maturely weighed and examined the chances of ruin and safety which resistance presented, and the result has been, the entire conviction that I should fall in the struggle. I am ruined, but I prefer the loss of my business, to that of my head. You see the public power is used by the elect of the people, only to improve their personal position. It is a settled thing."

The same evening I was seated at a corner of the fireplace,

conversing with Verdier on the events of the day, when some of his friends came to pay him a visit.

"Do you know the great news, Verdier?" said a draper. "To-morrow they will judge Agatha Lautier!"

"Poor saint!" answered my host with deep emotion.—"I hope they will leave her at quiet in her prison."

"Everybody hopes so!" resumed the draper,—"but it appears that some high personages, having presented complaints against her, the committee of public safety thinks it ought to inflict a punishment. All honest people in the city are in a commotion."

"Poor saint!" repeated Verdier, with an air of respectful commiseration,—"they will not pardon her! Her virtues speak too loudly against her. Another victim for the scaffold!"

"Who is this Agatha Lautier?" asked I of Verdier.

"Agatha Lautier is beloved by the whole city! She is a nun, scarcely twenty-three years of age, eminently handsome, exemplary in her conduct, and is never named but with veneration. Have you never heard her mentioned?"

"Never! and I shall be happy, if it does not disturb you, to hear the rest of her history."

"I ask nothing better," answered Verdier.—"This is it in a few words; It is five years ago that a deep sensation was created in the city, by the news that Agatha, for whose hand twenty rivals disputed, had taken the veil!"

"In vain did her friends supplicate her to renounce this project; neither prayers, nor remonstrances, nor exhortations, could move her from her resolution. In fifteen days, she entered the convent as a novice."

"We hoped that, deterred soon by the monastic severities of her calling, she would return to the world; nothing of the kind! Two years afterwards, all the city of Grasse were present at the taking of the veil by Agatha Lautier!"

"Upon the suppression of the convents, Agatha withdrew with her superior, to a little cottage, which the latter possessed at Antibes, where they both lived in such entire seclusion that their existence was hardly suspected."

"The superior had a brother, a captain, who had thrown himself into Toulon when that city raised the standard of revolt against the republic. This captain was wounded, and as soon as he was convalescent, took refuge with his sister. He had not been with her a fortnight before he was recognised, denounced, and arrested by order of the revolutionary committee. His sister and mademoiselle Agatha, both accused of having concealed an outlaw, shared his fate.—The captain perished on the scaffold, and his sister died with grief on the same day."

"Agatha Lautier, now alone in the world, became the benefactress of the prison—consoling the afflicted, sustaining the weak, and waiting upon the sick. The influence acquired by the admirable devotedness of the young girl, over her companions in captivity, was so great that the interior of the prison was no longer the same; they were almost happy there. The sentiments of charity and brotherhood, which she knew how to inspire in her companions, alleviated their captivity and rendered it bearable. You will comprehend that such a line of conduct would not long remain unpunished Therefore, Agatha Lautier appears to-morrow before the criminal tribunal."

"Faith! You have awakened in me such a desire to see this young creature, that I shall go to the tribunal."

"Well then, I will accompany you."

At the first ray of light that shot across my chamber, I dressed myself and went to find Verdier.

It was scarcely four o'clock, when we went out to go to the tribunal. The sitting was not to open till six o'clock, but the interest that Agatha Lautier inspired was such, that the whole city went in a mass to the tribunal; and although we were two hours in advance of the sitting, we had the greatest difficulty in getting into the hall.

Scarcely had I entered, when a violent blow on the shoulder almost upset me I turned about furiously,—it was Anselme. My host and I joined him.

"How is it then my friend," said I,—"that I find you here?"

"Faith! I might put the same question to you. I am come to see. It appears that the ogres of the committee are going to devour a poor young girl, whose whole crime consists in having too much virtue. I shall not be sorry to witness this monstrosity, which will only confirm me the stronger in my new opinions, for you know that I have changed them—"

After an interval of two hours, a bell sounded, silence was proclaimed, and the tribunal made its entry into the hall.

The members of the tribunal were scarcely seated, when the bell sounded again.

"There she is! There she is!" cried the crowd, and the young devotee appeared. A murmur of pity resounded on all sides.

For myself, I confess I was struck with respect and admiration at the sight of the young girl. Her round head dress, fastened by a band of black gauze, enclosed the most celestial and ideal countenance that can be conceived—a true type of the virgin of Raphael. A neck-kerchief of white muslin, on which shone a little cross of gold suspended from a black cord, completed the chaste toilet of the young martyr, as far as I could see it.

After the ordinary questions, as to her age, profession, domicile, &c., the president entered upon the gist of the act of accusation

"Do you know, Agatha Lautier," said he,—"that the brother of your former abbess was hidden in the house you lived in?"

"Yes citizen, I do know it," replied she without hesitation.

"Agatha Lautier," continued the president,—"was the house that you occupied hired in your name? Reflect well before you reply, for the words you are about to speak will decide your fate."

"I thank you citizen for your goodness," said the young nun.—"Yes, indeed, I well understand that to answer in the affirmative, is to confess to having given an asylum to an outlaw, and that that confession involves a condemnation to death! God has given me, up to this day of my life, strength to avoid falling into falsehood, and I will answer truly. After the suppression of the convents, our poor abbess had only her pension for the entire means of existence; but they soon ceased to pay it, and she found herself reduced, as well as myself, to work with her hands. We had believed, till now, that the humble cottage we inhabited belonged to my old abbess; but we were deceived. We hired that cottage. It was to my worthy abbess and to me, that its proprietor had let it, and it was I who always went to pay the rent."

At this reply a murmur of sorrow ran through the auditory, for they saw that Agatha was lost.

The president seemed to hesitate a moment; but soon resuming his examination;

"Agatha," said he slowly,—probably, in order to make the young nun understand the importance of this new question;— "with what funds did you discharge the rent to the proprietor; did not those funds proceed from the private resources of your ex-abbess, your part in that affair being reduced to that of a simple agent? Do not put yourself out; take time, and reflect before you answer."

N

"I thank you much citizen president," said Agatha,—" but truth is but one, and I do not want to reflect. The money with which we paid our rent, was the produce of the work, common to both my superior and myself; and as I was younger than she, it was naturally I who earned most. Yes, I understand quite well that this answer may be unfavourable to me," said she, on hearing a dull murmur rise from the benches of the auditory,—"for it renders me answerable for the asylum granted by my superior to her brother."

On hearing the murmur, or to speak more properly, the universal and spontaneous groans which arose from the auditory, the commissioner of the executive power rose hastily from his chair, and in a sharp voice,

"How is it," cried he, "that this scandalous sensibility is indulged for a wretched counter-revolutionist, who has concealed an assassin of the country? Are there indeed traitors in this court? Is there not to be found a single true republican? Simple citizens! who ascribe the words of that woman to the respect due to truth, cannot you perceive that a senseless and guilty passion has alone dictated these answers? She will not survive her lover, the defunct captain of the ex-regiment of Anjou!"

"Citizen," said Agatha, in the midst of a solemn silence,— "I regret on your own account, the words you have just spoken. Do not think that I yield to pride in repulsing your calumnies. No, the witness of my conscience is enough for me, and I would remain silent if I did not fear that the odious charge received without examination or reflection, might become a subject of scandal, a weapon in the hands of those, who unceasingly attack religion in the faults of its servants. Before God who hears *me*, and will judge *you;* before God who has given me the strength necessary to prefer death to falsehood, the captain has never been to me but a brother in Jesus Christ; an unfortunate outlaw, whom charity bound me to assist."

The commissioner, in spite of himself, cast down his eyes at this reply; however, thanks to a powerful effort of his will, he overcame his embarrassment. "Now the scene of the comedy is acted, let us go on with the debate," said he, in a brief and ironical tone.

The president then addressed, for form sake, some new and insignificant questions to Agatha, and then declared the debate terminated.

The commissioner, who spoke in his turn, did not belie the bad opinion I had conceived of him. After his speech, there prevailed amongst the auditory a deep and painful silence. The judges consulted together, but their deliberations were of short duration, and they scarcely rose before they were again seated.

The president rose, and after the usual forms, pronounced, in an indignant voice these words; "The tribunal condemns Agatha Lautier to the punishment of death, and declares her goods confiscated to the benefit of the nation!"

"The Lord be praised, may His holy will be done!" said the young nun, in a calm voice, after the pronouncing of this judgment.

"Have you nothing to add?" demanded the president.

"Nothing, citizen," answered Agatha Lautier; but soon bethinking herself, and raising her humid and grateful eyes to the president,—"yes citizen," resumed she, "it remains for me, before quitting this world, to thank the tribunal for the humanity it has shewn me. In a few hours, if God deigns to grant me mercy, I will pray for it in the abode of the elect!"

"Poor and generous young girl!" said Anselme to me, whilst big tears swelled his eyelids, and trembled on their lashes,—" she has not dared to thank the president personally, for fear of compromising him, for the kindness he has shewed her, and has therefore ingeniously addressed the tribunal

What delicacy and virtue, my dear friend! Enraptured by such an example, I feel that happiness is found only in the fulfilment of duty, and I have a great desire to strangle that beggarly commissioner! What do you think of the project?" Adieu poor saint! adieu!" murmured he, on seeing the gendarmes surround Agatha Lautier and lead her out of the hall.

A new prisoner now appeared at the bar. He was a stout robust countryman, with a face bronzed by the sun, clothes worn by labour, and a ringing voice.

At the first questions put to him by the president, he addressed the tribunal in a patois, and declared that he could not speak the French language.

"If I speak more slowly, do you think you will understand me better?" demanded the president, scanning his phraseology.

The prisoner opened his great eyes, shrugged his shoulders several times, as if in despair, and remained silent.

After a pause of some moments, the president resuming his address; "let them bring forward the witnesses" said he.

At this order five or six peasants advanced to the bar.

"What is this man?" demanded the magistrate, addressing one of them.

"That man is the advocate Lavaux, formerly of Marseilles, and now an outlaw for his federalist plots!"

"Are you quite sure of what you aver?"

"I can't be more certain. I swear it upon the republic."

All the other witnesses, being interrogated in turn, made the same declaration.

The pretended peasant turned pale. "President," cried he, exchanging his unintelligible patois for excellent French,— "I confess I wished to impose on the tribunal; but listen to me, I am innocent as a new-born child, of the infamous crime of federalism, of which they accuse me."

"We are ready to hear you; speak," said the president.

" Citizens," cried the prisoner, addressing the judges,—" I am glad of the opportunity of appearing before you, for I owe to it the power of freely expressing my sentiments. Citizens, there is but one truth in the world,—the republic; but one possible republic, that which we have this day the happiness to enjoy. Its intelligence, and its virtuous example, moralizes the people whom its genius produces. Still I will not conceal from you, citizens, that whilst acknowledging and admiring the sublime qualities possessed by the mountain, I have a cause of reproach against it. Yes, citizens, it is to be regretted that the mountain suffers itself to be moved by the sight of tears, caused by the arrests of justice ; for the tears of traitors fructify the soil of liberty."

" Prisoner Lavaux," said the president, interrupting the advocate, "I must remind you that it does not become you to make motions, but to defend yourself. Ten witnesses have sworn that you are the same Lavaux inculpated in the federalist plot of Marseilles, and outlawed. That is the point on which alone you must explain yourself."

" I a federalist!" cried Lavaux indignantly. " What calumny and falsehood! Accuse me, citizen, of being a thief, an assassin, and I will certainly defend myself; but to pretend that I am a federalist! Do you know, citizen president, that not one of these execrable criminals has been put to death without my being at the foot of the scaffold, enjoying the anguish of their last moments ? That I have assisted to massacre more than ten? I a federalist! Come then ; it is a mockery to pretend such a monstrosity."

" However, you are certainly Lavaux, the advocate of Marseilles. The despositions of the witnesses leave no possibility of doubt in this respect."

" Ah! Allow me. I understand it all now," answered the accused, pretending joy and surprise. " Yes I am an advocate;

I am called Lavaux, and I live at Marseilles. But there is also in that city, one of my profession, of the same name, which has caused the error of my being taken for a federalist."

The president then recalled the witnesses, and asked if it was true, as the accused pretended; but they all, without hesiation, declared there was no other of the name.

The advocate wanted to reply, but the president ordered him to hold his tongue, and the gendarmes forced him to sit down. Sentence of death was passed on the prisoner, with confiscation of his effects to the use of the republic.

"Wretches!" exclaimed he, addressing his judges. "May my innocent blood fall on your guilty heads! Yes, I am a federalist; yes, I hate and despise the mountain; yes, the republic has disgraced itself by wallowing in blood; yes you are—*you*, the representatives and servants of the mountain, are cowards and assassins! Yes, your memory will be held up to the execration of posterity."

Whilst the accused expressed himself thus violently, the gendarmes attempted to wrench him from a wooden bar to which he clung; it was only after long efforts that they succeeded in dragging him from the hall, foaming with rage; whilst cries of " to the guillotine, to the guillotine with the federalist accompanied him to the door of the tribunal.

It was very late when I re-entered the house of my host, where I found him absorbed in sad and deep reflections.

I passed a sleepless night, and rose the next morning with the first dawn. I had scarcely breakfasted, when one of the serjeant majors of my company presented himself before me.

"Adjutant," said he, "I come to inform you that the batallion has been required by the criminal tribunal, to take arms and mount guard at the execution of the two sentences to death which took place yesterday, and will be carried into effect to day. They will set out in a quarter of an hour."

I will not attempt to describe to the reader the regret,—

almost despair,—caused in me by this order; but I was a soldier and must obey.

Precisely at one o'clock, the drum beat, and the batallion, divided into two detachments, left the barracks; the first was ordered to repair to the square where the execution was to take place; the other was charged with escorting the condemned; I formed part of the latter.

Arrived before the door of the prison, the troops formed in double rank, and awaited the coming out of the prisoners.

A keeper of the prison, to whom I offered two crowns if he succeeded in enabling me to get to the condemned, bade me follow him.

After crossing a dark corridor divided by several doors, I at length arrived at the room which contained the condemned. Nothing could be more affecting and melancholy than the spectacle which presented itself to me. The advocate Lavaux, strongly bound upon a large and massy arm chair of oak, looked pale and livid, although his eyes shone with a feverish light, and his strong and husky voice was continually heard, now insulting his executioners, then, a moment after, imploring their pity.

At a few paces from Lavaux, seated on a chair, and surrounded with turnkeys and hangmen, was Agatha Lautier. When I entered, these subaltern attendants of the guillotine, were occupied in preparing the young martyr for death. One of them, armed with a pair of large scissors, the blades of which, gapped with too frequent use, tore, rather than cut off her magnificent locks. Another bound her hands with a cord. As to the chief executioner, a lean, bony, withered old man, he directed, with the greatest indifference, the proceedings of his valets.

Never shall I forget the sublime expression of resignation and mildness reflected from the celestial countenance of the young sister. From her beaming looks, I guessed that her thoughts were raised towards heaven. Agatha Lautier, I am persuaded, had lost, at that moment, the consciousness of earthly existence; and thought not of the guillotine. In a moment, however, I saw her turn pale, and her face betrayed the expression of acute physical suffering; for the executioner's servant, charged with tying her delicate arms, had exercised such brutality, that the blood had flowed to the extremities of her slender fingers.

" Take care there, wretch," said I, unable to contain my indignation.—The brute relaxed the cords with which he had bound his victim.

" I thank you sir," said Agatha in a soft voice, the sound of which still vibrates in my ears ; " I thank you sir for your humanity."

At this moment, the servant employed in cutting, or rather tearing off her hair, by a sudden and involuntary pull, displaced the muslin neckerchief which covered the shoulders and bosom of the victim. The man stooped to pick it up, when Agatha, with a fire and indignation, rendered more striking by the contrast with her habitual mildness, rose quickly from her chair, and throwing herself backward; " Sir," said she, her cheeks covered with a deep blush,—" My head belongs to you, but I am entitled to all your respect ! Touch me not !"

One of the women present, picked up the neckerchief, and put it again upon her shoulders, saying,—" Ah citizen ! there is not a better patriot than I; but on seeing you condemned, I, for the first time, cursed the republic !"

I thank you for your sympathy, my good woman," answered Agatha, with an accent which spoke from her heart;—" only, believe me, you ought not to curse."

" Let us set out," said the executioner, knocking out the ashes of his pipe upon his thumb-nail.

Agatha Lautier, since her condemnation, had several times expressed her desire to have the assistance of a confessor at her last hour. At the moment in which the signal for departure was given, a person employed in the prison, ran to inform her that a priest had offered himself to accompany her to the scaffold At this news, the countenance of the poor child shone with an expression of celestial joy.

The chief executioner, fixing his eyes upon a great silver watch, which he drew from his fob, gave unequivocal signs of his bad humour; turning a second time to his assistants, he re-iterated the order for their departure.

Agatha Lautier rose immediately, and proceeded towards the outer door with a calm and collected step. It was otherwise with the Marseilles advocate. Although his arms and hands were firmly tied behind his back, he found means to cling to the bars of the arm chair on which he was seated, and in a voice which fear rendered harsh and almost unintelligible; "I am innocent!" said he,—"there has been a mistake! Let them go and find the commissary of the executive power; Long live the mountain! Down with Brissot! Down with Danton! Long live Robespierre! Long live St. Juste!"

"Come my lads," said the executioner, addressing his assistants,—"take hold of this noisy fellow and carry him upon your shoulders."

The assistants threw themselves upon Lavaux, to execute the orders of their master; but the first who laid his hand upon him uttered a cry of pain and flung himself backward. The prisoner had set his teeth into his shoulder. "Ah wretch," cried the executioner,—"do you treat my men thus? Mind!"—and with his bony hand he struck him violently in the face.

Lavaux uttered a harsh inarticulate sound, scarcely human, then, with his eyes starting from their sockets, and grinding his teeth, he seemed to wait impatiently the approach of his enemies. It was a hideous picture that I shall never forget.

As to Agatha, relapsed into her reflections, a happy smile wandered over her features. She had seen and heard nothing of the brutal and bloody scene that had just passed.

The executioner himself, accustomed as he was to the passive courage of his victims, could not avoid remarking the striking contrast in the conduct of the two prisoners. "Are you not ashamed, you coward!" said he, addressing Lavaux,—"to show so much weakness before that child? You roar, you struggle, you bite and scratch for nothing;—your head must come off; take example from the nun."

Lavaux continued his cries, and ground his teeth with fury.

"Come! it is time to finish this game," said he, addressing his assistants,—"throw a coverlet over the head of this madman, and pack him up, so that he can neither bite nor speak, and let's be off!"

This order was immediately obeyed, and in two minutes, Lavaux and Agatha mounted the tumbril which waited for them at the prison door.

Lavaux having refused to hear the exhortations of the priest, was seated between two gendarmes. Behind him, placed beside the minister of God, was Agatha; another gendarme and two executioners completed the loading of the cart. In spite of the danger there was in showing any sympathy for those condemned by the criminal tribunal, the crowd, at the sight of the young girl, raised a murmur of admiration and pity.

Never had there been collected together at Grasse, so great a crowd as that which then filled the streets of that city. Stopped at every moment of its passage, the tumbril advanced extremely slow.

With my head resting on my breast for shame, and absorbed

in grief, I mechanically followed my company which escorted the fatal tumbril.

The multitude who awaited the arrival of the condemned in the square, uttered such cries when they appeared, that sister Agatha, disturbed in her devotions. cast around her a long and inquiring look. The first object which met her view was the scaffold. The sun shone full upon the keen blade, which sparkled in the rays. At this sight, Lavaux, whose fury had given place to complete prostration, began to sob. Agatha turned pale, and a nervous agitation shook her limbs.

"Courage, my child," said the priest "that iron which alarms you so much, will knock, in falling, at the gate of heaven." These words restored serenity to the victim.

In two minutes our detachment surrounded the guillotine, before which the tumbril stopped. "My brother," said sister Agatha, "you and I are going to appear before God!"

"There is no God,"—said Lavaux, "for if there was he would not let them cut my throat thus."

"Do you believe then, brother," answered she, "that if God had not given me courage, I should be so tranquil in the prospect of death?"

Hereupon, the executioner, assisted by his assistants, seized her, and pushed her before him towards the stairs of the scaffold; the young girl mounted them with a firm and confident step. Immediately the vile purveyors of death rushed upon her, and with brutal hands, laid her down upon the fatal plank. "Long live sister Agatha!" cried a sonorous voice, which rose in the midst of the silence—it was that of Anselme.

On seeing the poor victim thus mauled by the wretched butchers, I had shut my eyes. Never shall I forget the fearful impression produced in my mind by the fall of the hatchet. Lost in grief, I tried to persuade myself that I was the sport of some fearful dream; when an uproar near me, followed by a violent movement of the crowd, recalled me to real life.

"Ah the shabby fellow," cried a sans-culotte of the purest species; at least, if one might judge by his costume;—"Ah the blackguard; he rebels and will not make up his mind to the guillotine!"

I raised my eyes to the guillotine. Horrible! The blood streamed from it!

The spectacle which it presented, was the most hideous and striking that can be conceived. Lavaux, foaming at the mouth, struggled and uttered harsh and inarticulate cries, in the midst of the officials, striking, scratching, and biting them with the utmost rage, and thus kept them at a distance. At last the combatants, fatigued with such a resistance, called for the help of the soldiers of our detachment. I blush to confess it, but truth obliges me to say, that several of my comrades answered the appeal. The furious Lavaux was soon laid upon the plank, and in a few seconds he was dead! The crowd shouted,— "Long live the mountain! Death to the traitors!"

I then hoped that this bloody drama had terminated; but I was mistaken. When the cries of the crowd were a little subsided, the executioner seized the two heads of the prisoners, and hurled them into the middle of the square. The cries of "Long live the mountain!" rose again with greater strength. When the mutilated head of the unfortunate sister Agatha rebounded from the ground, an old woman took it up, kissed it in the forehead, and cried with a steady voice:—"Never did a more holy relic pass the threshhold of a church!" No notice was taken of this remark, which might otherwise have involved the death of her who pronounced it.

The drum beat and we were about to return to the quarters, when I saw the ranks disband themselves, and our men collected in a crowd, round a grenadier who had just fainted and fallen on the ground. I approached and recognised my friend Anselme. Every one attributed this accident to the heat; they little knew the heart of Anselme.

CHAPTER V.

Edmond and Gerard again; Their hiding place.—Gerard's narrative.—The chateau of Grand-boeuf; Its attack, and gallant defence.—A revolutionary peasantry.—The chateau abandoned and burnt.—Escape and revenge of Gerard.—He enlists.—Anselme meditates a change of party.—The camp at Saorgio.—We are reviewed by the General.—I smell powder for the first time.—Queer feelings.—I come off conqueror.—Life in the camp.—A deserter; His dinner and death.—A secret expedition.—Surprise and slaughter of the Piedmontese.—Anselme wounded.—I leave the camp on furlough.—Arrive at Messins.—Return to Grasse.—Transformation of Verdier.—Arrive at Toulon.—Massacre of a workman.—My own narrow escape.

During the four or five days succeeding the execution of Sister Agatha and Lavaux, I remained in a melancholy state of mind, shut up in my chamber, and saw Verdier but rarely.

"My dear friend," said he one morning on entering my chamber, "I have a service to ask of you, and one that will require all your coolness and energy."

"Speak," said I, "I am at your command."

"This is the case; I have received a letter from my cousin Edmond, who begs of you to meet him instantly at the ruins, will you go?"

I had no thought of refusing, and an hour after breakfast

I started. It was noon when I arrived at the old Chateau of the Templars: I had seated myself upon the same stone which had served me for a place of rest upon my first excursion into these latitudes, when a slight whistle attracted my attention.

" This way my dear friend," said the voice of Edmond ;— "pass along the postern before you."

I obeyed. The postern was so low, narrow, and obstructed with rubbish, that I had some trouble to clear myself a passage. At last I found myself in a kind of court, enclosed by the walls of the Donjon, Edmond waited for me.

" I ask your pardon my dear Sir," said he, clasping my hand amicably, for the trouble I have given you; but you know my position, and cannot blame the precaution that I take. Anselme is on the watch. Will you pass into the saloon?

Following him through a long, dark, and narrow corridor, I came to a spacious room, lighted by a lamp suspended from the roof.

Two bunches of straw which represented beds, two chairs roughly put together, and a board supported by four stakes representing a table, completed the household goods of the outlaws. A small cask of wine, some sacks of beans, and five or six bottles of oil, were all the provisions at their disposal. Four double-barrelled pistols hung up against the wall, constituted their arsenal.

As we entered, a shrill whistle was heard. " Tis my friend Gerard, who is coming to present his respects to you." said Edmond. The old soldier steward appeared almost immediately, and shook me warmly by the hand.

"Sir," said he, I cannot express the gratitude I owe you for your presence here. You have doubtless not forgotten the hope, you raised the last time I had the honour of seeing you."—He referred to a plan at which I had hinted for rescuing him from his present dangerous position.

"No Gerard! I will do all in my power to assist you.

"And you were good enough to add, that you had a very simple plan."

"Which I am quite ready to communicate to you! However, I confess I shall not be sorry first to know your history."

"Faith, I think it will only weary you."

"Fear not that; speak, I am listening."

I took a chair, Edmond threw himself upon one of the bunches of straw, and Gerard, seating himself between us, commenced his history.

"My life," said he, "dates from my entering the regiment in which I served fifteen years, with the Count de Grand-boeuf. The Count was colonel at three years of age, whilst at twenty I was still only brigadier. I taught him all that was necessary for a colonel to know, that is to say, five or six commands and three or four evolutions, which obtained for me the rank of quarter-master."

"The Count was sixteen and I was thirty-five, when he withdrew me from the regiment, and placed me as steward in his chateau of Grand-boeuf."

"I led the happiest life that can be imagined, when, about three years ago, the first clouds of the storm which now raged shewed themselves in the horizon. The Count was one of the first to emigrate. One night he arrived unexpectedly at the chateau. Gerard, said he to me, the rustics are turned fools, and dream of becoming my equals. I am going to join the Princes abroad, and we will soon return and bring these blackguards to reason! until my return I trust the defence of my chateau to you, and invest you with discretionary powers. All my people will be under your superintendence. If Grand-boeuf is attacked, I know your courage and energy, and I do not doubt for an instant that you will come out of this enterprise triumphant. On my return I shall know how to reward you amply for your courage and zeal. I swore to the Count that I would shew myself worthy of the confidence he had thus placed in me."

" I immediately set about purchasing a great store of arms, and putting Grand-boeuf into a state of defence. But I did not stop here; I went to all the most discontented vassals on the domain, and tried to conciliate them. I made myself acquainted with their embarrassments and wants, and generously assisted them. Success seemed to attend the effort, the grateful vassals promised to remain faithful to their Seigneur."

Some days passed without producing any incident, when I heard of the pillage and burning of a neighbouring chateau; and the same night the vassals of the domain came to look for me, and one of them, delegated by his comrades, entertained me with the following discourse.

" Monsieur Deputy, grateful for the goodness of Seigneur, we have decided to respect his chateau, we have therefore arranged with our friends of the neighbouring district, that they shall allow us to attack and destroy the chateau of their Seigneur, whilst they will demolish and burn that of Grand-boeuf! In this way, we shall not have the vexation of coming to blows with you. Now that you have been warned, you can take your precautions accordingly."

" My friends, said I, I would as soon have you for opponents as your neighbours, do not therefore oppress yourselves with your feelings of gratitude, come whenever you think proper, will be ready to entertain you."

" If its all the same to you, Monsieur Gerard, that we shall attack the chateau of our Seigneur, we will avail ourselves of your permission," answered the orator of the troop.

"Well then its all agreed, my grateful friends," said I, choose your time ; on my part I shall take my precautions."

" The night after I had received this singular deputation, there arrived at the chateau, one of the cavaliers of the Count's regiment. As no one had seen this man enter, I availed myself of the circumstance to spread abroad a report, that a detachment of thirty cavaliers, commanded by an officer of the regiment, had arrived at Grand-boeuf. To give more likelihood to this report, I ordered the cavalier whenever he perceived peasants in the neighbourhood, to shew himself as much as possible."

" The garrison I commanded, was composed in all of fourteen men. We were in no want of arms: our arsenal contained sixty double-barrelled fire-arms, besides one piece of artillery carrying a pound ball, and on the use of which we reckoned much."

"One afternoon we were going to sit down to table, when the sentinel came to warn us that the peasants were marching upon the chateau. On running to see, I beheld at least four thousand men, armed with pikes, scythes, and muskets, who were advancing with shouts towards us!"

" As we had been for a long time preparing to sustain a siege, we had only to repair to our posts, and await the enemy."

" Not willing to neglect any means, I presented myself at the iron gate of the court of honour, to enter into a parley. The peasants immediately surrounded me "

" My friends," said I, I have to caution you that we have decided, if the fortune of war turns against us, to blow ourselves up! Ten barrels of powder are stowed away in the cellars. See what you have to expect !"

" Unfortunately, my threat, not having reached the extremities of the crowd, the distant ranks pressed forward. I then sought to regain my post, but the peasants detained me."

"I am very sorry to occasion you any uneasiness, citizen Gerard," said one of the chiefs, "for really you are not a bad lad; but you must have the goodness now to let us shoot you! You understand that we are not such fools as to release so brave a man as you!"

"My friends," said I, "I see it is impossible to offer any resistance; let me return to my garrison, and try to prevail on them to lay down their arms. Promise me to respect the life of my sixty men, and I engage that they will abandon the chateau without defending it."

"My proposal was accepted, and they left me to withdraw safe and sound. My thirteen companions waited my return with great anxiety."

"Comrades," said I, "the peasants will grant us neither truce nor mercy!" Let us defend ourselves therefore, with the energy of despair, and if we must fall, let us not die unrevenged!

"I had scarcely finished my address, when the assailants enraged at seeing that we did not open the gates, uttered loud cries, and advanced to the assault, and a discharge of musketry sent thirty balls against the walls of the chateau."

"Fire, on all sides!" cried I.

"Immediately the windows of the chateau were lighted up with a girdle of flame. The cries of rage and grief which arose from the ranks of the besiegers, proved that our reply had taken effect."

"This first success put the peasants to flight, but having recovered from their panic, they soon resumed the attack."

"I shall pass by the several episodes of this battle, which lasted till the end of the day. Thanks to the excellent position we occupied, not one of us was wounded, except the ex-steward, who received a ball in the shoulder; while thirty of the ememy had fallen."

"Night came, and fatigued with the inutility of their efforts, the peasants, a little before sun-rise, withdrew from the chateau."

"We were thus victorious; but alas! it was evident that the vassals, instigated by the spirit of revenge, and the hope of pillage, would not cease their hostilities."

"Two days passed in a profound peace and tranquility, and I began to comfort myself with the idea that we had got rid of our enemies, when, on the third day,—a Sunday,—we saw them return, still more numerous than ever."

"This second assault was much more bloody than the first, we had the utmost difficulty in repulsing the peasants, who, intoxicated with brandy and rage, were killed in numbers at the foot of the walls."

"Thanks to a discharge of old nails, which we fired from our piece of artillery point blank upon them, we cleared not only the grand avenue, but the park of the chateau."

"An old housekeeper whose great age prevented her from following the Count abroad, beat the drum furiously during the whole of the attack, and made such a noise that the peasants withdrew, convinced that the chateau was defended by more troops than I had confessed to them."

"At length our ammunition failed, and we were forced to hold a council of war, It was proposed that we should take our sabres, and cut a passage through the enemy. I strongly represented that it was folly to think of cutting a passage through four thousand men. My friends, cried I, after reflecting a few moments, dress yourselves like peasants, cut off your beards, exchange your boots and shoes for wooden clogs, and hold yourselves ready to execute my orders."

"They all obeyed without hesitation. The old housekeeper alone came to me, and in a piteous voice: What is to become of me, Gerard? said she.

"Faith, good mother," answered I, "you must remain in the chateau, to do the honours to these gentlemen. It is at least impossible, unless they should be cannibals, that they would not respect your sex and age."

"My comrades soon returned, so well disguised, that a practised eye would not have detected them."

"Now my friends," said I to them, "follow my orders! You, Gervais, go and open softly the iron gate of the grand avenue, and the gate of the inner court. Mind,—if you let yourself be seen, all is lost."

"After a suspense of a quarter of an hour, Gervais returned, assuring me that he had opened the iron gate of the avenue and the door of the inner Court without being perceived."

"Now," said I, "load our little piece of cannon with old iron to the muzzle and take it to the vestibule."

"And what then, Commander?" demanded the cavalier."

"Then place yourselves in three ranks in the vestibule, behind the piece of cannon, and wait my orders."

"We soon saw the peasants advance in a crowd, and without any kind of precaution; the hinder ones pushed on the foremost, and in less than five minutes the court yard was so crowded that they were unable to act."

"Fire!" cried I, opening the door of the vestibule."

"At that instant twenty five musket shots were fired; the fish guard let loose a dozen furious bull-dogs, and our cannon sent its volley of old iron."

"Never, was panic more complete; mad with affright they trod one another under foot; and massacred each other without pity."

"Come comrades," said I, "the moment for saving ourselves is come; let us mix with this crowd, and lets each take his own course; Good bye, and may God protect you! Suiting the action to the word, I threw myself amongst the peasants, and soon opened myself a passage."

" In another hour, sheltered in a wood two leagues from the chateau, I perceived an immense sheet of flame, which rose to heaven, It was a fire of revolutionary joy; the ancient manor of the Counts de Grand-boeuf was burned by their vassals, amidst ries of " *Vive la liberté, L'Egalite et la fraternité!*"

" You may easily imagine what I suffered during the week that followed the burning of the chateau ; not daring to adventure myself out of the wood in which I had taken refuge, for fear of falling into the hands of my enemies, I had to, suffer all the horrors of hunger, thirst, and solitude."

"As soon as I dared, I abandoned the environs of the village and fled straight on, commending myself to God, Sleeping at nights in the ditches or the woods, and hiding myself in the bushes during the day, I led for many months the most painful and frightful life that can be conceived. Exasperated at length by being tracked like a wild-beast, I resolved to return evil for evil, and thus revenge myself."

" I began to make war on my own account against the republicans ; woe to the belated soldier, who passed within range of my firelock, which I had procured ! Woe, to the sans-culotte whom my arms could reach ! Both disappeared for ever from the world !"

" So," cried I, interrupting him, " when you had surprised me the first time, near this ruinous chateau, your intention was,"

" To kill you certainly ! answered Gerard.—" without the intervention of Edmond you would now be no more."

I requested him to proceed with his recital.

" 1 am come to the end " said he.—One day, a happy chance placed me upon the steps of Edmond who was also pursued, and I was fortunate enough to be of some utility to him."

" That is to say, that without your help I should have been taken and guillotined, Gerard," answered Edmond."

"I believe it," resumed the quarter master continuing to address me;" to start from that moment, sir, my existence, although still troubled enough, changed its aspect. I had a friend, and one upon whom I could depend! Judge then of my joy! Edmond and I at once concluded a *defensive alliance;* and we promised each other mutual help whatever were the forces that came to attack us. I may add, without boasting, that we have both faithfully kept this engagement. This sir, is the whole of my history."

"I thank you for your complaisance; your recital has exceedingly interested me. Now, let us not waste time, but consider in what way I can be useful to you, Would you have a great repugnance to take service again in the army?

" What a curious idea !"

" Not so curious! It is the only means of getting for ever out of your dangerous and false position. Follow me boldly to Grasse. I will present you to my commander, as one of my comrades of infancy; he will incorporate you in our batallion; and when once you shall have the republican uniform upon your back, I will consent to be shot to death, if ever they think of asking you who you are, or where you came from.'

The idea of quitting Edmond produced such an effect upon Gerard, that at the instant he was upon the point of refusing my offer, he could not bring himself to think of separating from his friend. At last, after much hesitation, and when Edmond had repeated many times that, being himself about to emigrate, his refusal would leave only a few days for their being together, Gerard concluded to listen to the voice of reason, and consented to follow me.

Gerard and I entered into Grasse about night-fall, the excellent Verdier received us with open arms, and applauded Gerard much for the steps he had taken.

The next morning I went to find my commander and presented the ex-quarter-master to him as an excellent acquisition to our batallion. My superior eagerly accepted his services. The same evening, Gerard, accoutred as a soldier, promenaded the city of Grasse, where, if he had been taken the night previous, he would have been guillotined.

A week afterwards the order came for our batallion to march for the camp, at Saorgio

The batallion was to set out the next morning,, and I was occupied in conversing with my host, when Anselme came to look for me.

" Ah ! there you are, deserter," cried I, "you have neglected me greatly for some time ! Are you fallen in love ?"

" In love !" repeated Anselme, shrugging his shoulders, no my friend, I am not in love, but I wish I had a fever."

" That's a comical desire ! In what respect would that serve you ?

" Just to obtain leave of absence, or rather to reform me."

" Does the service then lie so heavy on you, that you would sacrifice your health to get away from it ?"

" The military service properly speaking, is quite to my taste. What makes me so much desire to recover my liberty, is the shame I feel in thinking who are the people whom I serve."

" France, Anselme."

" Do you call it serving France to protect a scaffold, upon which a martyr is sacrificed ? Since the execution of sister Agatha, I have not enjoyed an instant of repose ; it appears to me that I have taken part with her assassins !"

" What do you wish to do, what profession do you intend to embrace ?"

" I intend to remain what I am, that is, a soldier ; but I wish to efface the blue and the red from my cockade, and serve the white."

"Then you will go to join the princes abroad?"

"No! cried Anselme quickly, I want rather to fight with Frenchmen against Frenchmen. It appears that La Vendeé and La Bretagne, far from yielding basely like the rest of France, resist the unclean tyranny of Robespierre and St. Just. I shall go to La Vendeé or La Bretagne.—But let us defer this subject."

The thought of quitting Grasse pleased me greatly; one thing alone gave me pain, which was, the separation form my excellent host, for whom I had conceived a warm and hearty friendship. The next morning it was scarcely daylight, when the batallion gathered upon the Grand square, and began their march to the sound of the drums: by seven o'clock we were nearly two leagues from the city of Grasse.

I dont intend to discribe, step by step, the march of the batallion from Grasse to Lantosque, the last village we entered, before reaching the camp at Saorgio, from which it was about two hours march distant. Still, I cannot pass over in silence the impression of deep sorrow produced in me by the sad and desolate aspect of the country; on all sides we saw only cottages in ruins, houses burned. granges riddled with balls or the hatchets of the military Flocks there were none! The inhabitants, on taking flight, had driven off their cattle. The weather was beautiful; the emerald carpet that spread itself to the sun, the flowers which cast to the winds their sweet perfumes, formed with this abandonment and melancholy silence, a painful and striking contrast.

Anselme undertook the business of foraging. Sometimes he procured a pullet; at others, a piece of beef, or a slice of a horse; and in short, our improvised camp-table was never empty. The ravens who scented carnage produced by the horrors of war, and seemed to have acquired a rendezvous in the bounderies of the camp, were not disdained by Anselme, who knew where to find a savoury part in them. He called them *(black partridges!")* We had slept about an hour in the abandoned cottages of Lantosque, when the report of cannon growling in the distance reached us. This was the first time I had heard the roar of battle, I could not resist a certain sensation.

" Do you know Anselme," said I, " that I have never yet witnessed an engagement! It seems to me, that the first time I shall make a pitiful appearance."

" Bah!" said Anselme, " you will do as everybody else does,—begin by being afraid of the bullets, and end by not regarding them."

" Does not the noise of the cannon hinder you from sleeping, Anselme?"

A hollow snoring from my comrade, replied to my question.

The next morning we began our march for the camp at Saorgio, where we arrived in two hours. An immense red cap, hung at the top of a pole, rose by the side of a tent occupied by the General, and served for a flag at the headquarters.

Never shall I forget the picturesque aspect the camp presented. Nothing could be seen but ghastly figures, whose clothing fell in shreds, and rusty arms.

We learned that a sharp engagement had taken place the evening before, with the Piedmontese, and that fifty of our soldiers were left dead on the field of battle.

On passing near a tent, or to speak more correctly, an old piece of linen stretched over four stakes which rose five feet above the ground, I heard cries and groans that froze the blood in my veins.

" What's passing there?" asked I of a soldier who came out with his arm in a sling, from under the cloth.

" That is the dressing room of the people who were slashed last night during the enterprise with the Piedmontese, and they are setting them to rights," said he.

P

In the afternoon the General passed us in review. In conscience he could not praise our appearance, nor did he indeed make any remarks upon it; but he enlarged much upon our courage and patriotism, praised us for the resolution we had formed of dying rather than surrender,—a resolution be it said in passing, that had never been thought of,—and finished by interlarding the word "country" with that of "tyrants" with such skill, that although that part of his speech was entirely destitute of sense, we were electrified, and applauded it with enthusiasm. He had scarcely finished his harangue, when one of his Aids-du-camp came to warn him that a corps of Piedmontese was ambushed in the wood that bordered on the camp.

"Soldiers!" cried the General, "considering the time you have lost, I will give you the preference in going to reconnoitre the enemy. It is a mission both difficult and dangerous to fulfil; shew yourselves therefore, by your conduct, worthy of the favour I have granted you."

The General then spoke a few words to our commander; after which he set off at a gallop.

"Adjutant!" cried our commander, addressing himself to me, "your promotion has been rapid, and you will hasten to win the epaulet you wear. Take thirty men with you, and go and reconnoitre the enemy."

A cold shudder passed through me, and I remained straight and motionless as a statue, without knowing what to answer.

"Are these men that are demanded, to be volunteers?" said I, addressing the commander,

"Yes, volunteers are required, for I do'nt wish to excite jealousy."

I then turned to the batallion, and in a voice which I tried to render strong and composed; "Who will volunteer and come with me?"

THE COMBAT.

" I ! I !" cried Anselme shouting aloud.

" I ! I !" repeated in chorus, the five hundred men of the batallion.

Five minutes after I set out at the head of thirty stout men to reconnoitre and beat out, if possible, the corps of the enemy whose presence in the wood in the vicinity of the camp, had been announced to us.

The borders of the wood into which we entered were covered with underwood,—thin, but thick enough to hide an ambuscade. I therefore ordered my men to deploy singly in order to cover the greatest possible extent of ground. Scarcely had this order been executed, than a discharge of musketry took place, and a soldier near me, struck by a ball, fell covered with blood at my feet.

Some suspicous whistling sung in the air near me, and made me shake.

" Do'nt mind them," said Anselme, " they are bullets : command us to advance."

" Come my lads," cried I, " be firm, charge these slaves, these satellites ! Forward ! Children of the country !"

The men obeyed my orders with unparalleled enthusiasm. Darting upon the Piedmontese before they had time to re-load, charged them boldly with the bayonet. The issue of the combat was not long in suspense. In less than five minutes we had killed two men, wounded seven others, made five prisoners, and put the rest to flight. We were conquerors!

Having secured our prisoners, we took our route back to the camp; but before leaving the spot, I ordered the men to construct a litter to transport the wounded.

" Do'nt trouble yourself about those slaves of the king, Adjutant," answered an old sergeant, who formed part of my detachment ; " leave them to me."

" Very well sergeant, I shall trust to you, to see them taken to the camp."

The sub-officer smiled in a significant manner, and went away without saying a word.

I was about to sound a retreat, when several musket shots which sounded from behind a bush at a few paces from where I stood, made me tremble; I thought it was a surprise.

" Give no heed to it," said Anselme, " they are the prisoners whom they have sent off."

" How! Cried I what do you mean by that?"

" I mean that the sergeant has shot the wounded men."

" Horrible and infamous! Can it be possible?"

" Come, don't put yourself out for such a trifling matter," said Anselme, what is done is a thing that occurs every day! Nay, you may knit your brows, and bite your lips, but you will never change the character of war; we must learn to accustom ourselves to cruelties which we are unable to prevent. Now, if you think proper, command the retreat "

Whilst we were returning to the camp, we conversed about the skirmish.

" Faith officer," said a young corporal who saw fire for the first time, " I will bet that you have had an affair with more than a hundred men!"

"Hold your tongue," said the old sergeant shrugging his shoulders; " you don't know what you are talking about, I am certain that the Piedmontese were our inferior in number."

"Ah then serjeant, that's a little too strong! what was the number of the enemy, according to your opinion?"

" Twenty-five or thirty men at most; we were nearly of equal strength.,"

This answer which considerably abated my triumph, did not please me much; and ordering one of my Piedmonese prisoners to come to me; " How many were you when you attacked us?" I asked.

"We were nineteen men," answered he; you have killed nine of them, five are prisoners, and five have saved themselves; that accounts for the whole."

This very exact information dissipated a little the vapours of vanity which got into my brain, but it did not wholly deprive me of the pleasure of victory.

The life we led in the camp was far from agreeable: the provisions we received, insufficient and of bad quality, only half supplied our wants. Our equipments and dress were still worse.

After the first two months in which I led this rough life of a soldier, I became accustomed to a camp life. Night surprises, skirmishes, and mounting guard, no longer caused that sensation which I had experienced at the commencement.

One morning at the distribution of the rations, we found to our great disappointment, that a convoy upon which we reckoned, had been intercepted by the enemy, and that we must pass the day without eating. As for several days already, our rations had been pared down to the starving point, and we were reduced to the pangs of hunger. This news caused a considerable effervesence amongst us. One poor fellow, a grenadier of the name of Noireau endowed with a huge appetite, incapable of longer supporting such stern abstinence, was arrested in an attempt at desertion.

Immediately a council of war assembled, and Noireau was condemned to be shot. My bad star ordered it that I was commanded to carry the sentence into execution.

When I went to find him in the tent which served for a prison, Noireau guessed that I was a messenger of death.

"Alas! Adjutant," said he, "you are come then to conduct me to the place of execution."

"You have guessed right, my poor Noireau," I answered, "I am in fact, charged with warning you that you have only an hour to live, and to ask if you have any last arrangements to make."

"Thanks my good officer, but how do you suppose a poor wretch like me, can have any arrangements to make?"

"Then good bye, Noireau,—have courage."

I was about leaving, when the prisoner seized me by the arm, and with a look half of shame, and half of entreaty;

"I want Adjutant," said he, to put a question to you, but I dare not."

"Speak my friend, and be assured I will do what I can for you."

"Is it true Adjutant, that when a man is condemned to death, they grant him before execution whatever he asks, pardon excepted!"

"Yes, Noireau, that's the custom."

"Well then," resumed the grenadier quickly, "if I require them to serve me a good dinner?"

"They shall do all they can to satisfy you."

"Well then quick! Let us have the promised dinner Adjutant."

Thanks to my zeal, I procured for Noireau a sumptuous dinner, namely, a slice of a roasted horse, twenty chesnuts, two apples, half a pound of bread, and half a pint of brandy.

The convict had finished his dinner, when, at the head of a platoon charged with his execution, I presented myself before him. I found him in high spirits.

"Faith officer," said he, "I have not perhaps acted so foolishly in deserting; this morning is one of the best in my life! I regret only one thing, that I can't retain the recollection of it longer. Come, I am not so much to be pitied; I have had a capital breakfast this morning! My mother died two years back, and will not feel the counter blow of my execution. Nothing retains me here below; adieu Adjutant, and many thanks for your goodness!"

Immediately after, five muskct-shots were heard, and Noireau fell with his face to the ground. In a few minutes, a little mound scarcely visible above the ground, shewed that the pioneers had, in their turn, fulfilled their sad task in this melancholy drama.

Towards the middle of *Prairial*, we received the order one night, to hold ourselves ready the next morning to take our soup at seven o'clock, and we conjectured that some important expedition was on foot; nor were we mistaken. The next day, towards eight o'clock we were on march with seven other batallions.

By three o'clock in the afternoon we arrived at the entrance of a beautiful valley, crowned on the right and left with a copse of oaks. Our division separated in two corps, nearly equal, and went to occupy the two sides. As to our batallion, we entered the coppice with orders to preserve the most profound silence, as we were placed in ambuscade.

When the sun rose above the horizon, we were worn down with fatigue. It had rained during the night, and the leaves of the trees covered with drops of water, shone in the sun's rays like caskets of diamonds. Aromatic plants and flowers exhaled delicious perfumes, which plunged us in a kind of soft intoxication. I was gazing on the landscape, when a strong pressure on the arm recalled me to the sentiment of real life.

"Look !" said Anselme, "there's the enemy !"

In fact at that moment a numerous corps of Piedmontese debouched at a distance of less than a mile. There were about fifteen hundred men.

The Piedmontese made their way cheerfully : the noise of their songs reached us, and I cannot express the deep pity I felt at that moment for those unfortunate people. All at once, the signal of attack was given : from the woods right and left issued a formidable discharge of musketry. Cries of despair and affright took the place of the songs, and a number of the Piedmontese were stretched bleeding on the ground.

Recovering from their surprise, they endeavoured to effect a retreat, but the outlets of the valley were occupied, and everywhere a shower of balls met the attempt. Already the ranks were exposed to our view, when the order was given to charge them with the bayonet.

We threw ourselves upon the enemy with the bayonet. The Piedmontese finding that all was lost, defended themselves with heroic bravery, and resigning themselves to death, thought only of revenge. The recollection of that hour of carnage follows me still at times in my sleep, and never will it be erased from my memory!

It was only after an hour of butchery,—for I cannot find a more appropriate word,—and when about a thousand Piedmontese corpses were lying at our feet, that I recovered my self possession.

As soon as my blood was cooled and recollection returned, my first thought was of Anselme. In vain I sought my friend, in vain I ran through the ranks which began to re-form, nowhere could I find Anselme. I ran at last in despair to the surgeon's quarters, which had been improvised for the purpose of relieving the wounded.

Alas! the first person I perceived was Anselme! A surgeon kneeling before him, shaking his head with an aspect of doubt, was sounding a deep wound which he had received in the breast.

" Do you think him in danger ?" I asked anxiously of the surgeon. He regarded me with a sharp expression, and then with the phlegm peculiar to his profession, replied, " Had not you better ask me Adjutant if he is dead ?"

" So then," cried I in despair, " Anselme is lost !"

"So far lost," replied he, "that I am going to lay him aside, and employ myself about other wounded. If you wish to have him buried, faith you are welcome to do it! He is not really dead, but it is all the same."

This barbarous reply exasperated me. "Citizen," said I, "I insist, do you hear, that you employ yourself about my friend!"

The surgeon judged it more prudent to obey than discuss. He unclasped the uniform of Anselme, and drawing a probe from his case, he searched for the ball that had entered his breast.

"It is really lost trouble to attempt the extraction of this projectile," said he, shrugging his shoulders.

"Do it, however," cried I.

The surgeon commenced the operation.

"Well!" said I, feeling myself ready to faint.

"Well, here's the ball," replied he, shewing me a small piece of lead of an irregular form. "Still it does not follow that the subject is out of danger. My opinion is, that he has only a few hours to live." He then bandaged the wound.

The sound of the drum called me away from my friend and I returned to my post, recommending Anselme to one of our friends, who promised to watch over him.

We were about to commence our march to regain the camp when I received an order from our chief of batallion to remain with a company, to overlook and protect the pioneers charged with the interment of the dead.

This mission gave me great pleasure, as it would allow me to remain near Anselme, whose desperate condition prevented his being transported to the camp. A car was sent for the use of the wounded committed to my care, and a surgeon was left with me.

The pioneers placed under my orders were actively engaged

in removing these traces of the conflict Some armed with mattocks, dug immense trenches to receive the victims of the day: others stripped the bodies. On all sides were heaps of shirts, gaiters, hats, muskets, cartouch boxes, and clothes, the spoil both of the Piedmontese and the French mingled in this scene of death.

One circumstance which with me was a cause of deep emotion, was the gaiety displayed by these pioneers in executing their sad office, which they enlivened with frivolous and indecent songs, and ill-timed jests.

Night began already to envelope us in darkness, when three cars arrived, sent from the camp to transport the wounded. Although my men and myself were greatly fatigued, I resolved to march at once, for I was anxious to see Anselme well provided for.

During the following fortnight, Anselme's condition remained nearly the same—between life and death. Every morning on going to see him I expected to find only a corpse, and it grieved me to reflect upon this sad termination of his sufferings.

At last, with the help of nature, for the care that my poor friend received, was almost nothing, a slight improvement was apparent; and a week after by the effort of a strong constitution, he became out of danger. All the time I could spare from my duties, I passed with him, and the diversion of mind, our conversation occasioned hastened his recovery.

"Well, my friend" said he " you see God has worked a miracle in my favour, to reward me for my good intentions. If they were to offer me a million to induce me to abandon my plan, I would refuse it without hesitation."

"Then, as soon as you recover your strength you will set out for La Vendeé?"

"Even before that; as soon as I can can drag myself away without danger. I shall gain strength on my route."

"I think your determination wrong, but you seem so resolved to carry it into effect, that I no longer dare combat it."

I resolved, come what might, not to remain with the army after Anselme had left, and concerted with him the means of getting away.

I commenced by procuring from the surgeon with whom I became acquainted in the rounds, a certificate which I presented to our Commandant, to whom I stated that having been attacked by chronic rheumatism; it was impossible for me to continue my service.

I shall omit the detail of the steps I took, and the mortifications to which I had to submit, before I could get access to the General. At last, after eight days of manœuvring and solicitation, my request was attended, and the General sent for me.

"Adjutant," said he, "you solicit leave of absence on account of indisposition, and you have produced a certificate from a doctor in support of your pretensions. I only believe what I see: shew me your disorder."

"But General it is rheumatism!"

"That's nothing; shew me your rheumatism then."

I had a great deal of trouble in explaining to the General that what he required of me was impossible. It was not till he learned that I had an uncle who had been nominated a representative, that the General began to give me credit for sickness. Then seeming to emerge from his reflections he said in an amicable way; "After all if the rheumatism cannot be proved, I suppose I must act upon the surgeon's certificate. See, here's a leave of absence for three months."

I took the paper with as much eagerness as pleasure, and ran to Anselme to announce to him the happy news.

The next morning, without further delay, I set out, after taking an affectionate and painful farewell of my friend.

"Farewell," said he, "do not forget that you have a friend in me, devoted till death. But who knows, perhaps we shall meet again sooner than you think."

An hour after, I fled, rather than left the camp, so fearful was I that a counter order might still retain me under the flag. It was not till I had cleared at least a league that I stopped to recover breath.

At four o'clock in the afternoon I reached the little village of Messino, and at once entered an indifferent Inn,-the only one in the place,—which appeared to me, in comparison with the camp I had just quitted, a sumptuous dwelling. There I dined at my ease, and slept,—the first time for many weeks in a comfortable bed.

The next morning, I left Messino and passed through several villages, the inhabitants of which, being Piedmontese, had, within the year, become by the fate of arms, French citizens. I met with several going to market to sell their vegetables and fruit. On perceiving me, they began crying at the top of their voices, "Long live the Republic! Long live equality!"

From Menton where 1 arrived the same day, I went to Nice. I hoped to find in that city, Italian manners and gaiety, but I was cruelly deceived in my hopes. Invaded by our armies, Nice resounded from morning to night with the beat of the drum, and its villas disfigured with decrees and proclamations resembled so many clubs. I hastened to quit it as soon as possible.

From Nice to Grasse, no new incident occured on my route, and I entered the latter city, before day break.

My first care was to proceed to the house of Verdier. Judge of my astonishment and disappointment, when instead of the stylish front of his shop, I perceived it black and dirty, covered, with dust, charcoal and stains of smoke! the door being wide open, I at once entered.

"Citizen Verdier!" cried I, in a loud voice, on seeing no one.

"Here he is, at your service, citizen," replied a familiar voice. A man then came towards me, who, from his shabby appearance, I took for a workman. A moustache, bristling for want of culture, like that of an angry cat, and a face well bronzed, were the first things I noticed in casting my eyes on the speaker.

"Citizen Verdier? repeated I, gazing earnestly at him. He threw himself into my arms, and embraced me warmly, crying, "What! Dont you know me friend? Am I then so much altered?"

The surprise this metamorphosis produced in me was such, that I remained a moment stunned, and could not pronounce a word.

"What! Verdier! Is it you?" cried I at last, recovering a little, my presence of mind; "What has happened! and what is become of your perfumery shop?"

"You well know," said Verdier, lowering his voice, "that my two rivals, the perfumers, elected members of the committee of the Popular Society, desired to see me quit my trade. I have been compelled to conform to their secret wish."

"Ah, I recollect; but what profession do you exercise now?

"I am a saltpetre manufacturer."

"A saltpetre manufacturer! What a queer idea that is of yours!"

"It is the love of my country that has inspired me in this affair," "answered Verdier, raising his voice, as if he wished to be heard at a distance. "Saltpetre, converted into gunpowder, represents the glory of the republic, and the humiliation of the aristocrats; that's why I am a saltpetre maker."

The more I heard and saw of Verdier, the more my astonishment increased. "My dear Verdier," said I, "I am terribly fatigued, and I wish much to sit down. If we pass into your parlour we can converse more at our ease."

As the localities of the house were known to me, I did not wait for my friend's answer, but went towards the parlour. On entering the old back shop, I found a dozen workmen, who were employed extracting saltpetre.

"My friends," said Verdier indicating me to them by a motion of his hand, "here's a true sans-cullotte, just returned from the army, whom I introduce to you."

"A sans-culotte never returned from the army! Cried one of the workmen, looking towards me, and shrugging his shoulders, with an expression of contempt.

"Why so citizen?" Demanded I coldly, repressing the anger his insolence raised in me.

"Because a good citizen never turns his back on the enemy; at least however, if his cowardice."—

"Enough, scoundrel, hold your tongue!" Said I, not being able to contain myself any longer.

Verdier, fearing an altercation, thrust himself between the workman and me. At the word scoundrel, which I had addressed to the man who had so gratuitously insulted me, his comrades were advancing towards me with a threatening aspect.

Laying my hand immediately upon the hilt of my weapon, I exclaimed, "The first who takes a step more is a dead man!"

At this threat, the workmen stopped, and Verdier hastening to speak:

"My dear friend," said he, "why put yourself out thus? These citizens who work for their country, are free to express their opinions! You are wrong, my friend, you are wrong; recover yourself I entreat you, and do not forget the sublime words inscribed at the head of the constitution,—'Liberty, Equality, Fraternity!"

I confess that on seeing Verdier, thus cowardlike, taking the part of my enemies against me, the strong affection I felt for him at once disappeared, and was replaced by a feeling of commiseration and contempt. Addressing myself therefore, to the workman who had so grossly apostrophised me, "It becomes you well scoundrel to talk of war, you who have never seen any other fire than that of a furnace! Scoundrel! to teach you to speak another time with more moderation, I shall denounce you for your conduct to the Committee of Public Safety!"

"Citizen," answered he, disdainfully, "we are too poor to be afraid of the Committee of Public Safety; it can do nothing against us. The revolution has been effected for our advantage. We despise your denunciation."

"If that's the case," cried I, "I shall go to the guard house and acquaint my comrades that there is, at the house of citizen Verdier, not saltpetre works, but a manufacture of defamation and injuries towards the soldiers of the republic You are above the laws! Be it so! We shall see if you will brave the swords of the defenders of the country."

This threat impressed the workmen much more strongly, and I think it was not without a certain degree of pleasure, that they heard their employer entreat me not to follow up this proposition—to which I at length consented with a show of reluctance. "I have forgiven you," said I, "no blood has been shed; but I swear to you that this is the last time I will allow my comrades, the defenders of the country, to be calumniated with impunity? Consider yourselves warned."

"After making this answer in a solemn tone, I left the back shop with a majestic step.

Verdier's garden which I crossed to come at the parlour

presented a scene of the most complete devastation. A few months before, it was the pride of my host, and was considered the richest in rare plants, of any in the city. Now there was nothing to look at but a bed of potatoes.

"You dont understand this change," said Verdier on observing my astonishment, "Flowers are aristocratic pleasures; potatoes feed the unfortunate."

"Verdier! Is it possible that you, whom I have known so independent, can thus have prostrated yourself before the mob!"

"Lower still!" said the perfumer, lowering his voice; Wait till we are in the parlour, and I will unfold to you my fate!

Verdier, being an old bachelor, prided himself much upon the elegance of his interior accommodation, even his workshop, a kind of mysterious *retiro*, was in perfect harmony with the delicious garden it was necessary to cross in coming to it. Judge then of my astonishment on reaching this room, at perceiving no longer, any of the elegant furniture which ornamented it on my first stay at Grasse. The paintings on the walls had been effaced; the portraits of the members of the Committee of Public Safety, and those of General Safety, ugly, and horribly portrayed, formed a most disagreeable gallery, among which Robespierre, Marat, and Lepelletier, radiated, as the three deities, in the midst of this pleiades of parvenue assassins.

"Is it possible, my dear Verdier," said I sorrowfully, "that you can have reached this degree of fear, and place the word to my sincere friendship,—moral meanness."

"Do not despise me," cried he. "Ah! my friend, believe well that my heart is not changed, but my courage has failed. That image of the guillotine, the nightmare of my sleeping hours, and the terror of my days, has made me descend to this hypocrisy. I swear that it was not death that frightened me, but the contact with the executioner, the cries and outrage of the multitude, the hatchet covered with blood, the horrible swing board, the hamper, the inside of which bears the traces of the bitings of the heads that have fallen into it. In a word, that ignoble and fearful agony which precedes the death of the condemned! I have suffered so much, that nothing more remains for you, than the right to pity me!"

There was such poignant grief in his voice, that I had no longer the power to accuse him. On the contrary, I attempted to inspire him with a little courage.

After having remained two days at Grasse, I affectionately embraced the unfortunate Verdier, and again put myself in route.

I had so often, during the siege, heard speak of the city of Toulon, that I had long promised myself, if ever occasion served, to visit it in detail. Although the accomplishment of this project would cause me to deviate from my route, I resolved to profit by my liberty, and proceed towards that city.

From Grasse to Toulon, I had to endure numberless privations; it is impossible to conceive the formalities, the vexations, the delays I was obliged to submit to, to procure a few ounces of bread, half mouldy and nearly indigestible. The scarcity that prevailed in these provinces, was frightful.

A little before arriving at Toulon I met with two fellow-workmen, who troubling themselves very little about politics, and more given to the study of their craft,—that of locksmiths,—were making the tour of France.

One of these workmen, a young man of twenty-five years of age, was a Picard named Antoine.

"Ah! there are the city gates," cried I, on perceiving one of the walls of Toulon.—"My friends, if you will believe me, we shall do well to maintain an absolute silence."

"Why so, soldier?" asked Antoine.

Because an observation made by us in jest, and wrongly interpreted, might draw upon us serious inconveniences.

"Truly!" said Antoine, "Well so much the worse for the authorities, who dont know how to distinguish good patriots from conspirators! What does it signify to me, if I am not afraid of these fools! I am an honest man, and I say what I think."

"You are wrong Antoine," said the other, "you will end by finding yourself involved in some scrape."

"Let me alone then, with your silly fear," cried Antoine, "I shall say what I please! That I am going to retake Toulon on my own personal account, for instance, and declare myself King of France!"

At the moment in which the infatuated locksmith pronounced these words, a man, wearing a greasy phrygian cap, passed near us. On hearing Antoine, he stopped short, and seemed undecided for a moment, as to what part he ought to take.

"Hold, there's a spy going to denounce us!" continued Antoine, bursting into a laugh. "You will soon take me for a Capet."

Not wishing to incur the risk of this imprudent fellow's society, I took leave of my fellow travellers.

An hour later, installed in the little dark hotel of the *Grand Cerf*, I waited in the common dining room, until they brought me the repast I had ordered, when several patriots of the city entered. "Do you know the news?" said one of them, addressing himself to the hotel keeper. "It appears that spies have entered the city; and they say too, that foreign satellites, disguised like republican officers and soldiers are here in great numbers."

"Is it possible!" cried the hotel keeper, "The scoundrels, let them be arrested at once.

I confess, that although my leave of absence was regular, I felt very ill at ease on this proposal. Fortunately, I sat retired in a corner of the hall, and the darkness hid my confusion. I bitterly regretted having yielded to my curiosity in visiting Toulon, and I determined to quit that city the next morning, if nothing prevented me.

I was about to retire to the miserable truckle bed in which I intended to pass the night; when all at once, a distant rumour, which appeared to proceed from a mob of people, reached us, and detained me in the dining room.

The uproar soon approached the Hotel du Grand Cerf: furious exclamations resounded on all sides.

"Death to traitors! To the lamp-post with the spies! Down with the satellites of the tyrants! To the lamp-post! to the lamp-post with them!"

Scarcely had these cries reached my ears, when, on looking over the balcony, I perceived two men, bruised and bloody, flying before the crowd. One of them, the youngest of the two, seriously struck by some missile, advanced with pain and a violent effort, and I saw that he was lost. In fact I had scarcely come to this conclusion, when a bludgeon flung with as much force as precision, struck the unfortunate fugitive in the legs, and knocked him down.

Before he had time to rise, the crowd, like a pack of hungry hounds, flung themselves upon him. In a few seconds, the unfortunate man, lifted by twenty arms, was elevated in the midst of the crowd. "To the lamp-post with the Piedmontese spy!" was shouted on all sides.

Let the reader judge of my astonishment and agitation, on recognising in the pretended Piedmontese spy, the locksmith, Antoine, my travelling companion. My first thought was, to raise my voice in his favour; but on reflecting a moment, I held my tongue I am persuaded that if I had undertaken the defence of that unfortunate wretch, my fate would have been the same as his.

"Detestable satellite!" cried one of the orators, "Confess your treason, and we may perhaps pardon you!"

"I cannot confess what does not exist," answered Antoine, in a voice, hoarse from fatigue, grief, and fear. "Why do you wish me to acknowledge myself a Piedmontese, when I am a Picard?

"A coward and knave, as well as a traitor!" resumed the orator. "Really citizens, does not this man imitate the Picard accent to perfection? Happily, we are too sharp to be taken in with such a ruse!"

"But citizens, but friends! Hear me I entreat you," continued the poor locksmith, in a supplicating voice. "Upon my honour, upon the head of my mother, I swear that I am innocent!"

"He persists in his falsehood, the scoundrel! Cried a man wearing a cloak, whom I recognized as the same person in whose hearing Antoine, from a spirit of bravado and opposition, had boasted as he entered the city that he would take Toulon alone. "He persists, the villain!" Repeated the informer. "Ah well! Citizen I swear by the head of Robespierre, by the altar of Liberty, by the Constitution, that I have, with my own ears, heard that satellite boast of retaking Toulon, and of fighting for the cause of the Capets. Will you dare to deny this, you wretch?"

"That was a joke," answered the locksmith in a dull voice, "I wished to amuse myself at the expense of my companions."

"Ah! it was a jest," resumed the orator with great vehemence. "In fact the slavery and degradation of the people, the triumph of the king, the misery of the peasants, the tythe, the vassals labour, the rights of the seigneur, are all indeed charming jokes for the servants and agents of tyrants! Ah!

to fight for the abhorred family of the Capets, appears a joke to you! To retake Toulon is a joke! Be it so, we also know how to joke! And to prove it we are going to hang you!"

A tempest of cries and shouting followed this speech.

"Here's a rope," cried a sharp voice at that instant, screaming above the clamour of the crowd. It was a child, one of those hideous vagabonds who, unfortunately, are to be found in all great cities; his offer was accepted with loud bravos.

Then succeeded one of those horrible spectacles, the sight of which appears a hideous dream, and the recollection of which lasts to the end of life. Antoine, seized by the crowd, beaten, thrown down, bruised, was noosed by the fatal rope, and soon his corpse, hung to the lamp-post, swung quivering in the air. As for me, I fled away frightened.

I learned afterwards, how much the punishment of this poor innocent man had been cruelly increased. The cord supplied by the little vagabond, being only a thick straw-band, was not sufficiently strong to perform the terrible office they applied it to, and the wretched Antoine endured an agony of half an hour.

It was scarcely daylight next morning, when I descended from my garret, and having paid my small bill, made all post-haste to get away from Toulon.

CHAPTER VI.

I enter Marseilles.—The theatre in revolution.—My cousin Jouveau.—His character and present occupation.—The sweets of political life.—The —illustrious N———.—The laceman, Levite.—I dine with the Representative.—Revolutionary viands.—The Gilder.—Jouveau's petitioners. —He refuses to be merciful; and I leave him.—Feast of reason at Aix. —Adventure at St. Cuna.—I am taken for a great unknown.—A practical philospher in an aristocrat.—I revisit Avignon.—Revolutions.— A company of honourable mendicants.—I visit Nismes.—Fete to the Supreme Being.

My imagination was so much bewildered and excited by this horrible nocturnal scene, that in walking, I sung the Marseillaise at the top of my voice. I am persuaded that had I been asked, I would have cried at that moment, " Long live Robespierre." It was only on arriving at La Ciotat that I recovered a little the tranquillity of my mind!

The girl of the inn burst out into a loud laugh when I shewed her my passport as an invalid. "I see how it is," said she, "some serious affair recalls you, without a doubt into the interior. Ah well! take my advice, in passing through Marseilles, pay a visit to my brother who is a gilder in that city, and he will arrange all that."

Not caring to excite her suspicions, I took the letter which she intrusted to me for her brother.

Arrived at Marseilles, I found that that city no longer existed! The houses seemed abandoned, and resembled so many tombs; one might believe himself in a colossal cemetery, if it were not for hearing, from time, to time the roll of the drums.

The evening of the same day, I went to walk under the Fort St. Jean, where I perceived, through the bars of a low window, several suspected persons who were detained there, and awaited judgment. There was so little hope in the downcast eyes of these unfortunates, so much pallor and suffering in their wasted countenances, that I could perceive they anticipated the scaffold. What a capricious thing is the human mind! At the moment in which I was almost weeping over the fate of these victims, I observed a play bill that announced for the same evening, the performance of the comedy of Accetophilé and the Dragon, and the Benedictines. In a few minutes after,—explain this action as you please,—I purchased a box ticket, and entered the theatre.

Scarcely had I set foot in the play house, when a powerful and nauseous smell assailed me, but my curiosity was proof even against the disgust, occasioned by the emanations of garlick that filled the place, and I determined to remain and see how the people of this terror-struck city amused themselves. I took my place in the pit, in the midst of soldiers, mariners, and workmen, and proceeded to light my cigar.

It was not till after I had become acclimated a little, to the dense atmosphere which surrounded me, that I could see what passed.

Some of the spectators had found a victim to amuse themselves until the rising of the curtain. He was a stout man clothed in green, having his powdered hair imprisoned in a bag, and occupying a box by himself, and he soon became the butt of the assembly, under the pretext that he half turned his back upon them. Seeing that he was insensible to their cries, their mockings, and their jests, they soon proceeded to threats.

" Down with the green dress! Down with the livery of the ci-devant brother of the tyrant !"

The stout man as immoveable as the pillar against which he leaned, seemed alone not to perceive this storm. His coolness and disdain, exasperated his enemies to such a degree, that forgetting all other considerations, they thought of surrounding the box, and threatened death to the citizen dressed in green. Already the most furious had risen to accomplish this design, when a municipal officer appeared in one of the front boxes, and commanded silence.

This pretention was received with hootings ; and an apple, —I beg pardon for this trivial detail,—thrown with great violence, reached the face of the public functionary, which was instantly covered with blood.

Bravos and enthusiastic vivas, expressed the pleasure this outrage afforded the disturbers.

" Fire the boxes! Demolish the theatre! Nail up the tyrants valet in the shape of a lustre !" cried several voices amongst the drunken sailors.

At these threats, rendered fearful by the pantomimic action of those who offered them, the women in the boxes rose precipitately, and the greatest confusion followed.

Seeing that the affair was taking a serious turn, I slipped towards the entrance door of the pit, and from thence to the corridor. The first person I saw, was the unfortunate municipal officer, who had been so badly received ; he was conversing with a very young man, whose rather elegant dress contrasted strangely with the rags of the crowd.

This young man on perceiving me, uttered an exclamation of surprise, then advancing quickly towards me, he took me in his arms, and almost stifled me against his breast.

"What! Ingrate! Have you forgotten me? Do you no longer know me?" said he.

"Is it possible! You my cousin Jouveau!" cried I.

"Myself, my dear friend! How happy I am now to see you again!"

"Citizen," said the municipal officer, addressing my cousin Jouveau,—of whom I shall speak more in detail by and by,— "Do you hear those cries? Those mad fellows are going to demolish the theatre, if you don't interfere! Perhaps indeed the city of Marseilles will be in insurrection to-night!"

"True, I forgot!" said Jouveau coolly; Lets make these boasters hold their tongues." Then addressing me briskly. "Have you about you, a large sheet of paper?" he asked.

"I have my passport."

"That will do: give it me at once, and follow me."

"But what do you think of doing?"

"A new uproar which shook the theatre, did not allow my cousin to reply. He hastened towards one of the boxes, the door of which was opened for him by the municipal officer, and into which he flung himself.

"The representative!" cried the municipal officer.

At this simple sentence, the storm that raged in the theatre, ceased, as if by enchantment, and there was a deep silence. Jouveau, then advancing to the front of the box, unfolded my passport, and intoned, rather than read, the following order:

"Equality, fraternity, liberty, or death! The representative of the people, sent by the national convention into the department of the Bouches-du-Rhone, with illimitable powers, learning at the present moment the disturbance that has now taken place;"

"Considering, 1st. The sovereignty of the people, violation of the law; Considering 2nd Plots, the offspring of the

R

conspirators, Pitt and Cobourg; Considering 3rd. The thunder of the people, sword of the law, the revengeful axe, the scaffold, the falling heads, the expiatory blood ;"

"Resolved :".

Article 1. The law upon the liberty of dress, the tranquility of patriotic exhibitions, will be scrupulously provided for, and enforced.

Article 2. The instigators, favourers, accomplices, partizans, and adherents of the disturbance, which has been manifested in the theatre, will be pursued and judged revolutionarily with all the rigour of the laws.

Article 3. All good citizens will be required, on pain of being declared accomplices, and punished as such, to come and denounce the individuals denominated in the preceding article.

Article 4. An extract of this present will be sent to all the communes, in order that they may conform themselves thereto.

Done and resolved at Marseilles, the 3rd Messidor of the year 2 of the indivisible, immortal, and imperishable republic.

The representative of the people,

Signed, N———.

A true copy.

Signed, Curtius, Secretary.

After having intoned this decree, which he extemporized for the occasion, Curtius, as Jouveau was called, gravely refolded my passport and sat down, The orchestra immediately commenced playing patriotic airs, and the curtain rose.

"Now tranquillity is re-established," said Jouveau Curtius, "I must go and see a little why this stout man dressed in green,—whatever he has done,—has provoked the public. Perhaps there is some mischief in it."

"When shall I see you again, Jouveau?"

"Wait for me here; I will return immediately."

Jouveau and I had been fellow-students at college, and as my good father, formerly connected with the family of my friend, acted as correspondent to this latter, our school-fellows had believed that we were actually related; and after having passed this off upon them as a joke, we finished by treating it as serious, and viewing each other as cousins.

Truth compels me to state, that my cousin Jouveau was anything but a scholar. Of a turbulent spirit, passionately fond of pleasure, and not overdelicate in the means employed to satisfy his desires, he displayed the most grievous and precocious disposition for dissipation. Forgetting as easily an injury as a benefit, according as his interest moved him; he saw in his friends, only the instruments of his ambition. Possessing a lively and ingenious disposition, and an inexhaustible fund of gaiety, he was a favorite with his comrades, who played upon him with the greatest impudence, and who best knew his extravagant egotism.

Perhaps I have been wrong, in point of gratitude, in thus recounting the defects of my cousin; for if Jouveau loved any one in college, it was certainly myself; he feared me much more than he feared our teacher; and a reproach from me, turned him pale. I had not seen him for seven years.

"Well," said I, when he re-entered the box, "Have you learned who this original is, that has thrown the theatre into an insurrection?"

"I know everything," replied he, smiling, "The man in green has been deaf and dumb from his birth, and did not at all suspect the uproar he had caused."

After the curtain dropped, Jouveau, taking me by the arm, drew me away with him.

"Cousin," said he when we were in the street. "I can now

satisfy your curiosity. You see in me, the secretary-general, intimate, and private, of a representative commissioner!"

"Receive my congratulations upon your elevation, I see that you know how to make your way."

"Why, yes, not badly. It is, however only six months since I entered into political life. My representative places absolute and unlimited confidence in me; he represents, but it is *I* who rule. 'Curtius,' said he to me, three months ago, after dinner, "I am a handsome man, and I represent better than anybody in the world; but I have an horror of work. Let us then divide the labour. I will shew myself to the crowd, receive the deputations, harangue the delegates. You shall employ yourself with all the administrative and political affairs, draw up all the resolutions, write down my reports. I shall leave myself entirely to your experience and patriotism. Does this plan suit you?" "Perfectly," answered I, for I am not such a fool as to refuse power. "In fact, since that conversation, his confidence in me is complete, and I manage everything. But it is late, and before I go to bed, I have to draw up a dispatch, respecting the disturbance which has taken place this evening at the theatre. Good night, Cousin, as soon as you are up in the morning, come to me, and we will breakfast together."

The next day at the hour stated, I found the anti-chamber of Curtius Jouveau filled with all sorts of people, and had a good deal of trouble to reach him. Seated near a desk in his office, Curtius had his nightcap on; he seemed to be undecided whether he would yield to the entreaties of two young women, who smiled in the most bewitching manner.

"Ah! Here you are cousin," said he on perceiving me; "you are welcome. My children" continued he addressing the young girls, whom my entrance had quite disconcerted, "return here to-morrow morning; to day I renounce business that can be postponed."

" But citizen," said the elder of the two petitioners, a girl of eighteen, " our poor mother is in despair! One day more of captivity is an age for the unfortunate who suffer."

" I don't like your insisting with me citizen," answered Curtius drily, " twenty-four hours are nothing; after all, if returning annoys you, no one compels you to come."

" Oh! That won't annoy us at all citizen," said the young girl hastily, " we will return;—farewell citizen.' They made an attempt to smile as they departed, but I saw the tears trembling in their eyes.

" What does your conduct indicate Jouveau?" Said I, " why have you shewn this harshness to these poor girls?"

" They worry me," said he, " and I have therefore sent them away; that's all "

As he spoke, a young man entered the office.

" Ah! Is it you Horatio Cocles!" cried Jouveau. "Go and tell Fabricus and the two Gracchi, when business is over to write fair copies of the letters for the Committee of General Safety. As for you cousin," said Jouveau, rising from his arm-chair and flinging his nightcap into the middle of the room, " follow me, I am going to present you to the illustrious N———, my very dear representative."

In passing through the anti-chambers, I observed that the petitioners saluted my cousin with profound humility and respect.

" Wait here a moment for me," said Jouveau, when we had reached the anti-chamber of the representative, " I am going to acquaint the great man with your presence." He then retired, and after an absence of a quarter of an hour, appeared again beckoning me.

" Come cousin," said he, " we wait for you."

The representative N———, whom I saw for the first time, resembled exactly a vigorous butcher boy in his sunday clothes.

He received me admirably, loaded me with caresses, and interrupting Jouveau who wished to begin my panegyric. "Your relationship with the citizen, and the friendship that you display towards him, speak enough in his favour, my dear Curtius," said he. "For the rest, from the frank, open, and martial air of your cousin, we cannot entertain a doubt that he is a good patriot! Adjutant," continued he, turning to me, " I count upon your taking a little family dinner, which I give to day to our good sans-culottes. I will not keep you now, for I am weighed down with business! They serve dinner at three o'clock precisely, be exact for I don't like to wait."

"Well!" asked my fellow student when we got into the street, "What do you think of N——?"

"I think it is fortunate for him that he met with you on his way."

"Why so cousin?"

"Because Hercules, who has accomplished at least a dozen labours, was never able to guess one charade. Thy representative resembles Hercules."

"The fact is, I am not altogether useless to him," said Jouveau. "What would you have? The Convention wants men like N—— to execute its will, they comprehend nothing and strike boldly."

On quitting my cousin, I took a tour in the city. After two hours walking, I went towards my inn, when I met a brigade of gendarmes, whom the few people abroad seemed to regard with terror. On observing their countenances, I soon came to the conclusion that they were going to make an arrest.

I had not deceived myself; arrived before the shop of a laceman, the brigade stopped, and the Adjutant who commanded it entered the shop alone. The brigade had not stopped a minute, before the street was already filled with a numerous crowd of people of all classes.

" Do you know what is taking place ?" asked I of a tradesman who, with open mouth, and outstretched neck, stood upon the threshold of his stall.

" I don't know citizen," replied he, " it appears however, that it is Lemite whom they are about to arrest."

" You ought to know this Lemite, as he is your neighbour ! What kind of a man is he ?" But I asked the question in vain, the man shook his head, and held his peace.

I had scarcely spoken, when a great uproar arose in the crowd, which increased in intensity continually. It was the laceman Lemite, who accompanied by the Adjutant of the gendarmery came from his warehouse.

Two young and handsome girls, the oldest of whom might be about twenty, and the youngest eighteen years of age, followed the unfortunate laceman. I learned that they were his daughters.

" Ah citizen, I conjure you," said the eldest, addressing the brigade. " leave us our good father, do not take him to prison, or at least allow us to follow him !"

" We have received no order to take you citizen," replied the Adjutant, " Come take yourself off."

" No we will never abandon our father !" cried the youngest in her turn ; " Force alone shall snatch us from his arms."

" We will employ force then," said the Adjutant coolly.

The poor child threw herself on the neck of her father, and covered his face with kisses and tears.

The Adjutant seized her in his arms, and sent her rolling several paces in the middle of the street.

When they raised the poor child, her face was covered with blood, and she had fainted, for her head had fallen upon the pavement.

"Citizen," cried the father, "my daughter is murdered! You have killed her."

"What of that? March I tell you!"

"Pitiless tigers! Stop, I will see my daughter!" Cried the laceman, who distracted with grief, flung himself with furious passion upon the gendarmes.

A struggle as short as it was terrible ensued The unhappy father, thrown on the ground, covered with blood and gagged, was soon borne away by the gendarmes. The crowd maintained a sullen silence.

The reader will easily comprehend the painful emotion which this scene of violence occasioned in me. Unable to contain my indignation, I entered the house of the laceman, and addressing the eldest of the girls, who was kneeling in attendance upon her fainting sister, lavishing on her, the most touching tenderness. "Mademoiselle," said I, "I think I am able to assure you, that I have credit enough to procure the restoration of your father. Dry your tears, and have confidence in God; your misfortunes, I hope will not be of long duration."

The poor child thanked me abundantly for the interest I took in her father. and I took leave of her, assuring her anew that the detention of her relative should not be prolonged beyond a few days.

I could have wished, after the sad event of which I had now been the witness, to dispense with being present at N——'s dinner; but his favour became indispensable for the accomplishment of my promise; since on him alone depends the liberation of the laceman, and I resolved to do as much as possible to engage his good will.

Precisely at three o'clock I arrived at his saloon, where they were to sit down to table. As soon as the representative saw me he advanced to meet me, and almost stifled me with his embraces. I augured well, from this reception; and my hopes now increased, when the representative took me by the arm, and placed me on his left hand at the table.

All the guests, with the exception of Jouveau and the President of the Revolutionary Committee, placed on the right of N———, were unknown to me.

The repast was exquisite; game, fish, early fruits, old wine, nothing was wanting on the table. I ought to add, that at this very period, the inhabitants of Marseilles had not the right of purchasing more than seven ounces of bread per day per man.

As soon as the first appetite of the guests was satisfied, and the soft and exciting warmth produced by the wines had begun to operate upon their brains, the conversation, consisting previously of monosyllables, took its flight, and shone in cheerful remarks.

The desert was about to be served, whan an orderly came in, and put into the hand of the representative a sealed packet.

Angry at seeing his pleasures interrupted by business, N——— knitted his eyebrows, and tore open the envelope with an evident movement of bad humour; but at the first lines he read, the expression of his countenance entirely changed, and he became animated.

" Share my happiness my friends. who are also those of the republic," said he; This morning I had given orders to arrest three abominable villains, three conspirators; two of them,—Roux, Judge of the Peace, and Lemite, a laceman have been found at home, and are now in the hands of justice.

" Ah !" cried one of the guests, a little bald man, with a squint eye and a restless look, "how can we sufficiently admire a representative who takes so to heart the interests of the republic? They talk of the energy I have shewn in the commission at Orange, but what is that in comparison with the holy and sublime love of liberty displayed by N——— ?"

The orator would undoubtedly have continued, had not two, servants brought in a little guillotine in sugar of a rose colour, which they placed before him. Then all the guests clapped their hands, with a transport and enthusiasm difficult to describe

"Citizens," said the representative, "shall we leave the guillotine in permanence?" At this question, which might conceal a snare, every one held his tongue, and an embarrassing silence prevailed over the assembly.

"Citizen," said a guest,—a place-hunter, under all regimes, according to Jouveau.—"Thanks to you, we possess two sorts of guillotines, one of iron, the other of sugar. We must use the first without relaxation, for the extermination of conspiraators; the second must nourish the patriots!"

"Let it be so;" replied the representative, who immediately distributed amongst us, the different pieces of which the hideous machine was composed.

Scarcely had this revolutionary dish, which constituted a practice very much in fashion at this epoch, been divided, than there was placed upon the table another, whose success was not less signal. This was an enormous basin, filled with figures in sugar, variously coloured, and representing Marquisses, duchesses, bishops, abbès, ecclesiastics, and financiers. I leave it to the reader, to guess, with what delicate jests, and good taste, the division that was made of these puppets by the representative, was accompanied, This task performed, the patriot leaned back and fell asleep in his chair.

Fearing to disturb the repose of so august and powerful a personage, the guests quickly departed in silence, walking on the tips of their toes. I confess that, for my own part, I was not displeased with this retreat, for I was suffocated.

As it was then, as I have already said, the height of summer, I resolved to go and pay a visit to the brother of the Innkeeper of Ciotat, for whom I had brought a letter.

The gilder lived in Rome Street. His name, inscribed upon the sign-board of a miserable shop, appeared to contradict the high opinion his sister had expressed of his power. I knocked at the glass door of the shop. An old servant all in rags presented herself.

"Is your master to be seen?" I asked.

That's as it happens." Answered she. "My master is too much occupied to lose his time with the first idler who presents himself."

"I have a letter from your master's sister." Answered I to the servant.

"Ah! You come from Ciotat, that's another matter; follow me."

Never have I seen disorder equal to that which prevailed in the work-room into which I was ushered. The mysterious gilder, seated at a table covered with paper, appeared to me, forty or forty-five years of age. He possessed one of those disfigured physiognomies which provoke antipathy and disgust. Without saying a word, he took the letter I presented, tore open the envelope, and scarcely throwing a glance over it, turned to me. "I caution you that if you have not cash, and hope to make me take assignats, you will be strangely deceived. Without ready specie, the thing is impossible."

" I have gold," answered I, desirous of knowing what he was driving at.

"That's the only mode of payment that pleases me! I ought however to forewarn you that the representative N—— and above all, his private secretary Curtius, are excessively severe, so that whatever may be the favour you ask, you must make up your mind to a heavy sacrifice. Come speak, is it an arrest or a liberation that you wish to obtain?"

"I ask nothing. Your sister who has been my hostess at Ciotat, gave me a letter for you, and I have brought you that letter, that's all; I understand nothing of your questions."

"Then what the devil brings you here! Why come to see me, and make me lose my time?" Cried the gilder in a violent passion, "I have nothing to do with your babbling; be off!"

"Your manners are not very captivating citizen," answered I coolly but as your coarseness arises rather from want of education, than an intention to insult me, I will certainly take no notice.

"Ah! Threats! Take care emissary of the royalists! Agent of the foreigner! I have a long arm!"

"To-morrow morning I will ask my cousin Curtius about that."

"Is Curtius the secretary of the representative N—— your cousin? Pray sit down, I beg of you citizen," cried the gilder, changing his tone at once, and handing to me a chair.

"I thank you, but as I still prefer your threats to your officiousness citizen, I have the honour to wish you a good evening."

Turning upon my heels, I hastily descended the stairs and went out, I already knew too much of Jouveau to be surprised at discovering his connection with the gilder. But I could not help reflecting with sorrow on the deep degree of debasement and degradation into which France was plunged. In civil affairs, as well as in the military department, the men invested with authority, saw, in their position, only the means of satisfying their avarice or their ambition.

The next morning I went at eleven o'clock to visit Jouveau. He had just risen.

Whilst he was dressing, several petitioners or friends sent in their names; and he ordered them to be introduced in rotation. Not wishing to inturrupt him, I went to wait the breakfast hour in the office.

Shortly afterwards, my cousin Jouveau entered, slamming the door after him with violence.

"What's the matter now, Curtius?" said I, "you appear to be quite in a passion"

"That's just what I am, parbleu!" replied he, "would you believe it, that I cannot take a step without being stopped by petitioners of all kinds. 'Citizen, return me my father!' 'Citizen, my poor innocent wife languishes in a dungeon!'—and so on. Sapre-bleu, I cannot go on thus much longer; My nerves are completely unstrung. To put a stop to this unbearable persecution, I must imprison two of the petitioners! that's the only way to have any peace. Will you go with me to the house of N———?" said he; "I shall scarcely stay there two minutes, and we will go to breakfast afterwards."

"Willingly," answered I; "for my part, I want to have a serious conversation with you. Come."

Jouveau went into the private office of his representative, and I remained in the anti-chamber, when I saw coming in a woman veiled, whose form and step indicated extreme youth. The stranger seemed agitated; and avoided the presence of the other petitioners. There was in her bearing such modesty, that I at once took a lively interest in her. Her appearance here, plainly indicated that some misfortune had befallen her, and I resolved if opportunity offered, to be of service to her.

"You do not recollect me, I believe," said she, advancing and raising the veil which concealed the most graceful and handsome countenance imaginable.

"Indeed Mademoiselle," I answered; "I honestly confess, never till this moment have I had the honour of seeing you.

"I beg your pardon citizen. I am the eldest daughter of the unfortunate Lemite, and you, citizen, are the only man who since the arrest of my poor father, has spoken words of

s

hope and consolation to my sister and me. In our accidental meeting this morning I see the finger of providence."

"Believe me, Mademoiselle," said I, "I will employ the little influence I may have, to procure the safety of your father; only I fear that that influence may prove less than my zeal and good will."

"Yet citizen, your presence here is a proof that you know some one connected with the representative N―――, or his secretary, Curtius."

"Yes, Mademoiselle, I know citizen Curtius, quite well. He is my old college acquaintance, and we call each other cousin."

"Well then," resumed the poor child, overcome with emotion, "you can save my father. A word from you to your cousin, citizen, will save a whole family from misery and despair."

"Have confidence Mademoiselle, Curtius will be here immediately. The first words that I address to him shall be to ask the liberation of your father."

"Citizen Curtius coming," repeated the young girl; Oh! I entreat you to present me to him! I feel that when it concerns the defence of my father, I should find words that a daughter alone could speak."

"On the contrary,—avoid seeing Curtius," replied I, alarmed, reflecting on her beauty, and the unscrupulous character of Jouveau. "Leave the defence of your interests in my hands, and believe that I will plead the cause of your father with as much warmth as if it were my own."

"And do you hope to succeed?" Replied the poor girl, attempting to read in my looks, the extent of my hopes.

"I am almost certain of it," said I. "Yet I cannot positively answer for my success. However I think I may say that we have twenty good chances to one bad one. Now go quickly, here is Curtius."

"And when shall I see you again?"

"As soon as I have obtained what you wish. Perhaps in an hour."

"Then if you do not come, after that time is over—"

"You must trust in God alone, for that delay will tell you that I am arrested myself, or that I have fled from the city of Marseilles."

Soon after, I was seated at table with Curtius, partaking of a sumptuous breakfast.

"Do you know the news of the day? said he; "We have just heard that a fleet of twenty transports loaded with grain, which we were impatiently expecting, has been captured by the English. This will have a deplorable effect in the city and the department. N—— fears a rising, and does not know what course to take."

"How have you learned this news?"

"By the report of the captain of the corvette which was charged with convoying the fleet, and who having, like a coward, taken to flight before the English squadron, has come safely into port. We calculate upon his execution, to calm and divert the public mind."

"But, tell me Jouveau, were the British force which took the fleet from the convoy, numerous?"

"Very so; they consisted of three ships of the line, seven frigates, and four corvettes."

"Well then, how could the unfortunate commander have been able to assist them with but a single corvette?"

"What does that signify to us? He ought to have sunk or blown up his ship; that would have allowed us to draw up a thundering bulletin, order a civic feast, and the people would have thought no more of the famine!"

"Jouveau," said I, changing the subject of conversation. "You know a man of the name of Lemite?"

At this question his countenance became clouded, and the

expression of his features altered as by enchantment. "Yes, I know indeed the man Lemite," replied he, in a short, dry voice; "What next?"

"That unfortunate man who has been incarcerated, doubtless in consequence of a mistake, is the only support of his family."

"Enough citizen," said Jouveau, cutting short the conversation; "that's an affair which does not concern you. Leave to the patriots who love the republic, the care of watching over its preservation and safety."

"My dear friend dont put on that mask; I know you too well. Tell me frankly whether you have any motive of hatred, revenge, or interest in this affair, and in the name of heaven lay the republic aside. Come, be frank!"

"Well, I agree to it. Lemite is a good republican and an honest citizen; but that will not prevent his head from falling on the scaffold."

"Wretch! I thought you only a thief; are you an assassin too?"

"My dear friend," said he coolly, and without appearing the least moved by my warmth, "I see you do not know me; a final explanation will I hope deliver me for the future, from your amazements and anger. Know therefore, once for all, that I acknowledge no other interest but my own, that I only countenance what may be profitable to me, and that,—thanks to my selfishness—you see how open I am with you,—I find myself placed above human passions. Envy, hatred, revenge, are sentiments which have no influence on me; I see only my well-being,—the rest signifies nothing."

"What interest then have you in hunting this unfortunate Lemite?"

"A very great one; Lemite has been imprudent enough to speak ill of N—— and the representative is furious against him. In promoting the revenge of this latter, I increase his confidence, and, consequently my credit. Now as this confidence and credit, represent for thy friend Jouveau, fortune.

pleasure, and power, you will see that I sacrifice this babbler Lemite, on the altar of ambition. Your protegè might have committed any other gross imprudence, and in consequence of the interest you feel for him, I would have saved him. But he has dared to attack the man who is all in all to me, and he shall die."

"Can nothing induce you to alter your resolution, Jouveau?"

"Nothing my dear friend, since I am not even angry."

"Well then, I leave you instantly. It will be impossible for me to live longer with you. The very sight of you makes me sick."

"I am sorry, my dear friend that you must go away, but as, upon the whole, you cannot always remain here, I will endeavour to console myself during your absence."

Judging that my supplications and threats would be ineffectual against a disposition so wholly selfish, I no longer insisted, and went away without replying to Jouveau."

Within an hour, with my knapsack on my back, and my walking-stick in my hand, I was traversing the highway from Marseilles to Aix.

I was much struck by observing that the miserable and ragged pedestrians whom I met inm y route appeared happy and sung loudly; whilst the horsemen, whose appearance indicated opulence, wore a countenance indicating inward care and deep abstraction of mind The conclusion I drew from this was, that the first, thought only of what they ought to be able to take, and the latter what they were in danger of losing. Uniforms of all kinds, delegates, gendarmes, prisoners, commissaries I met every moment. The road exhibited but one long train of disasters produced by the maximum accusations, and war.

I had scarcely been an hour at Aix, when a frightful uproar of drums beating to the field, and trumpets sounding to parade, caused me to put my head out of the window, when I saw the military body, the committees, the municipalities of the district, the judges, and all the other authorities, in procession. The soldiers and magistrates, singing loudly, walked before a green car, in which was extended with more freedom than decency, a very handsome woman. In a moment I joined the procession.

"What fête is this?" I asked.

"It is the fête of reason," was the reply.

Stimulated by curiosity, and observing that the crowd was peaceable, I joined the escort of the goddess of reason.

After a short march, we arrived at the spot fixed on for the celebration of this imposing ceremony, that is to say, before a church, the walls of which, blackened with smoke, and the doors riddled with balls, shewed that this holy place had sustained the ravages of the revolutionary storm.

The goddess descended from her car, entered the church, accompanied by all the authorities, and was seated under a dias of verdure which was prepared for her. Immediately the trumpets sounded furiously, and shortly after a municipal officer, wearing a tricoloured scarf mounted the pulpit to deliver an address. A perfect silence ensued.

"Brothers and friends," exclamed the orator of the feast, in a stentorian voice. "There is a power anterior to the creation, a power which ambitious hypocrites have managed to violate. I speak of reason."

"Misfortune to the people who forget it, hatred to the tyrants who want to defy it. The first fall into slavery, the second upon the scaffold."

A discourse commencing thus, promised much; the eloquence of the municipal officer was crowned with full success, and elicited thunders of applause.

Whilst the orator, ranting with furious gestures, made

the antique arches of the church resound with his formidable voice, a scene less solemn perhaps, but certainly more picturesque and curious, took place at a few steps from where I stood.

The goddess of reason, aware of the ogling of several fops, who had sidled to the foot of the dais under which she was seated, had ended,—a human weakness very pardonable in a woman of her age,—by forgetting her part, and abandoning herself to the pleasure of flirtation.

The sidelong glances were going on, when a large man about forty years old, and whose more than negligent costume denoted no great desire to please, appeared impatient of these delightful coquetries. At first he hummed, then seeing that his goddess was insensible of this warning, he began to swear moderately, in an under tone: at last, his monosyllables obtaining no success, he got seriously angry, and with rather an unparliamentary expression, disturbed the devotions of the admirers.

" Ah you slut," cried he, " you shall pay for this!"

" Hush!" and " Turn out the royalist" from several voices, certainly prevented the dirty fellow from proceeding, but was far from calming his anger.

" Ah the wretch! Ah the arrant brazen-face!" murmured he between his teeth, "Not to be more guarded than that! To insult me thus to my face! We'll see who laughs last!"

" What is it then citizen?" I asked in a low voice, "Is not the fete to your mind! Do you find the goddess unworthy for want of beauty, to fill the honorable post she occupies?"

" The brazen-face is only too handsome!" replied he, " and all these fops who insult me, they shall see if I don't know how to revenge myself."

" What do you mean by revenge?"

" Don't you know that the goddess of reason is my wife?"

" I was ignorant of that. Allow me to congratulate you."

The man shrugged his shoulders and knit his brows in such a manner, that I guessed my compliment was taken as an injury and insult.

The municipal officer at the close of his harangue, descended from his tribune, and the procession was on the point of resuming its march, when the husband of the goddess advanced briskly towards his too sensitive half, and apostrophized her with a warmth of expression that it is impossible to record.

"Stop!" replied she, " Wont they say that we are still living under tyrants, when a woman has no right to look before her, but she is threatened with being knocked on the head ?"

" What, you abominable jade !"—

" Ah ! let's have no foul words I beg, citizen husband. We come here to celebrate the feast of reason, and a voice tells me that an old and ugly owl like you who is always growling, is not to be compared to a handsome young man, whose lips utter only words of love. So if you are dissatisfied—"

Here the irritated husband advanced with his raised fist towards his better half. The goddess of reason for her part feeling herself too well supported by the presence of her admirers to submit to the gross correction with which she was threatened, rose with a bound from her seat, and with her head thrown back, her eyes sparkling and her talons displayed, prepared herself for an obstinate defence.

Immediately a terrible uproar, mixed with cries, laughter, and jests, made the nave of the large church tremble : the couple were at blows. If the husband was powerful, the goddess did not want courage, so that the combat soon took such a turn, that to prevent a misfortune they were obliged to separate the too animated pair.

This little incident greatly amused me, and did not displease the crowd; at the end of the ceremony, the husband, cooled by the struggle, and the wife, delighted at having so successfully resisted her spouse, soon recovered their dignity. The goddess remounted her car, and the procession defiled anew across the city, to the sound of drums and trumpets.

The cortege stopped before a fish merchants shop; the goddess descended, for the shop was hers, saluted the multitude, and all was over.

I rose the next morning and proceeded on my route. My first halt after leaving Aix, was at a large town called Saint-Cunard. There occurred at the inn at which I stopped, a comical adventure, which I think I ought to relate.

According to my usual habit of seeing everything in my travels, I went through the place, and returned harassed with fatigue and sighing with regret, at the thought of the meagre and pitiful dinner which awaited me; when, on entering the kitchen, I was both surprised and delighted to see upon the stove, a really very excellent dinner. The fire under the copper pans being deadened by a bed of ashes, shewed that this dinner was ready to be served, and I at once ordered the servant to lay the table.

The stupid girl looked at me with an air of astonishment.

" Is this dinner then for you?" she asked,

" Parbleu, for whom did you think it was?"

At this answer which certainly indicated no great matter, the wench opened her large eyes, looked at me with an expression of unutterable astonishment, and made a profound curtsey.

" If you will go into the dining room, I will do myself the honour of serving you," she replied.

" Be it so. Above all make haste, and don't keep me waiting, I am dying of hunger."

Soon after, installed before a table covered with a delicately white cloth,—a rare occurrence at that period,—they brought me an excellent soup, two bottles of wine, a leg of mutton, and two roasted partridges : I thought I was in a dream.

I had half eaten the dinner when the hostess bounced into the room with a cry of despair.—" Ah robber !" Said she, " what have you done ?" Then turning towards a young man of a severe and scornful cast of countenance who followed her:—

" Ah ! Forgive me citizen," said she, clasping her hands in a supplicating manner; " This vagabond is alone guilty. How could I possibly think that any man would be daring enough to take away your dinner ?"

I must confess that the anger of the hostess and the reproaches she addressed to me, did not astonish me much, for in sitting down to table, I had already entertained some doubts upon the destination of the sumptuous dinner which had been served up with so much attention. The idea of an equivoque occurred to my mind, but my hunger was such, that I resolved to profit by it before asking any questions. I comprehended at once, on perceiving the young man, that he was my victim. In the meanwhile, I thought it best to remain unmoved and put a good face on it.

" Do you know citizen," said the hostess calming herself a little on seeing my sang-froid, " do you know citizen that you have been very hasty ?"

" Citizen, I don't like my dinner to get cold."

" But this dinner was not prepared for you."

" To be candid, I will not deny that I begin to think so."

" It is the dinner of the citizen Commissary of the Public Safety that you have eaten."

" Well then," answered I, turning my eyes towards the young man, " the citizen shall eat mine."

" Don't you know then, what a Commissary of the Public Safety is?" Said the hostess emphatically.

"Perfectly" answered I laughing.

"Here's my commission," said the young man drawing from his portfolio a long patent, at the head of which was engraved a large radiated eye which took up half the page.

"I have not assumed that you were not in rule," replied I, preparing to cut up the second partridge.

The commissary, seeing that there was no time to lose, was about to seize the chair on which I had laid my knapsack and sabre.

"Dont touch that," cried I, "or I shall get angry,"

This stroke of audacity gave me the victory. The commissary stopped and stood motionless. However, not wishing to push it too far, which might have turned the table upon me, I instantly resumed a friendly manner.

"I am sensitive upon a point of honour, as all soldiers ought to be, who respect themselves, but although I am rather hasty, I am not a curmudgeon. If you will content yourself with what I call my dinner because I eat it, and which the citizen hostess called yours, because you ought to have eaten it, tell them to bring a chair, and sit down by my side, we will divide what remains like brothers. I am waiting your reply, and don't forget that I shall quickly get to work.' '

The citizen commissary, who was stunned for the moment by my off-hand manner of acting with so important a personage as himself, shook off his reserve, thanked me for my offer, —sat down, and in a few minutes, the commissary and I were the best friends in the world.

"Confess comrade," said I, "that you would have fared very slenderly, if I had not had a little fellow feeling."

"I do confess it," replied he, "but I comprehended at once, by your manner of acting, that you are not what you seem to be at first view; that is to say, a poor devil of an adjutant, on leave of absence for health."

"But I protest you are wrong."

"Come, a truce to modesty and discretion. I know now perfectly, what to believe about you my dear colleague. Yes, indeed, you have a perfect knowledge of your trade. One thing alone astonishes me in your conduct. Instead of dragging yourself thus painfully on foot as you do, why don't you go on horseback?"

"Ah, how young you are my dear friend," cried I smiling in a very serious manner, for I began to see the error into which the Commisary had fallen, and was not sorry to profit by it.

"Yes, I am young," repeated he, disconcerted by my firmness, "but that is not an answer to my question. Why, I say again do you travel the high road on foot, and with your sack at your back, as if you were an outlawed federalist?"

"Why, my dear friend? Just because I am very inquisitive of my species. Don't you understand me? Do you suppose, that to see and hear properly, one must be mounted on a horse or shut up in a post chaise? For my part I thought till to day, that my obscurity, by allaying all suspicion, and giving no umbrage, would assist me more in my study of manners, than a foppish train and imposing title, which would be considered as a challenge."

"Ah, I see, I see colleague. I am satisfied you are a man of no common stamp; I require no other explanation, Tell me,—I'll bet that you have been sent by that cunning sharper de Billaut de Varenne."

"No, you are mistaken, it is not Billaut who—"

"Then it is Couthon; confess it."

"Nor he neither; I can only repeat to you that I am what I have already said, that I am a philosopher and observer, that I am passionately fond of the study of manners, and that I fill no office under government,"

"Discretion amongst colleagues! After all, if it is in your instructions, you are right to act as you do, and I must affect to believe you. No matter! I am convinced that you play an important part, and are initiated into many secrets."

"Not the least in the world. I sometimes guess at what they would conceal from me, that's all."

"And do you guess the subject of my mission," asked my interlocutor slowly, and looking at me in a strange manner.

"Perhaps I do. I fancy to myself that you are entrusted with an important interest. The opinions of the national agents, districts, and great communities; arrests to propose, verbal and secret orders to convey to the representatives of the people. As to the plausible pretext you allege, as the motive of your mission, it should be the inspection of saltpetre-works and carriages—"

In proportion as I spoke, I remarked a singular change took place in the expression of my companion's physiognomy. When I had finished he saluted me with great politeness, and in an earnest voice;

"Citizen," said he, "I am quite ignorant who you are; however if you are questioned about me, I flatter myself you will not forget that I am quite devoted to the republic, and that we have partaken of the same bread and salt."

At this reply, I had the greatest difficulty to avoid laughing; but I preserved my gravity, and when my colleague re-entered his post-chaise, he shook me warmly by the hand, praying me not to forget, that he would always be my most devoted servant.

The next morning as I was preparing to resume my journey, I received the visit of the mayor of Saint Cunat. This functionary approached me with all the marks of profound deference, and saluted me humbly.

"Citizen," said he, "I hope that you will honour with

your presence, the civic banquet which the municipality are to give to-day in your behalf"

"What are you speaking of! What! The municipality make a feast for me? It's impossible!—"

"Citizen commissary extraordinary of the public safety—"

"What are you singing about now? I am not, and I never have been charged with such functions! I beg of you to consider me as only a simple sub-officer on leave—"

"Yes, I know, citizen! I understand. Fear nothing, we will respect your incognito."

"My incognito! What the deuce does that signify! I refuse to accept your invitation."

"But citizen," exclaimed the mayor with a comic look of disappointment, "The orders are given, the repast is commanded. Your refusal will plunge the borough in grief. Besides, I must inform you, that a deputation is already appointed to attend and thank you for your acceptance of it."

"Ah! Is there a deputation appointed? That's enough. Well citizen mayor, promise that this deputation will not come here, and I will engage to attend the banquet."

"Yes, I understand. Your incognito."

"You seem to understand everything here. It does not matter; only remember the formal declaration I now make, that I am quite simply an adjutant on leave of health, and that I hold no other title."

The mayor smiled with a knowing air, and undertook to report my declaration. With this precaution, and not fearing, in future, being accused of having appropriated to myself a title that did not belong to me, I resolved to profit by the error into which they had fallen, and to enjoy the homage they were heaping upon me.

The spot selected for the fête was about five minutes walk

from the inn; it was a platform carpeted with moss, and shaded by a row of olive trees. When we arrived, I found the whole population of the borough waiting for me, clad in their holiday clothes. My appearance caused a sensation, and the mayor, advancing to meet me, conducted me to the post of honour.

The banquet immediately commenced. Never in my life do I recollect being present at a spectacle so grotesque as that I then saw. Let the reader figure to himself nearly a hundred and fifty persons extended, in the same manner as the Romans, on the turf, and taking all the trouble in the world to appear at their ease.

There being no plates or dinner service, it was ludicrous to see the fingers of the guests plunged into the liquid dishes whilst the gravy splashed into their faces. And then, every moment, there were soup tureens overturned by the feet of neighbours placed before you; cries uttered by young girls, whose dresses had suffered from these injuries; groanings of old men, whose rheumatics made it painful for them to keep in that vertical position; in short, it was a pell mell and a confusion, that would certainly have inspired the pencil of Callot.

I had for a neighbour, I cannot say at table, but on the turf, a man, whose handsome countenance, satirical air, and intelligent eyes, had attracted my attention. I resolved to engage him in conversation.

"Citizen," said I, "I guess by the expression of your countenance, you feel very happy in attending this fraternal communion."

"The fact is, citizen," replied he, " I am greatly amused."

"Is this then, the first civic banquet you have attended?"

"Oh! not at all; I am too curious in studying the manners of our epoch, to miss any opportunity of observing them replied he; "I attend all the fêtes, all the sittings, all the gatherings, and in a time of quiet, I try to provoke a tempest."

"That's a confession, remember, that does not prove in favour of your patriotism."

"Why not? They have first pillaged and afterwards burnt my chateau, and I have applauded that popular justice, for it has proved to me that I was a tyrant. They have since told me, that the aristocracy was a monstrosity. that we were all alike, and I have not complained on seeing the dirty and ragged cloaks treat decent clothing with supreme contempt. They assure me that we are free, and I have not pretended the contrary, although the prisons overflow with captives. In a word, I have accepted without complaint all the ideas and the levities of the new order of things. You will agree with me, that having shewn so much docility and such deference for the opinions of others, the least they can do, is to allow me to indulge some fancies. Now my fancy is, to study on the spot, the happiness of those who have rendered us free. Thus, this civic banquet is full of attractions for me."

The irony which pervaded the speech of my neighbour was so visible, that it was impossible to avoid noticing it.

"Do you know citizen," replied I. "That without knowing who I am, you express yourself before me with imprudent freedom, of which I might take advantage."

"Bah! Said this singular personage, shrugging his shoul. ders. "Do you think me, because I have spoken freely, so denuded of common sense and reason, as not to know to whom I address myself? I know you perfectly."

"You know me! That seems very curious to me. Who am I?"

"First, my dear sir," said he, lowering his voice and applying his mouth to my ear. "You are not a commissary of public safety, as all these fools think. And further, 1 think I may add, that neither are you a man of violence."

"May I ask you,—for I confess that the originality of your mind excites my curiosity,—what have you formerly been, and what are you now?"

"Formerly I was called the Marquis de H———, and I was opposed to the court. To-day they call me citizen Gracchus, and I am a veterinary surgeon."

My conversation with citizen Gracchus was interrupted at this moment, by a patriotic chant, which the guests intoned with rare energy.

The banquet being finished, we rose from the turf, and a bal champetre closed this memorable day. I was about to retire, when I perceived the Marquis de H——— leaving the ball alone. I ran after him and holding him by the sleeve of his carmagnole;

"Citizen Gracchus," said I, " you leave very early. Are you not afraid of making them suspect your patriotism?"

"You must know, my dear sir, that I am a fatalist," replied he, and that consequently, I never trouble myself about the future. As I must start to-morrow, at break of day, I leave now, in order to get a few hours rest."

"Then you do not reside at St. Cunat?"

"No, I live at a small village called Remoulins, near Gardon."

"Indeed! Well it fortunately happens, that that village lies just in the route I have marked out for myself. If it is agreeable to you we will travel together."

"I can wish for nothing better than your company."

"Well then, come and sleep at the inn where I am lodging. In that case, we shall not have to wait for each other."

"I accept your offer with pleasure." Replied citizen Gracchus.

The next morning at an early hour, I awoke the hostess who was still abed, in order to discharge my bill. I had not left St. Cunat long, before I found reason to congratulate myself with having proposed to the Marquis de H., to travel with me. He was certainly the most original man I had ever met with, and his conversation divested the journey of its fatigue. Exercising the profession of a cattle doctor he was constantly on the road, and found great pleasure in the vicissitudes attending that life. From time to time he returned to the village of Remoulins, which was his quarter-general.

On setting out from St Cunat, we determined to quit the highway and travel by the cross roads, and we very soon entered the mountains. This mode of travelling presented a double advantage to us.—Affording delightful and picturesque prospects, and at the same time relieving us from the melancholy spectacle of the numerous captives which the gendarmery were conducting to the prisons in the large cities. I remarked at the same time the singular fact that the torrent of the revolution, had rapidly traversed the high roads, without invading those parts of the country removed from the great centres of population. Right and left of the frequented roads, we continually heard revolutionary or obscene songs; whilst in the isolated villages, the vespers and hymns of the church were still sung.

In the afternoon of the second day, we arrived at Avignon. My first care was to go to the house of my former host, the brave Marcotte; but to my great surprise, I found his house shut up and abandoned. I was retiring in disappointment, when a bookseller who lived opposite, called to me.

"Citizen Adjutant," said he, taking me into his shop, "Are you not the same soldier who stayed some time at the house of Marcotte?"

"You are quite right: but what is become of my former host?"

"Alas the poor man has fled."

"Fled! And what for?"

"Just because his cousin Pistache has denounced him to the committee of Public Safety."

"The scoundrel!"

"Citizen Pistache Carotte fell in love with the daughter of his cousin, the pretty Matilda, and as she did not return his passion, it follows that her father Marcotte has found himself transformed all at once into a dangerous conspirator."

"I will tell the villain a piece of my mind! Do you know whether he still lives in the same house?"

"Citizen," replied the bookseller, after looking round to see that nobody heard him, "If I may advise you, it is that you get away again from Avignon as soon as possible."

"For what reason?"

"Because you have been denounced to the Revolutionary Committee, as being the accomplice of emigrants and federalists. They have even demanded your immediate accusation and arrest."

"And how did the Revolutionary Committee receive this denunciation?".

"One of the citizens undertook to defend you as one whose blood, probably, at that moment, was flowing for his country. These words having elicited applause, the Revolutionary Committee passed to the order of the day. Notwithstanding, it is my opinion, that you will do well to get away from Avignon as soon as you can."

I thanked the bookseller for his information, and promised to follow his advice; and, accordingly started the same afternoon at night-fall. The next day, it was nearly eight o'clock in the evening, when the Marquis and I arrived at Remoulins.

"My dear Gracchus," said I to my companion, "Now that we are arrived upon your domain, I shall leave it to your superior knowledge of the place to procure me a supper and bed."

"You shall not want for either," replied he, "And I will also introduce you to excellent society."

"Nonsense! Where shall I find this excellent company? At the club?"

"No, at the Inn. Follow me in all confidence."

We soon after entered a miserable lodging house, the dilapidated appearance of which made me groan at the thought that I was fasting. In the common room into which we entered there was already a company of about a dozen persons. I never saw a more ragged set.

"Is this the good society you spoke of?" said I.

"Yes, it is."

"Truly!" replied I, laughing at this mystification. "Well, I forgot that you are an original and a philosopher. Will you present me to your honorable friends?"

"Willingly," said my companion, who, taking me with much stateliness by the hand, conducted me to a little old man, and raising his voice:—

"Viscount de F., I have the honour of presenting to you my excellent friend, citizen Alexis."

The mendicant,—for to judge by the old man's costume, he must have been reduced to a dependence on public charity for a living.—the mendicant, I say, rose immediately from the wooden bench on which he sat, and saluted me with much politeness.

"I am happy and flattered sir, to make your acquaintance," replied he, "For you want no other introduction, than that of being the friend of our excellent Marquis de H. Besides everything in your manners and language shews you to be a perfect gentleman."

I respectfully bowed to the mendicant, or rather the Viscount.

" If you desire it, my dear friend," said my singular companion, scarcely suppressing a sly smile, " I am about to have the honour of presenting you to the Duchess of O, whose name you ought not to be a stranger to. I must caution you," he continued, lowering his voice, " That although the Duchess is a woman distinguished both by birth and education, she is at this moment reduced to such an extremity that if I present you, she will certainly ask you for money. After all, by a twenty or thirty sous piece, you will render her the happiest of women."

The Marquis then conducted me to one of the most obscure corners of the cabaret, when I saw, seated upon a low stool, and half hidden by some one standing before her, an old lady of sixty-five or seventy years of age, whose immobility resembled that of a statue.

" My dear Duchess," said my companion, addressing her with great respect, " I have taken the liberty of bringing one of my good friends, who anxiously wishes to have the honour of making your acquaintance."

I thought I was dreaming.

By the manner in which the old woman, after I had been introduced according to all the rules of etiquette, rose from her stool and made me a curtsey, I could no longer entertain a doubt that she had lived at court, and was indeed the Duchess of O.

" My dear sir, " said she with a melancholy smile, " I guess by your astonishment, that you cannot conceive by what strange course of events and complications I am reduced to this state of destitution and misery in which you now find me. Look around you; observe the incredible metamorphosis and changes which are taking place in France, and my present position will no longer surprise you. Indeed, my history is very simple. Being seriously ill when the revolution burst out, I could not follow my friends abroad, and was fortunate enough in the devotedness of a poor old woman whom I scarcely knew, but who had for many years been attached to the precincts of my chateau, and now came to my aid. Alas! Scarcely had my protectress, on whose generous assistance I was now compelled to rely, saved me from the fury of Messieurs the patriots, who pillaged my chateau, than she died herself. How I have since subsisted I can scarcely tell. It appears that from time to time I receive small presents : at least that's what my steward informs me."

" How! Did you say your steward, Duchess ?"

" Indeed, that word must sound very ridiculous from my mouth," resumed the Duchess, smiling. " It is a habit of the past; as I have never in my life interfered in my affairs, I still call the worthy man my steward, who takes care of my interests. Hold, there he is, now coming in."

I immediately turned my eyes towards the door and perceived a little thin man, round shouldered, and wearing a carmagnole completely threadbare.

" Well Mons. Ferules," said the Duchess, " Have you brought me some good news ?"

" None, alas ! Madame la Duchesse," replied the little man bowing ceremoniously.

" Mons. Officer," resumed the Duchess turning to me, " I present to you the former preceptor of my children. I ask pardon for not telling you his true name, but I have never known it. My children called him Férules, and that soubriquet he has always retained."

" Your children have done me too much honour my good Duchess," replied the old man mildly.

In spite of the feeling of sadness, which the sight of the deep wretchedness of this woman produced in me at first, placed, as she had been, at the top of the social scale, but who now closed a life of luxury and power with so frightful and miserable an old age, I could not help smiling, on hearing the Duchess express herself in a tone of levity still befitting the great lady.

"Will you permit me to ask you Duchess, how it is that you are still at liberty?" said I; "I cannot conceive why they have not arrested you."

"Messieurs the patriots, pretend that I serve for an example, and that the life of a woman formerly rich and powerful but now fallen, (because she has been robbed and spoiled of her goods) into cruel indigence, affords a serious lesson for the people. If I had had my choice, between dying in good company with my former society upon the scaffold, or of spending the remainder in this cabaret, my choice would not be doubtful. After all, my faculties are so weakened, and I am so broken down, that I remain almost always in a lethargic sleep, which renders my lot supportable. My dreams make the present, my past, and I have not much to complain of."

The Duchess of O———, having thus expressed herself, saluted me with a slight inclination of her head. I understood that this long conversation had fatigued her, and immediately withdrew.

The day after my arrival, I left Remoulins to proceed to Nismes.

My companion the marquis refused to accept an assignat of twenty-five livres which I offered him at parting. He pretended, that since he had been reduced to poverty, he had experienced, like other people, great pleasure in gaining a livelihood by the labour of his own hands. If it had not been for the revolution," said he, " I should never have been sensible of my own worth. In the time of my prosperity and opulence, I was not considered capable of earning twenty sous."

The excellent Fèrules, having learned that I was about to start, announced his intention of being my guide. At day break I found him waiting for me on the high road. He accompanied me nearly two leagues, and reluctantly left me at last to return to the poor Duchess.

"My dear sir," said he at parting, "There's a letter for one of my friends, an old professor of rhetoric, who resides at Nismes, and who will serve you as a ciceroni. I will answer for him in all respects, he is the best man and the most trustworthy character I know. You may converse with him in perfect confidence."

"I thank you warmly for your kindness, Mons. Durand," replied I, "and shall avail myself of it. Will you in return, remit this letter to the Duchess of O———, and present to her my most humble respects."

In speaking thus, I slipped into his hand, the assignat of twenty-five livres that the Marquis of H——— had refused, and left him at a quick pace.

The hotel of "The Golden Pheasant," where I took up my lodging at Nismes, had, since the triumph of the revolution, taken the name of the "Hotel of Fraternity." "Formerly," said they, "it was only frequented by rich travellers." When I arrived there it opened its doors to all classes of society. Whatever might be the richness of the furniture, the rooms were indiscriminately given up to the first comers, and consequently presented a complete scene of disorder. One common table and one ordinary was provided for all customers and travellers.

At Marseilles, when I was there, the citizens had the right of purchasing seven ounces of bread each, per day. At Nismes, the ration was only four ounces. Fortunately, roots, fruits, and meat, were more plentiful.

I dined on the day of my arrival at the common table.

Near me was seated a man of about forty-five years of age, whose countenance, though insignificant enough, bore the impress of a facetious dignity, which led me to suppose that he had formerly filled some important function. His dignified gesture and decided tone confirmed me in that opinion, and made me desirous of engaging in conversation with him.

At the upper end of the table, a sans-culotte of the first water, that is, extremely ignorant, and proportionately violent, gave us a sketch, with much bawling and gesticulation, of his projects of reform for France. He demanded but five hundred thousand heads!—Scarcely a fifteenth part of the population, —in order to secure for ever, the welfare of the country.

"Ah! the wretch!" Murmured the stranger seated by me. "He would certainly do as he has said, if it were in his power."

"Sir," said I to him, "I have a letter to deliver to a professor of rhetoric; perhaps you can oblige me with his address.—So saying, I took from my pocket the letter of recommendation of Ferules, and handed it to my neighbour.

"This is a curious incident!" Said the latter, glancing his eye over the address. "That letter is for me."

"Indeed! Then I find we were destined to meet."

"The stranger, whose name was Jerome Bontems, read the letter, and afterwards gave me his hand;

"I am happy sir," cried he, "to make your acquaintance. From what the excellent Durand has said of you, I see that we shall at once understand each other."

On leaving the table, my new friend took me to visit the Arena, and several Roman antiquities which Nismes contains. At the close of the day he wished me a good night and left me, after spouting a dozen hexameter verses in Latin.

The next morning, it was hardly daylight, and I was in a deep sleep, when I awoke in surprise, from the noise of my

v

door opening violently, and saw the professor of rhetoric standing straight and motionless at my bedside.

"I ask pardon for awaking you so roughly," said he, "but I have just received an invitation to attend at the wedding of one of my old pupils, and I was unwilling to set out without informing you of my absence. But, now I think of it, the weather is beautiful and you have nothing to detain you at Nismes, why should you not accompany me." I promise you a hearty welcome.

"I thank you," replied I. "I see no reason why I should not at once accept your offer. By the bye, does your former pupil live in the direction of Sauve?"

"About five leagues from that city."

"That happens very conveniently. In accompanying you, I shall be so far on my route."

"In a few minutes I was ready, and we soon started. It was noon when we reached a large village, about five leagues from Nismes. I was overcome with fatigue, and proposed to my companion that we should stop and take one hour's repose.

"We are at the end of our journey," replied he. "Hold, do you see that large and handsome house, about five hundred yards off? That's the mayor's house—"

"What is that to me? I have nothing to do with it."

"I beg your pardon, you have to be present at a wedding, and my old pupil is just the mayor of this borough, and that is his house."

We were received by the municipal officer with a hearty politeness very unusual at this period. The dessert had just been brought in, when a man wearing a blue dress, and having round his body a leather girdle from which hung two drumsticks, entered the breakfast room, and saluting the mayor respectfully, asked him if it was time to begin to march.

"When you please," answered our host. "I am ready."

Soon after, we heard in front of the windows of the room in which we were, the sound of the drum, fifes, and cornets.

"Will you come citizens?" Said the mayor, smiling.

"Is it the wedding procession?" Cried Jerome, addressing his former pupil; "Hold, that's rather singular, I have not yet seen the bride."

"I shall not be married till to-morrow, my dear master. That music or charivari, announces the commencement of a civic feast."

"If it is that of reason, I have already been present at it, on two different occasions; and I must beg of you not to insist upon my accompanying you," said I earnestly, to the mayor.

"No citizen, the fête we are to celebrate to-day, in conformity to a decree of the convention, is that of the Supreme Being."

"Which means that, with pomp and noise they are about to perpetrate a sacrilege. Faith! I am desirous of knowing how far human folly will go. Let us set off.

We found at the door, the municipal officers of the borough, and a group of peasants, armed with pikes. On the arrival of the mayor, the cortege began to move, proceeded by a huge fellow who carried upon a brazen cross, the arms of which were cut off, a woollen cap of a dubious red.

We first crossed a cemetery, in which the tombs were overturned and the grave-stones broken and scattered about, and half hidden with tall weeds. We then entered an old church. This house of God had met with no more respect than the dwelling of the dead: it was the emblem of chaos. Let the reader figure to himself, a heap of slabs and tumulary stones, torn from the floor by the saltpetre-men, and obstructing the nave of the church; by the side of this wreck, stoves and baskets: to the right and left of the altar, a complete pile of human bones, fragments of saints, coats of arms, and broken sculptured benches; lastly, upon the table of the altar they had laid large boards covered with verdure; upon the boards, in the place formerly occupied by the tabernacle, was a chair, left vacant for the mayor. Scarcely was he seated, than the cortege, consisting of fifty persons, surrounded him, and he expressed himself in nearly the following terms.

"Citizens, spectators, assembled to celebrate the feast of the Supreme Being, the creator, but uncreated, whom the convention wills by its decree of Prairial, that we should honour to-day. Oh, that I had the harp of Rousseaù of Paris, and the genius of Rousseaù of Geneva, to sing worthily the praises of Him, who was before the world, and who will remain after it; of Him who gives us our harvests, and who instils into our hearts the love of our country, and of liberty! There are some here better qualified than myself, to fulfil this glorious and difficult task; let them come forward, and I will be the first to applaud their eloquence. In the meanwhile, and since my inexperience hinders me from expressing the holy enthusiasm which agitates me, allow at least, my voice, the echo of my heart, to intone the hymn composed by order of the Committee of Public Safety, in honour of the Great Creator of all things."

The mayor then drew from the pocket of his carmagnole, a roll of music: and after sol-faing in an under voice, he attacked in an outrageous falsetto the well-known hymn, "Father of the universe, Supreme Intelligence! &c.

At the end of each couplet, the drum beat, the fifes and cornets struck up with a most disorderly zeal, and the ex-clerk of the parish, the same comical fellow who bore the red cap on the brazen cross, rattled a large key lustily between the extended legs of a pair of tongs. Never in my life have I heard such a clatter.

When the hymn was finished, the attendants, adhering no

doubt to the prepared programme of the fête, began shouting, perfectly unconscious of the absurdity as well as blasphemy of their words,—"Long live the Eternal Being! Long live the Supreme Being!"

"What do you think of all this farce, officer?" Asked Jerome Bontems, in an under tone.

"I think, my dear poet," replied I in the same tone, "that the behaviour of the attendants is too decent to allow of the supposition that they are at all conscious of the sacrilege they have committed: they think they have done well. For the rest, I suppose the farce is over, and we are about to separate."

"I much doubt that," replied the professor; "it is rare in these days of eloquence, when France is punished by the rage for spouting, that amongst a company of fifty persons, one will not make an oration. We must wait for another discourse. I only hope that it will not be longer than that of the mayor."

Jerome Bontems was right. The cries of "Long live the Eternal!" had scarcely ceased, when a young man wearing large boots, rose from the bench on which he was seated, and advancing to the middle of the wreck which obstructed the nave of the church, demanded the word.

Silence not being readily established, the mayor began to ring one of the little bells which are hung on the necks of sheep, and after a time obtained a hearing.

"The word is with you, citizen officer of health." Said he to the new orator.

The young man immediately took off his hat, and put on a red cap which he drew from his pocket, and returning to his place where he first sat;

"Citizens," cried he in a sharp and piercing voice, "the superstition of Sunday formerly filled this place, which the

Decade has rendered lonely. That proves to us, brothers and friends, that formerly, the number of imbeciles greatly exceeded that of sensible men, and that the contrary is the case to day. In this temple, the walls of which are still black with the smoke of the wax tapers lighted by superstition, I wish to make the torch of reason shine in your sight. Till now, they have deceived you; I bring you truth and happiness. Brothers and friends, these words of God,—soul, —immortality,—hell,—paradise, have been invented, to make you pay the tithes, to draw money from your purses! These are tales invented by base men. Our grandfathers have had the simplicity to give faith to these ingenious and perfidious fables; their grandchildren will have the good sense to laugh at them."

"The plant, brothers and friends, has no other advantage over the earth that nourishes it, than its vegetative faculty; the animal, over the vegetable which feeds it, than the sensitive faculty: lastly, man, over the animal on which he feeds, than the faculty of touch and speech. What truth results from this observation? That the plant, the animal, and the man after their dissolution, become equal in a dust of the same nature! Banish then all fear of another world. Be happy here and obey,—so far at least as not to shew disrespect to the republic and the convention,—your desires and passions."

"We cannot deny, brothers and friends, that the convention has established the feast of the Supreme Being; but it is necessary for me to reveal all its thoughts to you. In thus acting, it has wished, in the sequel, to dethrone God. Soon, when that old and ridiculous superstition shall be uprooted, it will in its turn abolish that Supreme Being, which serves us as a transition in passing from darkness to light, and will then only recognise the fête of truth. I anticipate here, brothers and friends, in the midst of you all, who are or who will become philosophers, the celebration of that future feast, the only logic worthy of a sensible people."

"No more heaven, no more God, no more tales, no more Supreme Being! Long live the material enjoyments of life, the triumph of good sense, absolute liberty and fraternity."

After pronouncing this speech, the officer of health, who had been violently excited, wiped his forehead, which steamed with perspiration, and sat down upon his bench, to the noise of fifes, drums, and the plaudits of the mayor, the children, and the ex-clerk.

For myself, in spite of the sovereign contempt, which these monstrosities produced in me, I was indignant beyond expression.

"Why have you stenographed that infamous discourse? asked the professor of rhetoric, seeing me fold up my tablets. "I have heard that tirade to-day for the thousandth time."

"It is just because that speech affords me an exact and complete example of the eloquence of the day, that I wish to preserve it. In fifty years from this, it will present a valuable document for the study of our epoch."

I hoped that after the long exhibition of hatred and folly uttered by the officer of health, the orators, finding no other sacrilege to commit, would desist, and that this deplorable fête would have terminated : but I was mistaken. Scarcely had the officer of health seated himself, than a firm and accented voice, drowning the noise of the fifes, cornets and drums, demanded to be heard.

The new orator was a large and fine old man, whose calm and dignified countenance, upright and still flexible carriage, bespoke one of those simple and virtuous lives, which leaves to the mind all its intelligence, and to the body all its vigour to the extreme limits of life. Time had deprived his head of its hair, but had not extinguished the fire of his eye. His face presented one of those energetic and placid types which the pencil of Greuze has depicted.

Supported by a knotty stick, and his right arm extended, the old man remained a moment absorbed in his reflections; a profound silence was kept.

" Who is this old man ?" I asked of John Bontems.

" He is one of the notables of the consul-general of the Commune," he replied. " But listen, he is going to speak, I am deceived if the officer of health enjoys his triumph long."

Before the old man had spoken a word, I was quite prepossessed in favour of what he was going to say. The reader therefore will judge of my disappointment when I heard him deliver himself in patois.

" Why does he not speak in French ?" said I to the ex-professor.

" For the excellent reason that there are not in this meeting ten persons who speak that language. Do you think then that if our brave peasants had rightly comprehended the speech of the officer of health, they would have applauded him ? No certainly, far from it. The mountebank would have got his deserts. Let us listen I beg of you; nature falls short of art, it is true, but it produces at times, happy bursts of eloquence."

" Will you translate this speech to me as fast as he delivers it?"

" Very willingly."

As the notable of the council-general expressed himself with a solemn deliberation, it was easy for my friend to fulfil his promise.

The old man maintained the tone of language that I expected from him,—that of the heart. He began at first by describing the incommensurable power and unwearied goodness of God; then translating the discourse of the officer of health, he asked those present if it was their desire to tolerate such blasphemies?"

At this question, which was proposed without emphasis or anger, cries of rage rose from all parts, and the peasants, leaving the benches on which they were seated rushed like an avalanche towards the unlucky miscreant, who, pale and dismayed began to tremble all over and beg for mercy.

The exasperated country people would hear nothing, and the scene threatened a tragical termination in spite of the efforts of the mayor, who descended from the arm-chair, and interposed his authority between the fury of the auditors, and the object of their anger, when a man of about fifty years of age, clothed with a meekness very uncommon at that period, and of a stern and imposing carriage, advanced gravely into the midst of the squabble, and in a serious and severe voice called for silence. At the appearance of this unknown person, —whom I had not before noticed,—the calm was instantly re-established.

"My friends," said he, designating by an inclination of the head, his sovereign contempt for the pale and trembling officer of health. "It is not indignation, but rather pity that we ought to feel for the senseless. Send away that unhappy wretch who disturbs the ceremony, but do not ill-treat him. He says, he does not believe a God; you see he is already an object of pity."

The stranger, after having spoken thus, which the old man translated into patois, returned again towards the medical officer, and pointed with his finger to the door of the church. The atheist did not wait for entreaty. He saved himself in the midst of a concert of shouts and cries.

"What is that man?" I asked of my companion. "Is he

a Commissary of the Public Safety, that he possesses so much power? But no, the authority which he has just exhibited does not prove a revolutionary spirit."

"That man," replied the professor of rhetoric, "Is, like you and me, a plain citizen; but his eminently honorable character, and his private virtues, appreciated as they deserve to be by the country folks, give him great influence over them. Before the revolution, he filled the important office of Criminal Judge. His name is de N———, would you wish to be presented to him?"

"Faith, I cannot refuse. Honest people, who are not afraid to appear such, are so rare now, that when chance throws one in your way, you ought not to quit his company, without letting him see the estimation in which you hold him."

On leaving the church, the procession dispersed on all sides, and I returned with my companion the regent, to the mayor's house. The first person that I perceived on arriving was the Ex-Criminal-Judge, de N———.

This last, on seeing Jerome Bontems, smiled, and affectionately offered him his hand, calling him his master. My friend according to his promise, immediately presented me to M. de N———, and pronounced a magnificent panegyric on my private virtues.

The sun was sensibly declining in the horizon, when I proposed to the professor to get on my way to Sauve, but his former pupil the mayor, whose marriage was to take place the next day, would not allow him to leave. Somewhat annoyed at the idea of remainimg another day in this town, where I knew no one, and where no motives of curiosity or feeling detained me, I thought of pursuing my journey alone, when the Ex Judge N———, guessing probably my chagrin, proposed my taking a seat in his carriage, and accompanying him to his house.

"I live only a league from Sauve," said he, " And as that city lies in your route, I do not well see what motive you can have in refusing my proposal."

I gladly accepted this offer, and in a quarter of an hour we were rolling towards the country house of the Criminal Judge.

CHAPTER VII.

The Ex-Criminal Judge, and his family.—His high principle.—His nephew Maurice.—"Open in the name of the Law."—Arrest of N——.—His imprisonment at Sauve.—Scene in the house of Detention.—A protesting prisoner.—A quarrel for horses.—Jouveau again.—I bargain with him for the release of the Ex-Criminal Judge.—I arrive at Saint Hyppolite.—A sanguinary barber.—I wander among the mountains of Cevennes.—A fortunate encounter.—Supper, bed, and breakfast for nothing.—Citizen Rose, and the convent of Saint Benoit. Arrival at Mende.—My father's friend.—Citizen Larouvrette.—Charrier.—A royalist victory, and subsequent defeat.—Fate of Charrier.—A proposed excursion.

During the short journey, I had many opportunities of discovering and appreciating the character, and the extensive information of N——. Although our political opinions were not the same, we discussed, without anger, the opposite principles which we professed.

The country house inhabited by N—— and his family, was handsome, spacious, and indicative of health, "Follow me, my friend," said he to me, on throwing the reins to a servant, who had opened the great gates; "I am going to introduce you to my family."

Two females waiting for him on the ground floor, who on seeing him, advanced and tenderly embraced him.

"My friend," said the Criminal Judge, addressing the elder of the two ladies, " Allow me to present to you an officer whom I have met with to-day, and who has agreed to accept our hospitality."

Madame de N—— hastened to assure me, that she felt indebted to her husband, for the good fortune he had thus procured for her; and then invited me into the parlour. The daughter of my host, who had gone away, probably to give some orders, soon returned. I then certainly beheld the prettiest creature that poet'ever dreamt of. Scarcely seventeen years of age, she presented one of those splendid and modest beauties which it is easier to admire than to analyze, for everything about them is soul and sentiment.

"Will you please come to supper father," said she, tenderly embracing the Judge, who returned her caresses with warmth; "the cloth is laid."

I immediately offered my arm to the wife of my host, when many hasty knocks resounded at the street door, and caused us to start suddenly.

"Who can come to visit us at such an hour?" cried Madame N——, whose arm trembled under mine.

"Undoubtedly a friend," replied her husband quietly.

A minute after, the parlour door opened and a young man booted and spurred, and bearing in his hand a riding whip, presented himself to our view.

"Maurice!" cried Madame N——, advancing eagerly towards the new-comer; "What is the cause of this my friend? I am glad to see you; and yet I don't know, but a secret presentiment tells me that your visit here at such an hour, and without being announced, forebodes bad news! Speak, explain yourself, I am dying with anxiety."

x

"You disturb yourself unnecessarily, my good aunt," replied he, who Madame N—— called Maurice, "My business has conducted me within a quarter of a league of your house, and finding myself so near you, I did not wish to pass without paying you a visit : that's all."

"Is that true Maurice? Do you hide nothing from me?"

"Nothing Aunt, I assure you," said the young man blushing slightly.

I remarked that during all the time of supper, the restless eye of the young man, constantly sought that of his Uncle, and that this latter made a strong effort to avoid it.

"My good friend," said my host addressing his wife, when we rose from table, "I have several commissions to intrust to Maurice, and I shall appropriate your handsome nephew to my own use. To-morrow morning I will return him to you free from all business."

Mons. N—— spoke this with such complete tranquility, that his wife was reassured, and a little after she went out with her daughter.

"Well Maurice," said my host, turning to the young man, "Now we find ourselves alone, you may speak without fear. I am in danger, is it not so? You may speak before this officer, I will answer for his honour and prudence."

"Well then, my poor Uncle," cried the young man earnestly, "I must confess to you, that you are denounced again, and have no time to lose in taking flight, for if the intelligence I have received is correct, they must be this very hour in pursuit of you."

"That word is incorrect Maurice," answered the Ex-Judge, "They cannot be in pursuit of me, when I am not in flight."

"But Uncle, you will at least set out immediately."

"No Maurice, my conscience reproaches me in nothing, and I shall remain."

"Then you are lost!" cried the young man in despair.

"What! Do you wish me to abandon your Aunt and Cousin! No Maurice, as head of the family, my place is in my own house: do not insist, your entreaties will be useless! know the favorite maxim of my life,—Do what is right, and come what may, by the grace of God! But tell me Maurice," he continued, "This is probably a new denunciation, to which I shall owe my future arrest?"

"Alas, yes Uncle! Some wretch has laid before the Committee of Public Safety, a letter which was addressed to you by an emigrant, by which you are deeply compromised, and which he affirms has fallen into his hands by chance."

"That's a lie, Maurice, I am in correspondence with no emigrant. The informer himself is the author of that letter. I can perceive, in this dastardly method, the cowardice of a secret enemy."

The reader will have no difficulty in conceiving how much this dialogue between the uncle and nephew, unintelligible to me, but announcing an approaching catastrophe, must perplex me. I listened with intense anxiety.

"Will you," said I, "Put on my uniform, and take my letter of route? By that means you would be enabled to avoid your enemies."

"I thank you heartily for your offer," replied Mons. de N——— in a broken voice, "I can only repeat to you, that for no consideration in the world, would I withdraw myself by flight, from the false accusation which attaches to me."

"But still, do not forget that you are a father!" cried I, "And that your fate is bound up in that of your family."

"Enough! Enough! I beg of you to hold your tongue!" cried my host, interrupting me with extreme eagerness; "The temptations you present to me, can neither weaken my courage, nor make me change my resolution: but it may render my grief more bitter ; do not insist any more then, I beg of you."

"Hearken!" said I, "That is a troop of horse on march. Yes, I hear the noise made by the clang of the sabres." Alas, I was not mistaken, for soon in the silence of night we distinguished the step of the horses; and then a little after we heard violent blows struck on the outer door, which opened to the country.

Mons de N—— was going to open the door to the armed force, when the opposite door, pushed violently from the outside, opened, and his wife entered.

"What is the matter my friend?" said she, rushing towards her husband, whom she seized in her arms, "What are those knocks which are shaking the door? What is this noise of swords, and this murmur of voices which reach us?"

My dear friend," replied Mons. de N——, taking his wife's hand affectionately in his, "I know that your soul is great and strong, that you have always put confidence in God, and that, if ever misfortune overtakes you, you will know how to present your sorrows to him. Yes, my well-beloved, in an hour we shall be separated. But be of good courage! I need not tell you that I am innocent of the crime of which they accuse me, and soon, I hope, I shall come triumphant out of this trial."

"Is it then true that you are about to be arrested?" cried she, in so piercing an accent that it affected me to the very heart.

"Yes, my friend, but I am innocent, and God, in whom I place all my trust, will not abandon me. Now my dear wife, I entreat you to dry your tears, and resume your fortitude! You must not tremble and weep before my gaolers; do not suffer your tears and despair to depose against my innocence; for the sake of my safety be calm, I conjure you!"

Whilst Mons. de N―――― expressed himself thus, the blows against the outer door, redoubled in violence, and we heard a mournful voice, crying,—"In the name of the law, open!"

"Obey them " Said the Ex-Judge, to two servants who had just entered the dining hall to receive his orders.

He had scarcely finished speaking, when twenty gendarmes filled the dining hall in which we were.

"Which is he amongst you, who is called citizen N――――?" Demanded an officer, who held a roll of paper in his hand.

"You know well that it is I, lieutenant." Answered Mons. de N――――.

"The fact is, citizen, we have known each other a long time; but you know the law has nothing to do with individual and private feelings. You acknowledge yourself to be citizen N――――?"

The ex-judge made an affirmative motion of his head.

"In that case," continued the officer of gendarmery, "in the name of the law, I arrest you! Soldiers, surround this man, and do not lose sight of him."

"I am at your command, lieutenant," said Mons. de N―――― without losing anything of his serenity; "let us set out."

"Not yet! I must first set the seal upon your papers."

"Here's the key of my secretary. Will you permit me to open it?"

"Yes, citizen, for I know that you are an honest man!"

After having opened the secretary, Mons. de N―――― took a purse full of gold, and a portfolio stuffed with assignats, which were found in it, and held these two in his hand.

"Hide them," said the lieutenant of gendarmery quickly, in a low voice. "I cannot answer for my men, a denunciation is so easily made."

Turning himself about, Mons. de N―――― perceived me

at his side, and slipped the two articles into my hand, murmuring :—

"Ah! blessed be God! I feel more easy. I leave my wife and daughter above the accesses of destitution."

I will not speak of the distracting scene of the departure. Although Madame de N—— made the most heroic efforts to preserve her fortitude, at the sight of her daughter, who broke out in sobbing, she could no longer master the grief which wrung her heart, and she uttered piercing shrieks.

"Let us set out, lieutenant," said Mons. de N—— who, at this scene, probably felt his courage failing, and did not wish to be overcome.

"Truly, citizen N——," cried the officer. "I would give a year's pay to see you at liberty! after all," continued the gendarme, raising his voice, so that Madame de N—— could hear him, in spite of the sorrow which absorbed her;—"However, knowing the futile cause for which you are apprehended, I believe that you will soon be set at liberty! To tell you the truth, I look upon your arrest as a mere formality."

"Can it be true, citizen?" Demanded Madame de N—— with such an outburst of feeling, that I felt the tears rush into my eyes.—But no, I understand your generous falsehood."

"Citizen, upon my word of a soldier," said the officer, twisting his whiskers furiously, "Upon my word of a soldier, I will not deceive you, and have only said what I think."

"You see my good friend, that you are wrong to despair thus," added Mons. de N——, casting a stealthly look full of gratitude to the officer; "Come, embrace me for the last time, and say farewell; a few days hence, we shalt be again re-united."

"Let us set out! cried the officer, "I have left a convoy of prisoners at Sauve, and cannot remain longer absent."

"Maurice!" Cried Madame de N———, pushing her nephew gently forward by the arm. "I hope you will accompany your uncle."

"But aunt, I don't know that I ought to leave you alone."

"Oh! fear nothing. Now I know that my husband's absence will be but temporary, I am satisfied. Go, Maurice, you will bring back to me, the last orders of my husband. And who knows, but that you will find at Sauve, the order for his liberation, and thus return together!"

"It is possible, my good aunt," answered Maurice, in so broken a voice, that had Madame de N——— been less absorbed in the thought of the approaching deliverance of her husband, she would have perceived that all hope for her was lost.

Followed and preceded by gendarmes, Mons. de N——— at last went from that house, which an hour before, presented so perfect a scene of happiness, but which he now left, the habitation of despair. I followed him.

We crossed the court in profound silence; and it was not till the gates closed behind us, that the unfortunate N———, who had previously shewn so much strength of mind, paid his tribute of weakness to humanity.—The lieutenant addressing him, said,—"Citizen, I have known you for a long time, and I know that no man is more trustworthy. Will you promise me that you will not attempt to fly, and I will let you walk with your two friends, at liberty to converse at your ease."

"I engage not to attempt to fly," answered Mons. de N——— "Allow me to thank you for your generosity, believe me, that I cannot find words to express all the gratitude I feel."

After this reply, the officer pushed his horse on amongst his men, and we remained alone. Separated by about ten or twelve paces from the escort, it was easy for us to converse, without being overheard; but all three of us had our hearts so full, that we maintained a mournful silence.

It was near two o'clock in the morning, when we arrived at Sauve. A short time before reaching that little city, the lieutenant of gendarmery had caused Mons. de N―― to be placed in the midst of his soldiers. Maurice and I, after having given the last grasp of the hand to the unfortunate man, took refuge in an inn, to pass the rest of the night.

It is unnecessary to add, that we thought not of availing ourselves of the bad bed which we found in our room. Seated opposite each other, in our rickety and worm eaten chairs, we maintained a painful silence.

At the first dawn of day, we hastened to present ourselves at the house of detention, where the Ex-Judge Criminal had been added to the convoy of prisoners who had arrived in the evening. There I learned that the convoy were to march towards Paris, and that the prisoners were destined to appear before Fouquier Tinville, and that we could not see the prisoner untill two o'clock.

After a walk of some hours in the environs of the city,—for we were both so much agitated, that rest would have been impossible for us,—we returned to the house of detention.

"You cannot enter citizens," said the turnkey, "At least, not without an order from one of the members of the Committee of Public Safety; the warrant is peremptory in that respect."

The president of the Committee of Public Safety, to whose house we at once repaired, at first, formally refused giving us a pass, but having learned that it related to Mons. de N――, he immediately changed his manner, and gave us the authority we solicited.

The house of detention of the little city of Sauve, was an ancient convent, which, on the spur of the moment, was appropriated to this new purpose. When we presented our pass, we learned that the prisoners were at breakfast in common, in the ancient refectory.

After crossing a long corridor, divided by several strong doors, we reached the refectory where were the prisoners. Mons. de N———, on seeing us, rose hastily from the table, and advanced towards us, holding out his hand.

"Maurice! Sir!" cried he on approaching us, "I certainly cannot blame this last proof of friendship and devotedness that you wish to give me, in coming to see me here, but I confess that I should have preferred not seeing you again! I have been making an effort to detach myself entirely from earth, and anything that recalls an affection to me, weakens my courage." He then took his nephew by the arm, and drew him to the end of the refectory.

I employed the interval in noticing with more attention his companions in misfortune. Two of them attracted my more especial observation. The first was a man, still young, clothed in black with extreme neatness, who had an air of hauteur, —almost of dignity,—but little calculated to attract sympathy. Seeming to care very little about his companions, he appeared absorbed in his reflections; and from time to time, a disdainful smile passed across his lips. The second personage whom I remarked, was an old woman, dressed ridiculously in fashion, forming a striking contrast with the pitiable condition in which she was placed, who uttered in a loud voice the most anti-revolutionary discourse.

She spoke of that "good Mons. Robespierre" and that "excellent blood-letter Marat," with a rage and contempt incredible. The gendarmes present, not being able to impose silence on her, had concluded, by treating her as an old fool, and allowing her to exhaust her anger at her ease. It was evident to me, that the language of this woman was greatly opposed to the views of the other prisoners, who dared neither approve them, for fear of aggravating their position, nor blame them, lest they should pass for sans-culottes-

" That which vexes me," said the old lady, " Is to think that Messieurs the sans-culottes, having married our chamber maids, I shall be compelled, before mounting the guillotine, to suffer myself to be undressed by assistant executioners."

" Madame la Marquise," answered the man in black, who till then had maintained a haughty silence, " Our birth, places us above all these indignities !"

" Our birth sir !" repeated the Marquise sharply, " say *my* birth, if you please, but don't talk of yours. Nobody is ignorant of the fact, that your father, who was first a cloth worker, and afterwards a manufacturer, has bequeathed you a very plebian name, which you have thought proper first to disguise, and then ennoble, but you by no means belong to *our* caste."

" Madame !" cried the prisoner in a rage, " I should never have expected such an observation from you. Everybody knows, that if you have married the Marquis de C———, that does not prevent you from being the grand-daughter of an apothecary."

" Insolence ! My grand-father an apothecary ! Rascal ! Calumniator ! However, I am a great fool to put myself out about you. Truly, the idea, that, rather than sue to all the patriots and bare-foots of your family, you prefer mounting the scaffold, in order to pass for a ci-devant, makes me split with laughter, for you have absolutely stolen the punishment that awaits you."

We had been nearly an hour with the prisoners, when the gaoler came to warn us that we must withdraw.

The parting farewell of Maurice and his uncle was affecting. For the first time since his arrest, the Judge Criminal shewed symptoms of weakness, and could not withhold a tear, in pronouncing the names of his wife and daughter.

"Adieu sir," said he, embracing me, " May God reward by a happy life, the generosity you have shewn me."

I had only strength enough to hasten away, without replying.

On going out, we found the greater part of the inhabitants collected before the prison gates, waiting the departure of the condemned. We joined them; already the two carriages appropriated to this transport had arrived, and half the escort were wheeling about on horseback, when the gaoler came out with a look of alarm, and addressing the crowd :—

" Is there a doctor here?" he asked in a loud voice. " A miserable ci-devant, has plunged a knife into his breast, in order to avoid the punishment he deserves."

A doctor soon arrived, and entered the prison, in order to preserve for the scaffold, the ci-devant, who had attempted to save himself from it, by a voluntary death.

At the moment in which the provincial esculapius passed the threshhold of the house of seclusion, I seized the lappet of his coat, and asked him, who was the prisoner that had attempted to commit suicide, and if he had succeeded.

" I don't know him personally," answered he ; " He is a man dressed in black, and about forty years of age. He has just had his last struggle. and has not more than five minutes to live ! His companions are terrified, but there is one silly old woman ridiculously dressed out, who seems not at all affected by this spectacle. She only shrugged her shoulders with an air of pity, and repeated in an under tone :—

" Monsieur was afraid of finding amongst the assistant executioners, some cousin german of his, which might have compromised his nobilty ! That's the reason he stabbed himself so bravely !"

" Then," cried I, without leaving hold of the doctor's-coat, "it is not citizen N——— who is the suicide !"

"Not at all," answered he, "I know personally, citizen N———, who, in fact, I have just seen among the prisoners. He is a man of a great mind, who does not fear the scaffold, and whose religion will prevent him from attempting his life."

A movement which now took place in the crowd, indicated that the prisoners were coming forth; and a little after, we saw in the midst of the gendarmes, the victims devoted to the fury of Fouquier Tinville.

N——— appeared with a calm and dignified air, which never abandoned him, and raised his eyes towards heaven, with an undefinable expression of melancholy resignation.

"Come forward!" cried the officer of gendarmery, who commanded the escort. The calling over of the prisoners, which had already been done on their leaving prison, was renewed when they got into the carriages.

"The citizeness A——— R———. Said the officer, after having called a dozen names. No one answered.

"The citizeness A——— R———," repeated the lieutenant, fearing that one of the prisoners entrusted to his care had escaped.

The silence continued.

"Does no one answer?" Continued the officer turning pale. "But I am a fool to trouble myself," resumed he, "my list bears the names of four women, and I see four women here. It is bad temper and nothing else.

"But you have not called *me*, Mons. gendarme." Said the old marquise.

"Not called you? Who are you then?"

"I am called the Marquise A——— de R——— de V———, and not the citizeness A——— R———. I give you to understand, that I will not put up with any such insults."

"An old fool!" Come get into the coach."

"Not at all, gendarme. I will not get into the carriage. I protested the moment they came to arrest me, and I will continue to protest all along the road. I do not recognise in your Messieurs Robespierre, the right of apprehending in the name of the republic,—an illegal association of thieves and assassins, —a woman ennobled by a dozen quarterings. My head is in your power, but not my honour; you can conduct me to the scaffold, I know; but my duty, I repeat, is to protest, and I will protest.'

"Be it so, old lady, protest as much as you please; only make haste and get into the coach, or I shall be angry."

"My will is to remain; and I will not get into the coach.' Replied the old marquise, with ludicrous resolution.

"You must not be surprised, lieutenant." Said the brigadier of gendarmery. "This old witch always plays the same game. We have always been compelled to use force."

"Well! Do to-day as you have done on other days." Replied the lieutenant.

Three or four gendarmes immediately sprang towards the marquise; but the old woman taking from under her mantle a bloody knife, the same with which the son of the ex-cloth worker had accomplished his suicide,—placed her back against the gate and prepared for her defence.

At this theatrical stroke, the gendarmes remained motionless; there was so much ridicule united with so much danger in contending with the old lady, that they scarcely knew what course to take.

"Lieutenant," said one of them laughing, "must I go and procure a reinforcement of artillery? We shall never come to an end with this old Joan of Arc, without Cannon!"

"Indeed, I am wrong to threaten you," said the marquise; "on reflecting, it will be better to use this weapon against myself. If one of you take one step towards me, I will plunge this knife into my heart."

Y

"Let us see, Madame la Marquise," said the lieutenant, attempting to gain her favour by this concession. "What do you wish for? What do you require? I am quite ready, if it does not interfere with my duty, to grant you all the satisfaction possible. Speak—"

The marquise was about to reply, when a gendarme who had slipped behind the coach, threw a coverlet over her head: then rushing upon her, he seized her with all his force, before she could make any use of her weapon. Loud bursts of laughter rose amongst the crowd; in fact, it was difficult for me not to share in the mirth which it provoked.

"That's the same as being vanquished," said the marquise whilst they hoisted her into the coach. "I have only yielded to force, and the honour of the principle is saved. I still protest against the republic."

The crowd had already cleared a passage for the funereal convoy, when a new incident occurred to stop its departure. A stable-boy mounted, without a saddle, on a jaded horse, advanced towards the lieutenant and said some words to him in a low voice.

"Are you a fool?" cried the officer. "What! Do you suppose that I am going to take the horses out of my carriages and give them to you?"

"But lieutenant, there is no choice; it concerns the secretary, general and private, of the representative N——— of Marseilles, the citizen Jouveau."

At the name of Jouveau, a sudden inspiration crossed my mind, and although I had parted from him on very bad terms, I resolved to make an appeal to him, in favour of the Judge Criminal.

Addressing the officer of the gendarmery;—"Colleague," said I, "The citizen Jouveau is my relative. If you authorise me, I will do my best to arrange this affair."

"You will render me a great service," replied the gendarme. "Go, and I will wait for you."

I immediately jumped èn croupê behind the stable boy, and presently got off before the posting house, where stood a carriage, waiting for horses.

"Well!" cried Jouveau himself from the carriage window, addressing the stable boy; "Well, this new turn-out, where is it?"

"They cannot give it to you cousin." replied I. slipping off the horse, and running to the coach door. At sight of me, Jouveau made a grimace, in no respect flattering to my self love; I saw that he would willingly have cut me.

"What Jouveau!" said I, "Is this the way that you reqnite me! Ungrateful! You knit your eyebrows on perceiving me, whilst I run to you with open arms."

"Cousin," replied Jouveau, "if you are going to repeat your moral lectures, I shall treat you as an enemy; but if you are converted to the good principles, it is quite different, and I give you my hand with all my heart."

"Yes cousin," replied I, affecting a pleasantry far from my heart, "I am converted to the good principles:—Gold and gaiety for ever! That's my new motto."

"Ah! Parbleu!" Cried Jouveau, "I should never have looked for such a conversion. Cousin, a presentiment tells me, that neither of us will have to repent of the chance which reunites us in so unforeseen a way; that we shall do a good business together, you may from this moment make unlimited use of my credit."

"Faith my dear cousin," I replied with an air of indifference, "I accept your offer with so much the more pleasure that it could not have happened more apropos. I have just a favour to ask of you."

"Well, you lose no time! What is it cousin?"

" First to take away these horses which they have refused you."

" Refused *me!* You are dreaming."

"It is however, as I have the honour to tell you. An officer of gendarmery has taken the horses to effect the transport of several prisoners, whom he is escorting; and he will not yield them to you."

"Ah!" Said Jouveau, biting his lips, "But this officer may probably deceive himself. Cousin, do me the pleasure to carry him these two lines. If that is not sufficient, I shall have recourse to another method."

" And the favour I have to ask of you?" said I, taking the paper that Jouveau had written.

" We will talk about that presently. The business of the moment is, that I must have the horses. Make haste. If the officer is gone you must run after him."

I again bestrode the jade which had already served me, and darted towards the house of detention. The lieutenant of gendarmery, after having cast his eyes over the note, could not conceal his ill humour, but immediately taking his resolution :—

"We shall not start to day," said he, turning to the gendarmes ; "Take the accused back to the prison.

I stole away quietly, in search of Maurice.

"Maurice," I exclaimed, on meeting him, "Moments are precious ; ask no questions, I beg of you, but answer me at once ;—Is your uncle rich?"

" Yes," replied he.

·" Can he raise the sum of a hundred louis d'or?"

"Yes."

" Good ; not a word more. Farewell till I see you again; go, and wait for me at the hotel." Saying this I remounted my horse.

"Well," cried Jouveau as soon as he perceived me, "does the gendarme still hold out?"

"No, cousin; scarcely had he looked at your note, than he gave the order to unharness."

"Then I can continue my journey?"

"There's nothing to prevent it cousin, unless it be that I am dying of hunger. If you can stop at Sauve an hour, you will find me a guest worthy of your company."

"Agreed—I wish for nothing better; let us make the best of our time."

What I had foreseen, took place. When Jouveau had emptied a couple of bottles of wine, he was in excellent temper.

"Apropos, cousin," said he, "what is this favour you have to ask of me?"

"Oh, its no great matter," replied I, "you shall have it in two words: my purse is empty, and I wish to fill up the void."

"Ah! indeed!" cried Jouveau, "of course, then, you have a device for filling it; and it is a matter of business that you are going to propose."

"Yes, cousin, it is just a matter of business."

"For which you want my influence?"

"That's it! Of course your share of the profit will ever be much greater than mine."

"Well, cousin, let us hear the particulars: I am all attention."

"Hear them, then, in a few words Yesterday the Revolutionary Committee of the district, has given an order for the apprehension of the body of a certain Ex-Judge-Criminal of the name of N———."

"The deuce!" cried Curtius, interrupting me. "An Ex-Judge Criminal cannot be otherwise than guilty, for the mob love to see this kind of people executed. Truly I fear that you have bungled this business with a deplorable good nature, or that you have let them see the bottom of your empty purse."

"Cousin, you do me an injustice," cried I. "I protect my own interest and nothing else. The Ex-Judge Criminal N—— is an original, who prefers mounting the guillotine to entering into a compromise. It is therefore, with his nephew that I have to treat.

"Ah! Ah! we can't do better."

"This nephew, has promised, if I will obtain the liberation of his uncle, to pay me a visit at the inn where I am staying, and to forget, on leaving, a hundred louis left upon the mantle piece of my room!"

"In gold and not in assignats?"

"Jouveau," cried I in a tone of reproach, "you must have a very bad opinion of me, to load me thus with insults! I have stipulated for louis d'ors, and have ever taken care to observe, that not being a stock-jobber, I would not accept these louis except at a discount."

"Well, hear my resolution, which I shall not rescind. A hundred louis is not enough. If the nephew would bring the sum to a hundred and fifty louis, and you be contented with twenty-five, then I don't say—"

"I am much afraid they will refuse me," answered I, pretending to be in a bad humour; "However, I'll go and see."

Saying this, I rose from table, but just as I was leaving the room, Jouveau called me back.

"An excellent idea has just struck me cousin," said he, "To urge on the nephew, will you let me arrest him? I have several blank warrants about me!"

"Arrest Maurice!" cried I, scarcely restraining my indignation.

"Nay! Replied Jouveau. "It is a piece of civilty, that I wish to pay to you. You understand that, provided I receive my hundred and twenty five louis, I have nothing more to ask for."

"The thing is, you see cousin, this young man is as headstrong as his uncle, once arrested, he would pay nothing. Leave me to manage this affair in my own way."

Maurice, whom I found at the inn waiting for me, could not withhold an exclamation of joy on learning the bargain I had made. The money was not long in forthcoming, and in less than half an hour I presented him with the order for his uncle's deliverance.

Maurice took the order with an eagerness that the reader may easily conceive, and went away with it at a running pace.

"Farewell, cousin," said Jouveau, "I must get on my route. Do not forget that you have a friend in me, and that you will always find me ready to oblige you. I shall return to Marseilles in four days. Come and rejoin me as soon as you can; I will guarantee you good luck."

As soon as Jouveau had disappeared, I ran off to the prison; and the first person I met was the Ex-Judge, who was leaving it.

"Here's your liberator, uncle," said Maurice.

Mons. N———, with an eagerness I scarcely believed him capable of, threw himself upon my neck and embraced me several times.

"Ah! sir," said he, "you cannot imagine what I have suffered since yesterday. Believing my misfortune inevitable, I would not display a useless sorrow, which would have darkened the bloody recollection which my death bequeathed to those I love. But I suffered from that thought of abandoning my family; Ah! I suffered beyond expression."

The excellent N——— then left me to go to his wife, who had arrived at Sauve, and having been informed of her husband's release, was momentarily expecting him.

Having been instrumental in affecting this happy deliverance, I took leave the same evening of Mons. N——— and Maurice, in spite of their pressing attempts to detain me, and proceeded on my journey.

A few hours after leaving Sauve, having passed through a stoney, dry, and arid country, I arrived at the delicious valley of St. Hyppolite. An extensive meadow, and a forest of fruit trees which I crossed, led me to the city.

The distribution of bread, was taking place when I entered the inn. A long file of persons of both sexes and all ages, who, pale and extenuated by privations and fatigue, waited with a sorrowful resignation for the meagre pittance that was to save them from starvation. Young coxcombs, old gentlemen, fruit merchants, tanners, marquisses, blacksmiths, &c., pressed and elbowed each other pell-mell, to be ready at the calling of their names.

Armed with a large knife, and wearing a leather apron, the municipal officer superintended the weighing and division of the pieces of bread. Having carefully packed eight ounces in my sack, and had my passport viséed, I again proceeded on my road, and soon arrived at Ganges, where I found that all the shops were shut, and a dead silence reigned throughout the city. I entered a hair dresser's to get shaved. It was the "decade" day, and the barber's shop was full of customers of all descriptions. A dozen persons seated on a bench against the wall, waited their turns, whilst the hair-dresser, holding one of his customers by the nose, his head thrown back and his face covered with soap suds, flourished his razor in the air, and commented on the events of the decade.

" Ah !" said he, " I will not speak ill of the guillotine, but still I see much in that invention that requires alteration. We barbers would do more execution in an hour, than the guillotine will do in a day. Suppose for instance, the citizen I am about to shave at this moment, was an aristocrat and a federalist,—pshaw! A slight touch of the razor, and there's one dangerous rogue less." So saying, the barber, to give point to his demonstration rapidly struck the back of his razor across the throat of his customer, who, feeling the cold steel, uttered a terrible scream, and fell from his chair to the ground. Bursts of laughter succeeded this joke. The customer being served, an old man completely bald, took his place.

" Can you citizen," said he to the hair-dresser, " Put a little powder on my head to replace the wig, which my republican principles prevent me from wearing?"

" Powder!" Repeated the barber, " It is impossible. For six months past, not an ounce of powder has entered my shop."

" Well then citizen," resumed the old man, "Put a little flour on, instead of the powder."

" Flour! Do you fancy that I am going to lavish the food of the people in order to gratify your ridiculous foppishness.'

" But citizen, the air, striking upon my bald head,"—

" Hold your tongue, conspirator! Bring me some mill-dust and then I will powder you to your satisfaction."

Not relishing this fellows treatment, I left the shop without saying a word, and proceeded on my way. On leaving the charming little town of la Vigeva, I came to a fertile country, covered with a rich vegetation. Disgusted with the centre of population, which presented only the melancholy spectacle of evil human passions, I determined to avoid the town as much as possible, and, in fact, on leaving Morneys, I plunged at once into the Cevennes.

I cannot describe the exciting impression of happiness I felt, when roving free amidst the solitudes of these mountains, and thinking that whilst around me reigned treason, violence and espionage, tranquil and careless, I surveyed the beautie of nature. That contempt of human ambition, fury and violence, which the sight of nature produced in me, explained how and why it was that the mountaineers of the Cevennes had opposed to this day, with unshaken obstinacy, the principles of the revolution. Still, they had perceived, that to oppose by force, the march of the new ideas, would have drawn upon their country, persecution and ruin. Therefore they received the delegates with all the appearance of delight, entertained them well, and at last sent them away perfectly satisfied with their patriotism. The reader will be unjust however, if he attributes to them falseness of character; they displayed only their acuteness, or rather perhaps, a sovereign contempt for these agents.

Although my uniform of a republican soldier might have induced them to mistrust me, wherever I went I was received with a sincere and frank hospitality.

I set out one morning early, in order to arrive before nightfall at Mende, where I intended to sleep. About noon, I found that I had missed my way. Exhausted by fatigue and hunger, I flung myself at the foot of a huge rock, which screened me from the sun's rays. I drew from a napkin, a piece of bread weighing about five ounces, which, with a few figs, constituted all my provisions, and then sat down to dinner by the side of a limpid spring. I began to attack my bread and figs, when I heard a slight noise in the briars and ferns which surrounded me; and almost immediately I saw, coming from the thicket a very young man, elegantly dressed, and who, on perceiving me, could not repress an exclamation of surprise.

Remarking the hesitation of the youth :—"Citizen," said I, " I am an officer of the regiment of la Cote d'Or. If you wish to partake of my repast, sit down at my side, there are still four figs and nearly two ounces of bread; if you delay for five minutes, there will be nothing at all."

Encouraged by my freedom, the youth began to smile. "I will not deny, citizen," he replied, "That you frightened me. May I ask what route you are following?"

"I intend to sleep to night at Mende."

"You cannot think of that. Do you know what distance you are from that town?"

"Faith, no! Two or three leagues I suppose."

"You are far from the mark. Seven leagues."

"Is it possible? Then I must have gone backwards since the morning, instead of advancing."

"That's very probable; you have got out of the way. You ought, in fact, officer, to thank the accident which has brought us together, and to follow me."

"Follow you! Faith, with great pleasure; only allow me to ask you where you are going to take me to?"

"I regret not being able to answer that question. All that I am permitted to tell you is, that you will meet with a hearty reception, will run no danger, and that they will charge you nothing for your entertainment. But, I must beg you, supposing you accept my offer, to ask no more questions on the subject."

I accepted the young man's invitation, and we proceeded on our way. After a walk of more than four hours, we arrived at a wood of fir trees, which, placed upon the plateau of a mountain, covered a large extent of ground. We entered the wood, and following a foot path, the firm and beaten soil of which showed that it must have been often trodden by passengers, I perceived at about a hundred paces before us, a fixed and brilliant light; and almost at the same instant I found myself in the midst of a vast glade of the wood, where stood a large edifice.

"Where are we now? And what is this chateau?" asked I.

"We are arrived," he replied, "at the end of our journey. As to this chateau, history pretends that it was built by the Counts de Gèvandau; and tradition, by the devil: choose which of these versions suits you best."

My companion now pulled an iron chain which hung alongside the grating. The sound of a bell vibrated in the air.

A huge knave of a sans-culotte,—as far as I could judge from his costume,—came forward with a dark lantern in his hand.

"What can I do to serve you, citizens?" he inquired in a stentorian voice.

"Tell citizen Rose, that two travellers ask his hospitality for this night."

"I have no need to trouble citizen Rose," replied the sans-culotte roughly. "Are you patriots?"

"Enthusiastic patriots!" Said my companion; "Ultra Revolutionists."

"That's enough, we will open the gates to you. Vive la Republique!"

The iron gate receded before us, creaking on its hinges, and we entered the court yard of the chateau.

"My friend," said my companion, again addressing our guide; "in spite of fraternity and equality, we generally like to know who we receive. The citizen, as his uniform indicates, is an officer; and belongs to the battalion of the Cote d'Or. As for myself, I am nobody, but I am called Abel."

"Ah, are you Mons. Abel?" said the sans culotte, in a familiar tone. "My goodness, sir, how sorry I am that you are come so late,—for I am afraid those ladies are gone to bed and cannot receive you,—will you come for a moment with me, whilst I go to learn whether I should introduce you?"

The man led us into an apartment handsomely fitted up,

on the ground floor, where he begged of us to wait, and then went away.

He soon re-appeared. " Mons. Abel," said he, addressing the young man, who seemed much abstracted ; " If you will take the trouble to follow me, citizen Rose is waiting for you.' Abel disappeared with the sans-culotte, who in a few minutes returned. " Citizen," said he, " If you will do me the honor to share with me my humble supper, I am about to lay the table."

" That's an honour which the keen air of the mountains that I have breathed all the day, will render most welcome to me," I replied, examining him with more attention than I had hitherto done.

He was a stout robust youth, with broad round shoulders, athletic limbs, and a very marked physiognomy. However, in spite of his formidable moustaches, thick eyebrows, sabre, carmagnole, and long, black, rough, and matted hair, his whole person indicated contentment and simplicity, rendered still more striking by that revolutionary display of which I have spoken.

In a very short time, he unfolded a very white table-cloth, and placed two covers opposite, and several bottles of wine on the table ; then, going into an adjoining room, he returned bearing a soup-tureen, from which a delicious odour exhaled.

" Shall I offer you some of this soup, citizen ?" he asked, taking off the cover.

" Offer everything citizen," replied I, " You run no risk of getting a refusal."

I made a most admirable supper, and, my voracious appetite appeased, questioned Antoine, as the sans-culotte was named, on the subject of citizen Rose ; but though he would evidently have laid down his life in her defence, he was very chary of imparting any information respecting her.

z

When the repast was nearly ended, the youth Abel returned, and I besought him to satisfy my curiosity.

"I! I am almost asleep," said the young man, "And I aim at nothing just now, but to go to bed. Finish your supper at your ease, and at the same time, I will plant myself in that great arm-chair, and take an instalment of the night."

In fact, my companion, after placing himself comfortably in a vast fauteuil of carved oak, was very soon asleep. In half an hour, I rose from table, and awaking the young man, I proposed to him to retire.

Antoine, taking a flambeau with branches, in which were several wax candles, walked before, to shew us the way.

Stopping at the first floor, he opened a door, and I perceived two pretty rooms neatly furnished, and each containing a bed.

"This is your lodging," said Antoine. "I hope you will have a good night. If you want my services, you will only have to pull the bell-rope, and in less than a minute I will be at your side."

Alone with Abel, I endeavoured to obtain some information of him; but whether my companion was really overcome with fatigue, or wished to avoid all explanation, he begged me to defer our conversation till the next day. and hastened to go to bed.

It was broad day when I awoke, and getting out of bed, I called Abel, but received no answer. On lifting the curtain of the bed in which he had slept, I found that he was gone.

I went to the window, which commanded a view of a large garden; on one side of which was a forest of lofty trees, which I concluded fenced a park. There seeing Abel offering his arm to a young and very handsome girl, I withdrew hastily, and hid myself behind the curtains. Presently I saw a second female, who appeared to be watching the young man and his companion. This lady, who might be twenty-five years of age, appeared to be a person of distinction. She was dressed in a costume of a grave colour, and a formal cut. Her countenance exhibited a union of resplendent beauty, with rigid severity. Her mouth smiled, whilst her fixed and deep look, indicated important pre-occupation of mind, and her firm and decided step, was wholly destitute of that kind of nonchalance which sits so well on a woman. The young girl hanging on the arm of my friend Abel, was what a pretty child at her first entrance into life should be,—timid, excitable, and modest.

I left my post of observation, and ran down the stairs to proceed to the garden. At the sight of a soldier with large moustaches, a face bronzed by the sun, and a uniform torn by the brambles, the companion of Abel drew back hastily, and uttered a slight exclamation of terror. As to the other lady, her look was directed towards me with perfect composure, and without indicating the least surprise.

"Madam," said I, saluting her respectfully, "Have I not the honour of addressing her who is called the citizen Rose, and whom I must call my benefactress, in gratitude for the generous hospitality that she has granted me?"

"You are not mistaken," replied she, "I am the citizen Rose; but you owe me no thanks. The hospitality that you have met with here, is in no respect exclusive; it is accorded to all. I therefore repeat, that you owe me no thanks." She bowed to me, and continued her walk, leaving me lost in my conjectures. I walked about the garden, till Antoine came to tell me that breakfast was ready.

Having fully satisfied our appetite, I asked Abel if he intended to pass the day at this mysterious chateau, my intention being, in that case, at once to resume my route.

"Nothing detains me here," replied he, "And we will

start immediately." In a few minutes we found ourselves again amongst the mountains, and proceeding towards the town of Mende.

"Well! my dear dear officer," said Abel, "I hope I have kept my word, and that nothing of what I promised to you last evening, has been wanting. And now I will gratify your curiosity. Know then, that this mysterious chateau, thus concealed in the midst of the Cevennes, is a convent of nuns, of the order of Saint Benoit, and that citizen Rose, is absolutely the lady Abbess of that community.

"A convent in full power in the year 2 of the republic! I cannot take such a joke seriously."

"I assure you that I am not joking. Listen a moment, and you shall see what a firm and upright character, like that of citizen Rose, is able to accomplish. Citizen Rose,—whose true name is de H———, entered this convent of the daughters of St. Benoit, about six years ago, in quality of novice, in consequence of a disappointment in a love affair."

Four years after, being named abbess, she consequently filled that high office when the revolution commenced. Guessing the result, citizen Rose, with the sagacity of a statesman, saw that her convent was destroyed, if she espoused the cause of the noblesse against the citizens. She therefore took the heroic resolution of sacrificing her prejudices to the safety of her community. Without waiting for the orders of the municipality to take down the weathercocks from the roof, the wolves heads and tusks from the doorways, demolish the battlements, &c., &c., she proceeded at once, herself, to grant these puerile concessions to the new ideas which now overran the country, and at once acquired the character of a good citizen. Then came the order for the suppression of convents. Not at all alarmed, she immediately bought up assignats at a minimum price, and thus obtained a large nominal property.

Then came the day of sale of the conventional estate : she became the highest bidder, under the name of a poor goatherd, in whom she had the fullest confidence ; so that she again entered into legal possession of the fields, woods, and chateau."

"Did no one come forward, to dispute this fine property with her?"

"No one. They say, that the district authorities had received large sums of money to prevent competition. Now, as I know citizen Rose to be very prudent, I am inclined to believe in the truth of these assertions. As to the peasantry, they are too much attached to the excellent abbess, their providence in misfortune, to think for an instant, of appropriating this property to themselves. On the contrary, they would have destroyed without compunction, every one who had opposed the designs of the abbess." When once legally installed in her convent, she exchanged the monastic costume of the sisters, for clothing of serge. She suppressed the bells which announced the different religious exercises, and adopted noisy rattles instead. Lastly, in order to account for the assembling of so great a number of women, she established a boarding school for young ladies—"

"I doubt," said I, interrupting my young companion, " whether this boarding school obtained many pupils."

"You are mistaken. The generality of the revolutionists, enriched, or on the point of making fortunes, were anxious to place their daughters with citizen Rose, in order to complete their education, and give them good habits."

"In fact," said I, "I am not at all surprised at that. In revolutions, the rising plunderers, when once they have amassed riches, finish by reflecting, that they are destined to form part of a new aristocracy. They therefore, are anxiously desirous that their descendants and heirs should possess that education which they denounced, and treated as useless, when it was exclusively the privilege of the children of the wealthy whom they had plundered."

"That's just what happened to the citizen Rose. Most of her pupils are the daughters of the authorities of the district, or the superior functionaries of the department. This will explain how it is, that they let her remain at quiet. For myself, I have been sent by my uncle, to see his daughter, who lives at the school, and whom they wish me to marry."

"I thank you heartily for your account. This history of a convent flourishing under the year 2 of the republic, appears to me a unique circumstance."

On arriving at Mende, nearly at nightfall, I left my companion to go to the inn. It seemed to me that the young man followed me some distance, and I presumed that I might shortly receive a visit from him.

The next morning, I was fast asleep, when the hotel-keeper opened the door of the room, awoke me suddenly, and beckoning to a stout well dressed man, whom the darkness,—for it was scarcely day,—had prevented me from perceiving before. "Here," said he to the stranger, "is the person in question."

The gentleman advanced quickly towards my bed, looked at me a moment attentively, and then in an imperious voice; "I am one of the district administrators," said he, "show me your papers; you appear to me a suspected person."

"Citizen administrator," replied I coolly, "be so good as to give me my knapsack. Thank you; here's my passport, read it and allow me to go to sleep again."

"These papers appear regular enough," Said the gentleman, addressing the inn-keeper. "You may withdraw, my friend, and if I want you, I will call for you."

"Citizen officer," continued he, when we were alone,

"your passport is of very old date. I am therefore resolved to learn who you are, what is your family, and what are your means of existence?"

"Before replying to your questions," replied I, looking steadily at him. "I beg to know first, if you are not the father of a charming young lady, and the uncle of a thoughtless young man, whom I have recently seen?"

"Come, I see that you are a sensible man." Cried the administrator, whose air of gravity disappeared, and gave place to a frank laugh. "The fact is, my nephew in confessing his imprudence of yesterday, caused me some alarm. I see now that the young man has had more good fortune than he deserved, and I no longer insist on knowing who you are."

"I do not intend to be surpassed in generosity," replied I, also laughing, "and as my passport does not inspire you with confidence, so much the worse for you, for I must bore you with the recital of my genealogy."

I then explained to him in a few words, how I had been the victim of the requisition, and then made him acquainted with the position of my family.

"Well! exclaimed he with surprise, in the middle of my recital. "This is truly a singular accident! Do you know citizen, that I have been intimately connected with your father?"

"You! Is it possible?"

"Quite so. Do you remember a journey your father once made to Paris, about twelve years ago, to prosecute an important lawsuit?"

"Which he gained. That circumstance had too great an influence on the destiny of our family, for any of us ever to forget it."

"Well, I was your father's advocate."

"Then you are Mons. de la Rouvrette."

"The same, young man. Only I beg of you to call me simply, Larouvrette."

"I will bear it in mind, citizen."

After an interesting conversation, the administrator retired, and left me to repose! but not without having made me promise, that as soon as I rose, I should repair to his house, where he was going to prepare an apartment for me.

It was not without slightly blushing, that his nephew Abel met me again. The day having passed, I wished to take my leave of citizen Larouvrette, my intention being to set out on my journey next morning; but he strenuously opposed my resolution.

"You shall pass the whole week here," said he, "and if it is necessary to employ force to detain you, I will do so."

It was useless protesting and arguing; citizen Larouvrette would not consent to set me at liberty. All that I could obtain of his obstinacy was that he would not keep me beyond four days.

"Since you are fond of travelling," said he, "this delay will admirably suit your tastes; I must go to see my eldest brother who lives in the Gevaudan, about a dozen leagues from hence. Will you accompany me? You will pass through a curious country." I accepted his proposal; and the day fixed for our departure having arrived, citizen Larouvrette and I set off on our journey after breakfast, and my companion informed me that the brother whom he was going to see was an ultra royalist.

"Only look at the obstinacy of my brother," said he. "He opposes the marriage of his son with my daughter, under the pretext that my republican sentiments are too violent. Now you must know, that my brother's whole fortune amounts to only a couple of thousand crowns of income at the utmost, whilst mine equals at least three times that sum. I therefore represent wealth against poverty, and truly, if I did not love my daughter and Abel so well as I do, I would never think of setting my foot in my eldest brother's house."

The Gevaudan is a very arid and barren country, and the deepest misery and poverty everywhere prevailed. In a cabin, whose cracked walls and torn thatch denoted the wretchedness of the owner, we found one of those fine old men we sometimes meet with in the country, an admirable type of practical philosophy, who represent the stoical resignation of the labourer broken down by fatigue, and waiting for death without fear. On seeing us enter, the old man saluted us with a slight inclination of the head, and as soon as we had made him acquainted with our wishes, he placed before us two broken cups, the only earthenware his cabin contained, and raising with difficulty a wooden bowl, standing in a corner, he filled the cups with milk.

"Father," said I respectfully, "The dilapidation of your cottage tells me that the requisition and spoliation have extended their ravages even to you. The revolutionary troops must have passed here."

"Alas!" replied the old man, "They have robbed us of our children, and forbidden us to worship God :—that is to say, they have deprived us of the arms that procured us a living, and of the religion which enabled us to suffer."

To the questions I put to him, the old man replied with frankness and simplicity. I was glad, on going out to see that citizen Larouvrette left a crown by the side of his empty cup. It was almost night when we arrived at the end of our journey. The dwelling of the elder Larouvrette was a mixture of the country house and the farm, combining the useful with the ornamental.

Mons. Larouvrette might be from fifty to fifty-five years of age. His expressive physiognomy indicated an extraordinary energy of mind. Of the middle height, and well made, he must have been endowed with remarkable muscular power. It was easy to see by his simple and easy language, and his natural and quiet manners, that you had to do with a man to whom the usages of good society were familiar.

He received his brother without any exaggerated demonstrations of friendship, but with a cordiality which assured me that he was not so fanatical a royalist as he pretended. The sight of my uniform occasioned him an involuntary movement of bad humour; but he received me with extreme politeness, mixed with a coolness and reserve, which, without being offensive, from the first moment, raised a barrier to our intimacy.

The next morning, being summoned by the breakfast bell, I entered the parlour, when Mons. de la Rouvrette came briskly to meet me and taking me by the hand; "I beg your pardon, my dear sir," said he, in a friendly tone, "for the coolness I shewed you yesterday, but I had not the honour of knowing you, and you are aware that at the present time it is necessary to be cautious. My brother on informing me who you are and the excellent lesson of prudence which you have been so good as to give to my hair-brained son, makes me regret having lost a good evening of conversation. I hope that you will still stay with me some days."

The next day, citizen Larouvrette set out for Mende, Not being able to resist the cordial advances of his brother, I determined to remain some days with him.

Never in my life do I recollect meeting with a man so polite and complaisant as my host. He served me as a guide, and accompanied me to the mountain. One day we were passing near a farm, when I remarked upon the front of the rustic building, many traces of shot.

"Has there been a battle here?" I asked.

"Yes," he replied; "and that battle was near changing the whole destiny of France."

These words astonished me greatly, and I begged him to explain himself more clearly. He at once proceeded to satisfy my curiosity.

"There are events," said he, "which are not noticed in their passage, which nevertheless, have scarcely failed to change the face of the world. The most invincible conqueror stumbles and falls like the lowest of his soldiers, on meeting a stone in his path. A grain of sand or gravel, which chance throws into a powerful machine, suffices to stop the wheels, and neutralize the power. History, in relating great events, often takes no account of the futile and leading causes, which have produced them. We mountaineers are not of an aggressive disposition; but we possess a remarkable obstinacy in resistance. Our ungrateful and arid soil, in condemning us to almost inevitable privations, has instilled into our hearts, the love of order and religion. If at any time government touches our property or our faith, it commits an irreparable fault, for which we have no pardon. Our peasants, who saw without alarm,—perhaps even with a degree of sympathy,—the coming revolution, soon changed their sentiments, when they felt the weight of certain monstrous decrees of the Convention. The violence exercised against the clergy, the requisition, the patriotic, but forced taxes, soon cured them of their weak enthusiasm, and made them dream of means to relieve themselves from so odious a tyranny."

"A people which suffers and reflects, is soon ready to appeal to physical force, the chances of arms, and violence. At least this was what I persuaded myself; and, faithful to my lawful princes, I resolved to seek them, and ask if they thought it would serve their cause, —which I considered that of France,—to give a direction to this discontent."

"Having with great difficulty procured a passport, I was about to go to the frontier, when one morning, I received a visit, which certainly, I was far from expecting, and which reduced my projects to nothing. A Mons. Charrier was announced, whom I immediately ordered to be introduced."

"He informed me that he had been created Field Marshal and Commander-in chief, by Mons. the Regent of France, and that he was about to head a rising of the peasantry in favour of the royalists. As I discovered that he had formerly been a grenadier in the regiment which I commanded, and that he was practically unacquainted with military tactics, I refused the brevet of colonel which he offered me, and declined to serve under him. Still, I gave him good advice, which he rejected with scorn. At my expostulations, he grew insolent, and I was compelled to request him to leave the house. I will give you the history of his exploits, if you wish it.

"Certainly," said I, "it interests me greatly, and I beg of you to proceed."

"As soon as I had shut the door upon Charrier, who, be it said, in passing, was rather a conceited puppy, blinded by a foolish ambition, than a rogue, I hastened to forewarn all the royalists of my acquaintance that they should not engage in the wretched and impossible scheme in which it would be attempted to enlist them. Thank Heaven, the generality of them listened to my advice."

Very few days had passed from the visit of Charrier, when I learned all at once, that he was coming at the head of a corps composed of five or six thousand men, to carry Mende, and was marching upon our town of Marvejols. The patriots took to flight; the old bourgeoise reappeared, and assembled at the Hotel-de-ville. The deliberation was long, and it is probable that it would have ended in nothing, when one of the scouts sent out, returned to announce that Charrier with his army, was not more than a quarter of a league from the town."

"Immediately, one of the bourgeoise snatched up a brazen dish, threw into it five or six large rusty old keys, and proposed going to meet Charrier, and surrender the town, on the condition that the lives and property of the Marvejols should be respected. They were again about to deliberate on this, when the sound of the trumpets of Mons. the field-marshal and commandant was heard. The bourgeoise and notables took to their heels at once."

"Never, my dear sir, shall I forget the burlesque tableau which the entry of the royalist army into Marvejols presented."

"At the head marched first Charrier, mounted on an enormous cart horse, with the carcass of an elephant and the gait of a rhinoceros. The costume of the governor presented the most ludicrous assemblage imaginable, of tinsel, feathers, and broidery mixed; no quack doctor has ever exceeded him. Immediately after Charrier, came his artillery. Goodness! What cannon! they were made of wood bound with iron, and drawn by the peasantry; resembling the primitive engines which followed the first discovery of gunpowder. As to the royalist army, comprising fifteen to eighteen hundred peasants, who advanced, marching on their toes, in affectation of marking the time, neither pen nor pencil can depict the fabulous collection. Armed with muskets unfit for use, sticks, stones, even cooking utensils, they resembled a troop of masks on Shrove Tuesday, or a company of travelling comedians."

"Roosted upon his horse-elephant, Charrier listened graciously to the deputation of bourgeoise who brought him the keys of the city. He even condescended to harangue them in a complete discourse which he closed by declaring that he and his invincible army were ready to shed the last drop of their blood for the defence of their religion and their sovereign."

"During the first days of the occupation of Marvejols by the
2 A

royalist troops, all went on well. From morning until night, Charrier received delegations and deputations, which afforded him opportunity for the display of his eloquence; whilst his peasants eat, drank and sung to their heart's content. Everybody was satisfied. The greater part of the neighbouring mountaineers who really believed that France reckoned only two cities, Mende and Marvejols, seeing the counter-revolution complete and perfect, eagerly ranged themselves under the flag of Charrier, in order to share in the rewards which Louis XVII, or the Regent would not fail to bestow on them."

"Alas! these sweet illusions were of short duration. One morning, the scouts of Charrier ran in great haste to announce the arrival of the patriot army at Avignon. The ex-grenadier caused the generalè to be beaten, and having left the care of the city to fifty poor devils, commanded by an old barber, who took the title of governor but who was more commonly called major, he himself opened the campaign and marched against the enemy."

"The patriots of Avignon, were personally brave, and furnished with real artillery, well served, and would have proved formidable adversaries, if they had been headed by a good general. This was just what was wanting with them. It was between that old chateau you see on the left, and which was formerly used as a summer residence of the bishops of Mende, and that farm upon which you observed traces of balls, that the two armies met. The patriots began by a general discharge of their artillery, to which the royalists replied by a fire of musketry, and then immediately after this fine exploit, the two armies ran different ways, as fast as their legs could carry them. I must do Charrier the justice,—for I had mixed with his men as a volunteer, and was present at the whole affair,—to state that he was the only one of his party who displayed, if not presence of mind, at least courage. Abusing, striking, and rallying the fugitives, he managed to collect a hundred of his combatants, and ran in pursuit of the patriots. A slight skirmish ensued, in which the royalists were completly victorious."

"I will not attempt to describe the joy of the conquerors when they re-entered the city. Marvejols was illuminated and the whole night was spent in perambulating the streets, shouting in the patois, ' Bibe le ré !' or 'Long live the king !' In the meantime, those distant districts which had saved themselves without fighting, sounded the alarm on their passage, and magnified the victory of the royalist army, which they also increased to ten thousand men."

"The government therefore hastened to send large bodies of troops against the insurgents, who, however, had dispersed of themselves after the battle, and abandoned their chief. Charrier, who had taken refuge in one of his farms, which we shall pass in a few hours, upon the arrival of the detachment sent against him, threw himself into a trench made to preserve potatoes, and which, for greater security, was covered with a large slab of stone. The detachment after having ransacked the farm house from top to bottom, and discovering nothing, was about to withdraw, when Charrier, suffocated for want of air, and the exhalation of the fermenting potatoes, could not suppress his groans. They soon snatched him from his hiding place, and dragged him to Rhodez, when on the day after his arrival, he was beheaded in the midst of a vast concourse of people. I must acknowledge, that in spite of the consummate incapacity he had evinced, he died with true courage. Monde and Marvejols were retaken without any fighting. The peasants who hoped that their humble station would protect them from the consequences of their peurile rebellion, met with a sad fate. During the two following days, the republican troops tracked them from house to house, on the plains, in the streets, everywhere, and massacred without pity, more than fifteen hundred of them. Thus ended this deplorable enterprise, which, if it had been matured and combined with care and directed by a skilful man, might have given an immense development to the Vendécan war and broken down the convention."

It was scarcely one o'clock, when Mons. de la Rouvrette proposed returning to Marvejols.

"It is not then your intention to continue our walk to the end of the day? I think you promised to shew me the house and farm where the unfortunate Charrier had hidden himself and was arrested."

"In fact," said he, "I hoped to be able to keep you company a longer time; but I have reflected, that as I have to start early to-morrow morning, I have need of taking some rest to-day."

"Are you setting out for a long journey?"

"Not at all; merely a simple excursion, but wearisome from the obstacles which it presents, and only accessible on foot. It is attended with some danger and requires all my strength. But now I think of it, will you accompany me?"

"I am wholly at your command, and will blindly follow you where you may think proper to take me."

"I thank you for your confidence. You shall not find it misplaced. I can promise that you shall witness a novel phase in the social aspect of our time."

CHAPTER VIII.

The mountain solitudes.—A houseless republic.—Everything al-fresco.—The wounded Count.—Brother Peter and the Spy.—Confession of the Assassin.—The Count's story.—Laura and the ex-cartwright.—I leave the encampment.—Saint Flour.—Durand and his wife.—Poison.—Marital tenderness.—The Count's fearful revenge.—I am arrested and marched off to prison.—An awkward reacontre.—A mean vengeance.—Locked up in my cell.

On our return to Marvejols, we supped early and soon retired for the night. The next morning we got on our route, before sun-rise. I found the mountains I traversed after my entrance on the Cevennes, grand, majestic, and picturesque in the extreme. On descending again into the plain, we saw immense flocks, under the care of shepherds.

It might be near three o'clock, when my companion and I reached the edge of a vast and dense forest, which we had for some time perceived in the distance.

" We are now nearly arrived," said Rouvrette, " A few more minutes, and I shall clasp my good brother in my arms."

Beyond the first limit of the forest we had to climb a hill exceedingly steep, and covered with high broom. I had stopped a moment to gather a plant, when an exclamation uttered near caused me to raise my head; when I saw Mons de la Rouvrette embracing a sturdy peasant, who had emerged from the thicket.

On perceiving me, the countryman could not withhold a movement of surprise; and he put his hand hastily under his vest, where I perceived the bright barrels of a pair of pistols.

"Make yourself easy Prior," said my host laughing, "This gentleman is my friend, and you may place entire confidence in him."

The Prior then politely saluted me, and excused his suspicions; "Too well justified," he added, "By the persecutions he had endured." He then asked if I had any political news, worthy of notice to communicate.

Before I could reply, a young peasant, dressed in a ragged jacket, and carrying a double barrelled fowling.piece on his shoulder, suddenly presented himself. Mons. de la Rouvrette embraced him affectionately, called him Mons. de la Chevalier. At last, on arriving upon the summit of the hill, we found a middle aged man dressed in a cloak, and also armed with a fusil, whom my companion saluted respectfully, saying "Monseigneur, I am exceedingly happy to find you well again." This man with the cloak was nothing less than a bishop.

The Prior, the Chevalier, and the Bishop, after having agreed to meet us again, as soon as they had fulfilled their duty, left us, and we pursued our way alone. We arrived in a few minutes, at the limits of a vast platform, where a spectacle I shall never forget, presented itself to our view. A dozen men, kneeling, were listening to a priest, who, clothed with his cape, recited the breviary: near them their firearms were piled.

I must do this pious auditory the justice to state, that not one of those who composed it, disturbed themselves on our appearance. The voice of the priest continued to resound calm and sonorous.

The service being over, Mons. de la Rouvrette immediately presented me to these outlaws, as one of the victims of the requisition, and I was at once as much the object of their pity; as if their lot had not been worse than mine.

"Console yourself, young man," said one of the canons "The monstrous excesses which desolate our times, cannot last much longer. In a short period, France will re-establish the ancient order of things."

"I ardently desire the fall of the cowardly and sanguinary Robespierre, and all his abominable accomplices," replied I to the canon, "But I am a republican, and in no respect, wish for a return of the ancient regime. I believe in the possibility of founding a good republic!"

"My friends," cried Mons. de la Rouvrette, who now interposed, "You see that in presenting this gentleman to you as a man of principle, I have not deceived you; his frankness proves his integrity. I am acquainted with his family, which is most estimable: I therefore entreat you to place every confidence in his honour and discretion, and I will answer for him with my head."

"His being in your company, my dear Rouvrette, is sufficient to give us entire confidence in him," replied one of the canons, "No one is better qualified to judge, in a question of honour, than yourself."

Several of the outlawed priests, now employed themselves in preparing the common supper. Dry leaves were heaped up under sticks, placed against a large flat stone, and soon the flame rose high in the air. From a thicket of black thorns, a little old man brought out a large quarter of veal, ran a spit through it, and addressing his companions in misfortune, asked:—"Which of you, gentlemen, will take the duty to-day?"

"It is the reverend provincial Father,' answered several voices.

At the same instant, a fine old man of threescore and ten, arrived, and having made an excuse for being so late, began immediately to turn the spit.

The joint was beginning to exhibit its gilded tints, and exhaled a very appetizing odour, when a young brother, brought a fine hare which he had just killed with his fowling piece.

This wind-fall produced a general exclamation of joy. "I vote thanks to the citizen," said one of the canons, parodying the style of the period; "it is the second *Jacobin* he has brought us within four days."

The veal being cooked to a nicety, the outlaws seated themselves in a circle upon the mossy turf; the brother who had killed the "*Jacobin*," brought a large pitcher of spring water, and the little man who had lighted the fire, distributed to each, a slice of bread, dipped in gravy. I learned that this represented the soup.

Never did more frank cheerfulness reign amongst a party of friends, than that which prevailed at this repast.

After supper, the bishop, whom I had met disguised as a peasant, returned thanks, and the proscripts strolled about in detached groups.

I remarked that the same brother who had killed a hare, placed carefully in a wooden porringer, a slice of roast veal, and some bread and cheese. "Is it for one of your sentinels you are preparing this repast?" I asked.

"We have indeed, sentinels and spies set to guard us and survey the enemy," he replied; "but this portion is not for them. I am going to take it to a curè who has been attending a poor young man, who was wounded eight days ago."

"A young man of your party, and wounded by some republican soldier, I conclude?"

"Yes, the Count de L———, who received a ball in the shoulder, in venturing alone in the streets, of St. Flour. It is a miracle that he was not killed."

"Will it be inconvenient to you for me to accompany you?" said I.

"Not at all," replied the brother, whose name was Peter, and whose frank and cordial manners had captivated me; "on the contrary, your society will be quite a treasure, I so rarely find an opportunity of conversing."

We descended the hill; then following a foot path scarcely discernible, we reached a narrow glade lying between two ravines in the very depths of the frost. Removing with his hand, the high broom which surrounded us, brother Peter advanced a few more paces, and then in a soft and kind voice said, well monsieur Le Compte, how do you find yourself to day?"

I then perceived in a kind of fosse, a large hazel hamper six feet long, and filled with tree moss, which served for a bed for the wounded man.

"My wounds are quite healed brother," answered the Count de L—— in a firm voice, " and if it was not for the fever which burns in my veins and racks my limbs, I should get up to day. But who is that soldier?"

"That soldier, Mons, Le Compte," replied I, "is a moderate and conscientious republican, whose head will probably be cut off by the Jacobins one of these days, but who, in the meantime, will be happy to be of service to you, and to place himself completely at your proposal."

"I should never have guessed your political opinions Sir,'' replied the Count; "I should have taken you for one of ours. As to the offers of service you make me, I thank you from the bottom of my heart. But first; one question; is it not as an outlaw that you are come to the forest?"

"Certainly not; I came here with my friend Mons. de la Rouvrette?"

"Will you allow me to finish my question. If you are not

a proscript. you have the liberty of going where you please. Now pray, what is the precise route you are taking?"

" I am going first to St. Flour."

" You are going to St. Flour!" cried the count with eagerness; heaven has sent you to me, and you may save my life! Listen to me attentively I entreat you."

" That is the way Mons. Le Compte, that if you add another word, I will beg of this gentleman to take himself off" cried the old curè, who took care of the patient "what! you are just recovered from a crisis of twelve hours, and are still burnt up with fever, and yet you will trouble yourself with business. Lie down, sleep, and to-morrow if you are completely recovered, I will give you liberty of action."

The old curè spoke this with so much decision, that the invalid saw he must submit; and in a quarter of an hour he was in a deep sleep.

I was about resuming the conversation with the curè, when I saw him hastily snatch up his fusil, and then lay his ear to the ground. He appeared to me to distinguish the noise of several persons coming from the neighbouring thickets, who were advancing towards us with precaution and in silence.

The mournful cry of an owl rose in the silence of night; upon which the old curé laid down his fusil, quietly resumed his place, and turning towards me; "There's nothing to fear," said he, "they are friends coming to pay a visit to the Count."

In fact, I immediately saw Mons. de la Rouvrette coming arm in arm with a man about a dozen years older than himself. I ran to meet them.

"My dear sir," said he to me. "Allow me to introduce my eldest brother, the archdeacon."

"Ah! you have terribly frightened me," I replied, after having respectfully bowed to the archdeacon; "I thought for an instant, that we were surprised by a detachment of revolutionary troops."

"Oh, there is no danger of that," said he, smiling, "my precautions are too well taken." The new comers then inquired with much anxiety, after the health of the Count: they thanked and complimented the old curé who had the care of him, for his devotedness, and proposed to him, if he felt himself too much fatigued, to take his place and watch the invalid during the night.

"I thank you heartily," he answered, "but I cannot avail myself of your kindness. The young Count is now quite out of danger; his mind alone is diseased: and as it is to me alone he can speak without reserve, I am quite indispensible to him."

Mons. Rouvrette did not consider it proper to persist, and after having remained about half an hour, was about leaving, when the curé spoke to him a few words in a low voice, which drew forth an exclamation of surprise.

"You ought sooner to have apprised us of this circumstance, Monsieur le Curé; it appears to me very important," he replied.

"I was withheld by the fear of uselessly alarming the station."

"It is far better to frighten our friends, than to let them fall into danger! We will see to it to-morrow, and have a battue in the forest. In the meantime, I shall visit the sentinels and urge the most vigilant inspection.

"Sir," said 1 to the curé, when Mons. Rouvrette was gone. "The invalid cannot hear us: tell me what you meant by saying, that you were afraid of alarming the station?"

"The proscripts shut up in this forest, and amongst whom there are federalists, also outlawed, who do not live together. They are divided into five churches or stations."

"What! have you federalists amongst you? I am curious to know how you manage to live on good terms with them!"

"We are not so blinded by the spirit of party, that we don't know how to acknowledge honesty wherever we find it. If the federalists, instead of being the minority, composed the majority of our governors, the French republic would not have become an object of execration to the whole world; they might perhaps have rendered it possible! Have you any other question to put to me?"

"I beg your pardon, but what is that fact, so serious, that you dared not divulge it for fear of alarming the station to which you belong?"

"The day before yesterday," replied the old curé, slowly, "it might be about two hours after midnight, and I was asleep by the side of my patient, when I heard a noise of broken branches at a few paces from me; it appeared as if a man was advancing cautiously through the ferns and brushwood. I seized my fusil, and placing myself between the Count and the direction from whence the noise proceeded, I cried, with the whole strength of my lungs, '*Qui Vive!*' All was again silent. Convinced that I had been deceived, I resumed my repose. Judge of my anxiety, when, half an hour after, the branches began again to shake, and the same noise was repeated. This time, it was no longer possible to doubt, and my resolution was promptly taken. I sprang in the direction in which I supposed an enemy might be hidden, then, a man, whom the darkness did not allow me to recognise, and who seemed to rise out of the ground, fled before me with such swiftness that I soon lost the noise of his footsteps. I leave you to judge in what a state of anxiety I passed the rest of the night; the thought that the son of my benefactors might fall into the hands of revolutionary troops, froze my blood in my veins. Yesterday the same incident occurred again, in nearly the same manner as on the first occasion; only this morning I found, hanging upon a thorn bush, a piece of red wool of the stuff of which the phrygian caps are made."

"And have you not then communicated your fears and suspicions to anybody?" I asked.

"To only one person," he replied, "Brother Peter, who has promised me to pass this night in rummaging the environs of the place we are now in. But hold, I hear him now coming towards us!"

In fact, the curè had scarcely spoken, when brother Peter, with his fusil on his shoulder, crept towards us.

"Mons le Curè," said he, "I think I am near finding out the mystery. If you hear a noise to night, remain motionless till I call you, and trust yourself to my judgment, not to expose the count to the least danger." So saying, he bowed to us, and disappeared.

Complying with a hint from the old curè, I squatted myself amongst the broom, and held my peace.

Two long and gloomy hours passed without any incident to disturb the silence of night, and I began to think that the priest had been the sport of some hallucination; when I heard at a short distance from my hiding place, the branches shake with considerable violence. I was about to rouse the old curè when a light flashed across the darkness, and the discharge of a gun, followed almost instantly by a cry of agony, proceeded from a spot a few paces from me.

Sabre in hand, I immediately darted out of my hiding place, to defend the good old curé against the revolutionary troops. Fortunately, he ran no danger, as we learned from brother Peter, who, with a dark lantern in his left hand, and his fusil in his right, presented himself before us.

"Fear nothing gentlemen," said he, "And follow me; the spy must be dead."

2 B

A few paces from the place where lay the Count, we found a man, clad in a shepherd's dress, and struggling in a pool of blood."

"Who are you? And what do you come here for, wretch?" I demanded.

"Alas, citizen, I am a poor father of a family, whom distress has led to commit a crime, and whom the justice of heaven has punished! For mercy's sake have pity, if not on me, at least on my poor wife and unfortunate children."

"You have received money to betray us to the executioner, you villain," cried brother Peter.

"No my good sir, do not think that," replied the wounded man, in a voice that grew weaker and weaker. "I wanted, —or to speak more properly,—my master wanted only one person amongst you."

"What person? Come, don't attempt to deceive us!"

"The Count de L———," replied the wounded man.

Brother Peter was about continuing his questions, when the Count, whose name had just been pronounced, suddenly appeared himself upon the scene. Advancing slowly towards the wounded man, and in a voice, which his closed teeth rendered hoarse and nearly unintelligible,—

"How is Mademoiselle Laura?" he asked, fixing upon him a look of almost magnetic intenseness.

"Mademoiselle Laura!" repeated the wounded man, "You must be speaking of the citizen Durand!"

"Is Mademoiselle Laura then married?" resumed the young Count, with an apparent indifference that alarmed me, for I saw at once that it was only a cloak to his redoubled rage.

"Certainly! To my master, the citizen Durand," replied the peasant.

"Laura married to a citizen! To a cartwright!" cried the Count, darting upon the wounded man, and seizing him by the throat; "Wretch, you have belied her! Say you have lied, or I'll strangle you!"

It was with great difficulty that the old curè, Peter, and myself could snatch the wounded man from his hands.

"Come Edward, calm yourself," said the curè, "Do not afflict yourself thus about a falsehood. I assure you, I do not at all believe in the marriage of Mademoiselle Laura. You know well that you are her affianced husband. To morrow I will go with you to St. Flour, and we will bring her here. But for mercy sake, moderate your passion, or you will destroy yourself."

The Count uttered a heart-rending cry, and fell to the ground. By degrees however, his transports diminished in violence, and ended in a flood of tears.

"Mons. de la Rouvrette now appeared, accompanied by a dozen of the outlaws, who, attracted by the noise, had run to our help. In a few words, I put them in possession of the events which had occurred ; and after committing the wounded man to two of their party, they took the Count to the encampment. The rest of the night passed without any new incident.

I was about to rise in the morning, when I saw the hero of the night, brother Peter, advancing, and made haste to meet him :—" Tell me," said I, " Who is this man whom you have wounded, and why did you shoot him? What has he done?"

" I do not know the man," he replied, " And I am ignorant of what was his intention. All I can say is, that I fired at him, because I saw him put a pistol to the head of the young Count de L———. Now you know as much as I do on the subject."

A few minutes after, we reached a narrow glade, situated not far from the encampment, where I found the shepherd who had attempted to assassinate the Count. He was guarded by two postcripts, and was securely bound,

Although he had lost a great quantity of blood, he was in full possession of his senses; and his examination commenced soon after our arrival.

"My friend," said the bishop to him. "What motive led you to attempt the abominable crime of which you are guilty?"

"Alas! Monseigneur," replied the shepherd, "it is distress! I am married, and the father of three children, very young, and my whole resources amount only to a hundred crowns a year, which my master pays me in assignats."

"And who is your master?"

"My master is the citizen Durand, formerly a cartwright, but now president of the district of Saint Flour."

"And is it by his order that you attempted to assassinate the count?"

"Yes, monseigneur, by his order."

"Explain to me how you have penetrated into the midst of this forest, without being detected by one of our sentinels?"

"You forget, monseigneur," replied the wounded man that I am a shepherd myself. It was on that account alone, that my master selected me to assassinate the Count!"

"And how much has your master paid you to accomplish this bloody mission?" resumed the bishop, addressing the wounded man.

"My master, monseigneur, has given me three crowns in silver."

"Three crowns! What! Is it for so small a sum that you have agreed to commit so wicked and odious a crime?"

The examination of the prisoner was continued at some length, and his guilt being fully established, he was sentenced for immediate execution.

Before the fatal moment, the Count drew from him a

confirmation of the fact of Laura's marriage, and the further information that she was the victim of her husband's unmitigated brutality.

When the assassin had fallen dead upon the sward:—

"Sir," said the Count, taking me by the arm, "yesterday, you kindly offered me your services, which I have accepted; are you still in the same mind in that respect?"

"I have only one word to say, Monsieur le Compte. To-day, as yesterday, I am at your command. Allow me even to add, that I have the greatest desire to be of service to you. Speak, then, what can I do?"

"You can lend me your passport and thus enable me to enter St. Flour without being noticed and pursued."

"Before complying with your desire, allow me to impose on you one condition. It is that you will take some days of rest before you set out."

"I consent to it," answered he. "In fact, I require all my strength and energy for the accomplishment of the project I meditate."

During our walk, the young man related the history of his misfortunes in the following narrative.

"My cousin Laura, the only daughter of my father's eldest brother, had not reached her seventeenth year, when I quitted her about a year ago, to join the army of the Princes, but she was already an accomplished beauty, and my affianced bride."

" In the small city of St. Flour, lived at that time, a man named Durand, whose dissolute life was branded with disgraceful antecedents, and whose violence was dreaded by all his neighbours. This Durand, who had had many opportunities of seeing my cousin, fell desperately in love with her. I had scarcely been gone two months, when I received a letter from my cousin, acquainting me with the persecutions she had suffered from him. On reading her letter, I thought I should go mad with shame and rage; and at once resolved to go without losing a minute, to the help of Laura. Unfortunately, being pursued and tracked from my first entry into France, I was compelled to conceal myself, and I could not reach St. Flour. A skilful cmmissary, whom I accompanied, informed me on his return, that this infamous Durand had been nominated Administrator of the District; and had caused the Marquis de L———.—my uncle and Laura's father,—to be arrested. Two lines written in haste by my cousin, confirmed to me this sad news. "I owe it to my father," said she, "that after having saved him, I shall have the right to die."

"There was no time to hesitate, and my part was soon taken. Abandoning the shelter this forest afforded me, I instantly went to my uncle's chateau, which is situated at about a quarter of a league from St. Flour. Alas, I found it in ruins! Rendered insensible to danger by my sorrow, I boldly entered St. Flour, where I learned that my cousin was residing with citizen Durand, the ex-cartwright, and the actual President of the District, and the patriot,—*par excellence*—of St. Flour. I determined to go at once, and seek him."

"It was almost night when I arrived at the house occupied by the President. My heart beat with violence, and it was not without extreme excitement, that I let fall the knocker of the door."

"Judge of my despair, my rage, at seeing my cousin Laura in the first room in which I entered."

"You here cousin! cried I, and was then silent, for my heart was so swelled, that I could not speak."

"Pale as death, Laura looked at me with fixed and haggard eyes without replying. She seemed neither to see or hear me, when, uttering all at once a heart-rending shriek, she fell heavily on the ground."

" To spring to her aid, to raise her, and overwhelm her with assurances of friendship and tenderness, was to me the work of a moment."

"Already I saw the blush mantling in her face, already I felt her heart beat, when the door opened, and a man of a brutal aspect entered the room, uttering frightful blasphemies. This man was citizen Durand."

" For a moment disconcerted by my presence, which he was far from expecting, he was nevertheless, not long in recovering his coolness, or to speak more properly, his impudence."

"It appears, said he, addressing Laura sneeringly, that you are not much better than your class, the other aristocrats. What! On the eve of our marriage, do you receive young gallants, who come to entertain you with amorous nonsense? Know that the honour of being the lawful wife of a good patriot, involves serious obligations, and grave duties. Retire!"

" Citizen Durand then turned to me, and measuring me from head to foot, with an impudent look—,

"As to you my fine spark, continued he in a contemptuous tone, I know you; you are the ci-devant Count de L———. In the name of the republic, which has outlawed you, I arrest you."

"Infamous rascal," said I, "If you take another step, I will blow out your brains, and I drew from my pocket a pair of double barrelled pistols, with which I had provided myself, and placing one to his ear :—On your knees, I continued, on your knees before Mademoiselle de L———, and ask of her before you die, pardon for these outrages."

" Unable to speak a word, the villain did not hesitate to obey me; he fell on his knees.

" Laura, continued I, addressing my poor cousin, leave the room I beg of you, for a moment."

"Why so cousin? she asked in a voice so broken, that I guessed rather than heard what she said."

"That I may do justice upon this scoundrel."

"Laura took two steps towards the door, stopped a moment undecided, and then returning towards me:—

"Cousin, said she, casting down her eyes, as if overcome with shame; If the affection you have entertained for me is not now quite extinguished, respect the life of citizen Durand whom I love, and who will soon be my husband."

"Poor and magnanimous child! How cruel and unjust was I towards her, when, driven mad by grief, I answered her bowing deeply:—Citizen, I see that you have profited by the leisure the incarceration of your father and my absence have afforded you; nor can I compliment you too much upon the exquisite tact and delicate taste you have displayed in choosing the citizen Durand for your knight!"

"I departed without turning my head, without reflecting that I was an outlaw, and that behind me I left an implacable enemy in the citizen Durand."

"Absorbed in grief, I passed through the city slowly, when cries, or rather furious howlings, caused me to turn my head. Five hundred paces behind me, I perceived a hungry pack of sans-culottes and revolutionists in pursuit of me. I felt such a disgust of life, that this spectacle, far from frightening, produced in me almost a sensation of pleasure. I continued therefore to advance without quickening my pace, when the idea of revenge presented itself to my mind. I resolved that the infamous president of the district should fall by my hand. I ran with the utmost speed; only one ball reached me in my flight, and it is from that wound I now suffer. Such, my dear sir, is my lamentable history."

"For so young a man as you are, you have already had much suffering," said I, after a moments silence. "I can imagine that your cousin's treachery has broken your heart. But what I cannot comprehend, why you can still think of her, and call her a poor magnanimous child! Nothing in the conduct she has displayed towards you, seems to justify this admiration on your part."

"Isolation and reflection are excellent counsellors," replied the Count. "1 have coolly reflected, during my long illness, on the events that I have related ; and I have arrived at the full conviction that my poor cousin, in affecting to reciprocate the hideous tenderness of that Durand, has devoted herself to the safety of her father. Did she not write, that she would have the right to die, only after having saved her father?"

"Ah, you are right!" cried I, "I understand it all now! That poor young lady is silently performing an action, which involves the highest heroism. Tell me now, what are your projects and hopes? Why have you asked me to lend you my passport? What will you do when you get to St. Flour?"

"My projects are very simple," replied the young man; "I possess gold with which it will be easy to corrupt one of the gaolers of the house of detention, and thus get my uncle away. When once this object is accomplished, I will carry off Laura, and bring her with her father into our forests, where we will wait a propitious moment for passing the frontier. Your passport, in permitting me to remain freely at St. Flour, will greatly facilitate the accomplishment of this project."

"And when once you shall have reached a hospitable country ?"

"I will marry Laura," he replied, " What signifies the sacrilegious tie, which unites that angel to the bloody revolutionist. I shall recollect the past, only to admire her filial devotion, and to curse her intended executioners."

As the Count finished his recital, we reached the camp, where the bishop, clothed in his sacerdotal vestments, was celebrating mass.

The third day after my excellent friend Mons. de la Rouvrette proposed to me to commence our return ! "A longer absence," said he, may awaken suspicions about me, and prevent the intercourse I kept up with the proscripts."

After taking leave of the proscripts, we departed. I had agreed before hand, with my new friend the Count, that I would wait for him the following day at night fall, at the gates of Saint Flour. I intend to avail myself of this interval, to get information of Laura and citizen Durand, to visit the prison, and to collect all the information necessary to the success of our enterprise.

When we had once reached the high way I parted from Mons. Rouvrette. I took the road leading to Chaude Aigues where I arrived only a little before night fall. No incident worth relating marked my stay at this little town. I had appointed a rendezvous with the Count at the gate of St. Flour, but my embarrassment was extreme, when on reaching that city I perceived that it was separated into two parts, the one situated at the base, the other at the summit of a height, and that, it had no gates. I determined to await my young friend at the entry of the suburbs, but conjecturing that the count would not arrive till the next day at night-fall, I decided to go and see this Durand, the sole cause of his misfortune.

The house occupied by the great patriot Durand, formerly a poor cartright, and now a rich proprietor, was one of the handsome dwellings in St. Flour.

I perceived, seated in the first into which I was shown, a young female whom I presumed must be Mademoiselle Laura de L——. Two old gossips kneeled at the foot of the arm chair in which she sat, making her inhale salts, calling her by name, and rubbing her hands without obtaining any answer.

"What do you want citizen?" asked one of the old women.

"To speak to the citizen president of the district;" I replied.

"He is absent and will not return in less than an hour."

"Very well, I will return : but tell me, citizen, is not this young woman ill? I possess some knowledge of medicine; If you have need of me, you have only to speak, and I am at your command."

"I thank you," answered the old woman, "and accept your offer with pleasure. Here's the fact in two words; this young Citizen was married only a week ago."

"She appears to me very young to be married."

"Oh no, she is near seventeen. This morning a babbling tongue has told her bad news which has much troubled her,"

"What bad news, Citizen?"

"Well, she has learned that her father was guillotined a week ago to-day, in fact the same day and just the hour that she was married."

Judge of the grievous sensation these words caused me. Still I had enough presence of mind and command of myself to conceal the violent shock I had received.

I advanced slowly towards the chair, and taking the arm of the unfortunate young person, I felt her pulse with all the gravity of a consummate practitioner. That pulse was so feeble, so insensible, that for a moment I thought it had ceased to beat.

"Was it immediately after she had learned the tragical death of her father, that she fell into this kind of lethargy?" I asked of the old woman.

"Yes citizen," she replied.

"Reflect well, I beg of you before you answer, for the question I put to you at this moment, is very serious, has not this young woman being left alone? has she spoken."

"No indeed, she has said nothing: she has contented herself with sobbing and drinking from a little vial which doubtless contains a portion ordered by the doctor who attends her.

Then, after having swallowed the contents of that vial, she seated herself in this arm chair. A quarter of an hour after she was such as you see her now, like one dead."

" And that vial, of which the unfortunate lady has drank the contents, where is it? Have you preserved it?"

" The vial was broken in falling from the hands of the citizen to the ground, and we have swept away the pieces," answered the old woman.

"Well, find those pieces at once," cried I, " And try, above all, to procure the label which was attached to it."

One of the women,—she who had not yet spoken,—went out grumbling, and returned in about a minute.

" Here are the pieces you want to see citizen," said she. " As to the label, I have found it whole, and have also brought it."

I eagerly seized this last object. Let the reader judge of my despair, when I read in printed characters, *External use*; then a little lower, written by hand, these two terrible words, *Laudanum, Rousseau.*

" Why wretches," cried I, addressing the two old gossips, who drew back with fright, " wretches, do you know that your mistress is poisoned?"

" Is the citizen poisoned?"

" Why yes, a thousand times yes! Come, quick, fetch a doctor as soon as possible."

" Nay, citizen," replied the old woman, "if she is poisoned, it is probably because she has had enough of life, 'tis a matter that does not concern us."

" Infamous hag! you deserve to "—

" Dont put yourself out citizen; if you knew, as I do, the upshot of the thing, the interest you take in that handsome child would not be so strong, Oh! You need not roll your eyes in that way; I am the aunt of citizen Durand, fancy to yourself, that my nephew is fallen in love with this chit, I don't well know why, but the more's the pity; and yet that girl is actually the daughter of the Ex-Marquis de L———."

"And is it this ci-devant who was guillotined a week ago?"

"The same. Marry! You may guess that weakness has its limits. My nephew is fond of his wife, but he is a good patriot, and in spite of the love he bears to this girl, he has not yet fallen so low, as to consent to become the son-in-law of a ci-devant. The day of his marriage, he therefore had the spirit to send his father-in-law to the guillotine."

The deep indignation, the unspeakable horror this confession caused in me, almost deprived me of consciousness. I was still under this influence when the doctor arrived. He ordered coffee and mustard plasters, and gave me the promise of returning again before the end of the day. As for me, fearing that the horrid and wicked aunt of the President would leave the unfortunate girl to die for want of assistance, I installed myself without ceremony in the house, and began to prepare the doctor's prescriptions.

In the first instance, I ordered that the patient should be put to bed. I had then just poured the coffee into a cup, and was about taking it to her, when citizen Durand arrived. He had been out since the morning, and was ignorant of the fatal accident which had be-fallen his victim. The first word was not one of pity but of rage.

"Ah, the wretch!" cried he in a hoarse and sottish voice "Is it thus that she acknowledges my kindness? a race of vipers is that of these aristocrats! they are all alike! may the devil carry me away if I put myself out for this duchess; she will die will she! well! let her die! what do I care?"

"What do you want citizen officer?" he continued, turning to me, and looking at me with an insolent and suspicious air.

"I come," replied I, "in the absence of the commissary of war, to bring my passport to you to be viséd."

"What does that concern me!" he cried. "Address yourself to the District, the office is open till night, and you will find the secretary there. Go, be off!"

"Do you know citizen," I answered, "That you have a way of expressing yourself, that does not in any respect please me. The want of manners you display in addressing a defender of the country, gives me a very bad opinion of your patriotism. I will just speak two words about you, to my cousin of the Convention. Farewell." At this answer, the citizen President of the District lost all his assurance, and entirely changed his tone.

"But citizen," said he, "I assure you that you deceive yourself respecting me. If I have answered you with a little roughness, it is because my wife is in the last extremity, and I scarcely know what I say or do."

I should have wished to have stayed longer, to be certain that Mademoiselle de L—— wanted for nothing; but fearing to awaken the suspicions of Durand, I resolved to leave. Instead of going at once to the District office, I went down again into the suburbs of the city, and took a room at the inn of the " Niveau-Egalitaire ; for it was possible that the young Count de L—— might arrive the same day, and I wished to announce to him the sad news I had learnt.

I was leaning sorrowfully on my elbow at the window of my room, when all at once I recognised, in the person of a peasant, the Count de L——, coming towards the inn. I cleared the staircase at two leaps, and ran forward to meet him.

"Ah! here you are," cried I, tenderly embracing him," I did not expect you before to-morrow evening."

" The fact is," he replied, " That the restlessness and anxiety which consumed me, were such that I could delay no longer. I will not ask you whether you have learned any news concerning my cousin, as you have yet had no time to take any steps."

"You deceive yourself, my dear friend," said I, in a voice broken by my tears; "I have news and very sad news too, to give you. Follow me to my inn."

In a few minutes, we were shut up in my room. "My dear sir," said I, with a sorrow I could not conceal, pledge me upon your honour, to support like a man of courage, the fearful news that I have to communicate."

"I swear to you," he answered, with a firmness and indifference which I did not expect in him. "Speak fearlessly! My cousin is no more, is it not so?"

"Mademoiselle de L—— still lives, but I ought not to conceal from you that her state is nearly desperate."

"I understand. The misfortune which overwhelms her, has, for a moment overcome her religious feelings; she has committed suicide."

"Yes," answered I in a stifled voice. "But alas! that is not all."

"Ah! that is not all" repeated the Count, preserving the same impassibility. "What more can have happened?"

"You forget, my dear and unfortunate friend, your uncle, the Marquis."

"True. Well! he has killed himself also?"

"No, but he has been assassinated by the hand of the executioner! His head fell at the same moment that his daughter, your cousin, married citizen Durand."

My excellent uncle!" said the Count calmly; "He at least, is now happy!"

I confess that at the sight of this extraordinary indifference displayed by the Count, on learning the fearful misfortunes that had befallen his family, I felt thrilled with an icy coldness. I regarded the young man with surprise, mingled with fear, for I fancied for a moment that his reason had given way. But nothing in this examination occurred to confirm my fears.

"Faith, I cannot comprehend you!" cried I, "your conduct and your attitude are to me a mystery, beyond my reach."

"My conduct is very simple and very logical, nevertheless; the ties that attached me to life, being broken, human griefs pass off without affecting me. To-morrow at furthest, I shall have rejoined my cousin and uncle. Adieu my dear friend. Hold, take these two hundred louis, of which I shall no longer have need. You are good and sensible, and this money will serve you in comforting the unhappy. If you meet with an unsworn priest, beg of him to say some masses for the repose of my soul. Let us again embrace, and again, once more, Adieu!"

The count then took a pair of double-barrelled pistols from his pockets, carefully examined the priming, and went towards the door, without saying a single word.

"What are you going to do, unhappy man?" said I, darting towards him and siezing him by the arm; "to destroy yourself without resource, or advantage to any body."

"Let me alone, my friend;" he replied, attempting mildly to disengage himself from my grasp. "Your exhortations and remonstrances can have no effect upon my resolution. My destiny it written in heaven, and it must be accomplished."

"Take care my friend," cried I, still retaining him; "don't you see that you are falling into blasphemy! Can you believe that a crime,—for that's what you meditate,—can be written in heaven?

"My dear sir," replied the Count, with the utmost coolness, "I repeat that human considerations have no longer influence over me. I am in pursuit of an end which I will attain before I die. I will therefore sacrifice every obstacle that lies between my will and that end.'

"This is a threat, Count?"

No my friend, it is not a threat, but a warning. I esteem you and love you; but if you persist in opposing my departure I shall be under the hard necessity of blowing out your brains!" Every thing is indifferent to me, except my vengeance. Now, and for the last time, adieu."

"No! I will not abandon you to run thus foolishly to death," cried I, "since my remonstrances have no effect upon you, I will accompany you and share your dangers."

"You will do wrong," said he quietly. "The best thing you can do, is to forget that chance has ever thrown you in my way, and to banish even my name from your memory."

"I have said that I will follow you, and not abandon you;" said I, "what I have said, I will do!"

"Be it so," he answered, "I no longer oppose you. But follow me at a distance, that those who may meet us, do not perceive that we are together."

"I will remember; let us go out."

After a ten minutes walk, we reached the house inhabited by Durand. The young man knocked, and the aunt of Durand opened the door. Half a minute later I entered in my turn, but saw no one.

Crossing the dining hall and guided by the sound of voices, I pushed open a second door, and entered a large bedchamber, where I perceived the citizen Durand and his aunt, Mademoiselle de L———, and the Count her cousin. It was a perfect drama.

The young man, with his pistols in his hand, looked fixedly at the poor child, whose colourless countenance, already overcast with the shades of death, outdid by its extreme paleness the whiteness of the sheets. On his cheeks no trace of a tear was seen. Huddled against the wall at one of the angles of the bed room. citizen Durand and his amiable aunt were crouched one against the other in the most extreme terror.

" My friend," said the Count almost smiling, " You see I have lost no time in making myself master of the place ; I hold the murderer in my power! Faith, since you have determined to follow me, it is but justice that you should share my laurels; will you have the goodness to go and shut carefully the street door, that they may not surprise us." I did not hesitate to obey, and hastened to shut the door, and for additional security I pushed before it a pile of furniture.

" My dear sir," said the Count when I returned to the room, " Take this pistol, and on the least movement that that wretch and his accomplice shall make to escape, blow out their brains, whilst you hold them in your keeping, I shall go over the house ; my absence will not be long."

" Citizen Officer," said the President of the District in a low voice, as soon as the Count had left us, " If you will set us at liberty, I swear upon the salvation of the republic, that you shall have no reason to repent of it."

" Do not fear that we shall denounce you," added the old aunt ; " Assuredly our gratitude will guarantee both our discretion and silence."

" I would ask nothing better than to listen to your entreaties," I replied, " But I have given my word to my companion, and I cannot break it."

I had scarcely finished speaking, when the Count returned.

"I have found what I wanted," said he, "a cellar without any opening to the street, vaulted with cut stone, and closed with a door so thick, that I think it must be cannon-proof. "Come, follow me," continued he, addressing the prisoners. The president and his aunt did not wait for a repetition of this order, but obeyed immediately.

As soon as I found myself alone with Mademoiselle de

L—— I hastily approached her bed, and raising her in my arms, first awoke her from her lethargic sleep, and then prevailed on her to take a whole cup of coffee. "Well cousin, how do you find yourself now?" asked her lover, whom I had not heard return, but who then had placed himself behind me, straight, motionless, and with fixed look and arms crossed.

At the sound of that voice which was so dear to her, Mademoiselle de L—— uttering all at once a terrible shriek and closing her eyes, cried with affright, "Mercy, Gaston! mercy! Do not curse me! I must save my father!"

"Laura, my beloved, my only love!" said the young man in a mild voice, and falling on his knees at the foot of the bed where the poor girl lay. "Speak no more of the past! We are about to be re-united for ever! God waits us in heaven."

The Count seized one of his cousin's hands, and raised it respectfully to his lips. I could not refrain from weeping.

"You forgive me then, Gaston," resumed Mademoiselle de L——, whose countenance, already altered by the approach of death, was covered with a slight blush, and became resplendent with beauty and youth.

"Forgive you, my sainted Laura! What have I to forgive you for? The sacrifice of your happiness which you have had the courage to make to duty? Your martyrdom, your long agony?"

"How good and noble you are, Gaston," murmured the young girl, regarding him with an angelic look. "Your appearance has so much affected me, Gaston, that I have not yet had time to wonder how you came here!"

"My presence proves to you, my beloved Laura, that God never abandons those, who believe and hope in his goodness."

"But alas!" said Mademoiselle de L——. "Is not my

death a crime? Will God forgive my having made an attempt on my life?"

"Set your mind at rest my beloved," said the young man, softly grasping her hand; "when you drank the poison which destroys you, grief had deprived you of your senses. You have not yielded to a guilty thought, but to delirium!"

"Gaston, might I not see a priest?"

At this question from the poor unfortunate girl, a cloud passed over the countenance of her lover.

"That is impossible!" said he. "No human being must again penetrate into this dwelling. Why look at me with wondering eyes, Laura? Cannot you perceive that I am jealous of your last sigh?"

At that moment, a nervous spasm agitated the frail and delicate frame of the young girl, and Gaston, rising hastily, began to lavish upon her every attention in his power.

I shall not relate the tender and sweet conversation of the two lovers. Many times during their discourse, when they recurred to the happy days of their youth, and spoke of the games and the troubles of their childhood, I felt the tears flow, down my cheeks, in spite of myself. Alas! This discourse was to be their last. The unfortunate girl turned pale and again fell into a dreadful fit. I then left the corner where I had remained till then motionless, and ran to her help. My appearance seemed greatly to astonish the Count. "What! Have you not yet gone away?" said he, "I believed you were already far from hence, and thought no more of you. Come, follow me."

Gaston then took me roughly by the arm, and without giving me time to answer him, dragged me towards the outer door.

"But my friend," said I, whilst he hastily destroyed the kind of barricade which I had formed with the furniture against the door; "But my friend, what are you going to do? Listen to me I conjure you."

Without replying to me, the Count continued his work, and opening the door, pushed me gently into the street.

"And your gold that you have left with me," said I abruptly, "Take it again!"

On hearing these words, the Count raised his shoulders with an air of pity. "You well know that I have nothing further to do with earth; keep that gold," said he, shutting the door sharply upon himself.

It would not be easy to make the reader understand the extraordinary impression I felt, on finding myself again in the street.

It was to a selfish feeling, the instinct of self preservation, that I owed the recovery of my presence of mind. A detachment of revolutionary troops, who debouched at the moment from the end of a street, recalled me, to a true appreciation of my position. I fancied myself arrested, and I hastened to get out of the way at a quick pace, towards my hotel.

On arriving at the *Niveau Egalitaire*, I shut myself up in my room, for it seemed to me, that during my walk, many persons had looked at me with astonishment. I consulted my glass and it showed me a face so pale, and features so disordered, that I was afraid of my own picture. I threw myself upon the bed, and found by my watch, when I awoke that I had slept an hour. This refreshing rest completely restored me to my usual condition, and I thought I might proceed, without danger of awakening suspicions to have my passport viséd at the district. Thanks to the accidental meeting I had with an honest and obliging Citizen, who offered to be my guide I soon arrived at the district and obtained my visé. In another hour I again entered my inn, more and more uneasy respecting the fate of Gaston. At every noise of a step, at the least creaking of the worm eaten staircase I jumped off my chair, and placed my ear against the door. In vain my reason, in accordance with my presentiments, told me that Gaston would never return, that I had seen him for the last time. I fought against the reality, and strove to persuade myself that all hope was not yet lost.

Night soon came. A heavy rain began to fall and drove violently against the cracked window panes.

Every one knows how much the objects which surround us, the physical atmosphere in which we find ourselves enveloped, influence the imagination and weigh upon the thoughts. The rain, the profound darkness, and the icy cold which prevailed, sunk me at the end of an hour, into such a condition of discouragement, that I could not restrain my tears. I am persuaded that if the innkeeper, had not come to tell me that supper was ready, I should have remained up without thinking of going to bed during the rest of the night. Fearing however to excite suspicion, by remaining thus shut up in my chamber I replied to my host, that I had fallen asleep from fatigue, and then hastened to go down.

Whenever it begins to rain at St. Flour, the air becomes very cold ; I was not surprised then, on entering the kitchen, to see a dozen persons sitting before the fire place in which, although it was the height of summer, blazed up an enormous faggot of dry vine branches. The conversation turned upon the events of the day. When I entered the kitchen, a man whose spatterdashes, all covered with dust, showed that he was just off a journey began to tell us what he had seen during his travels.

He was suddenly interrupted by a boy who entered the kitchen quite out of breath, and in a hoarse voice cried '*Fire!*'

"Follow me," said the newcomer, whose panting proved that he had run rapidly ; " Follow me, the line is formed; and there is not a moment to lose !"

"But whose house is on fire?" asked one of those present.

"That of citizen Durand, the President of the District."

The reader will readily comprehend the deep concern this answer produced in me. I rushed like a madman into the street The direction taken by the crowd whom I met, soon confirmed the terrible news which I had learnt. A few minutes later, the sight of a sheet of flame which illuminated the darkness of the night, made me redouble my speed. When I reached the street in which the burning house was situated, I was stopped by so compact a crowd, that it was impossible for me to advance nearer than within two hundred paces of the burning house, I hastened to join the line, formed by the inhabitants.

"Do you know," I asked of my neighbour, in taking from him the pail full of water, he held to me to pass to the next, "Do you know if there is any one dead or wounded?"

"I don't know exactly," he replied. "The most strange and extraordinary reports are circulated on the subject of this fire. They say that citizen Durand has barricaded himself with his wife and his aunt in his house, and that he himself is the author of the catastrophe."

"That seems very extraordinary! How can you suppose that a man, unless indeed he is mad, could commit such an act?"

"They add, that citizen Durand, jealous as a tiger of his wife, had surprised her with a young man, and that then, quite beside himself, and having lost his reason, he has set fire to his house."

I left off talking with my neighbour, for I had no reason to doubt the origin of this drama. It was evident that Gaston after the death of his cousin, had no wish to survive her, and that before following her, he had, to revenge himself, accomplished this act of destruction, which so much alarmed the city.

Next day, greatly agitated and disturbed at the melancholy end of these noble young people, I was about to leave the town, when I felt myself seized by the collar. Turning round, I perceived at once that I was arrested by a lieutenant of gendarmes followed by his troop.

"I am a soldier of the republic," I said, "And carry my passport. Beware how you meddle with me!'

"You are in correspondence with the aristocrats," he retorted, "and were seen to-day in company with a ci-devant who has escaped us. You must answer for that at the bar of the tribunal."

"I am innocent," I cried, "As you will learn to your cost,"

"That remains to be seen.—Come, march! said the leader of the troop. Thus, in a few minutes I traversed as a prisoner, the streets of St. Flour. Scarcely any persons turned about to see me pass. After a rapid march, we arrived at the District, and I was ushered into the presence of the vice-president.

" Who are you? where do you come from? what crime are you accused of?" demanded he.

"I am an officer, returning from fighting on the frontier against the enemies of the republic, and they accuse me of corresponding with aristocrats. Here's my passport which your secretary has viséd only yesterday."

The vice president seized the paper roughly, cast his eyes over it, and resumed his interrogatives when a carriage driven at full gallop stopped in the court of the district. A little after a nervous and rapid step was heard in the antichamber, and soon a young man with a proud and resolute air entered the room where I was.

At the sight of this new comer I could not repress an exclamation of surprise, for I suspected that I was lost. The stranger, whose appearance, so unforeseen and ill-timed caused me such a sensation of fear, was no other than the same Commissary of Public Safety, whom I had met at St. Cunat fifteen days before, whose dinner I had involuntarily eaten, and who had taken me for a colleague.

Scarcely had he announced his title, than the vice-president rose with a haste quite un-republican, and offered him the arm chair on which he was seated.

I am come to the District merely to throw a glance over the register and ask some information," said this eminent personage, looking at me with a fixedness and attention that it required all my efforts to sustain with indifference. "But no, I cannot be deceived," added he, continuing his examination of my person. "It is certainly he. What! Colleague, don't you recollect me?"

I saw that impudence alone could save me, and calling up all my sang froid to my aid, I resolved to push the game to the end.

"I recollect you perfectly," replied I.

"Well then, why do you remain thus silent and motionless without offering me your hand?"

"Because, as you ought to recollect, it is my system never to make any demonstrations that may compromise the incognito that I wish to preserve," replied I, affecting singularity.

"Faith, I am wrong, I confess. I had forgotten, on meeting you again, that you proceed mysteriously. After all, there is no great harm done. The citizen vice-president is probably the only person who knows your position, and he will be cautious. What are you about in this District? Don't put yourself out, if my presence annoys you, say so. I have occasion to go to the popular society, and will return when you have finished your business."

"The fact is," said I, increasing in impudence and audacity, for the decisive moment appeared to me arrived, "the fact is, your presence does disconcert me."

"That's just what I guessed. In that case I will run to the popular society. Without saying adieu, I hope we shall dine together to-day,"

"I cannot promise you that, but I will use all my endeavours to do so. Au revoir."

During this dialogue, the vice president had evinced unequivocal signs of astonishment. Nor can I even now recall without laughing, the comic expression of stupor in his face when, for the first time, he saw the Commissary of Public Safety treat me as a colleague.

"Pardon me, citizen," said he, retaining him for a moment, as he was leaving the hall, "I don't comprehend your discourse. Why do you treat this soldier as a colleague, and tell him that he may reckon on my discretion?"

At this question, the commissary looked at me, smiling and shrugging his shoulders in pity, as much as to say, "Truly, these provincial gentry are not very knowing." Then without deigning to reply, he walked towards the outer door. My heart beat violently; a few more steps and I was free. Alas! my destiny was written, and fulfilled! The vice president, who had not lost a single gesture of this pantomine, ran towards the commissary, and placing himself before him at the door; "Citizen," said he, "I entreat you to answer me. Have I then in arresting this officer, involuntarily failed in respect to a friend of the illustrious and incorruptible Robespierre? Never shall I forgive myself for this contempt. Speak, I entreat you."

"How! Have you arrested this officer?" repeated the commissary, with an astonishment which augured evil for me.

"I have, and I was interrogating him when you arrived."

"And did he reply?"

"He showed me his papers, which are all correct, and prove that he belongs to the army of Piedmont."

"At this reply of the Vice President, the countenance of the young revolutionary delegate changed; his smile disappeared, and gave place to a grave and severe expression, his eyebrows contracted in a threatening manner, and in a dry and haughty voice:—

"Let me see your papers," said he abruptly.

I was lost! My audacity having failed, there was nothing left for me but to submit with resignation to my unhappy lot; and I instantly obeyed.

The Commissary of Public Safety examined my papers with great attention, and then, turning to the vice-president:—

"Citizen," said he, "You must answer with your head for this spy."

"What! Is not that officer then, a government Commissary?"

"The wretch, I repeat, is a spy, an emmissary of the foreigner, a royalist, a federalist, an English agent, perhaps even an unsworn priest, or better still, a ci-devant, an aristocrat!"

In proportion as the Commissary advanced in this nomenclature, the vice-president recoiled from me with horror.

"Citizen," said I calmly to my old acquaintance of St. Cunat, "All these crimes of which you accuse me, may be reduced to a single wrong, that of having taken you for a man of spirit, and having joked with you; if you will be just, consult your memory, and you will see that I never represented myself to be a Commissary of the government; on the contrary I always refused to accept the title of colleague that you persisted in giving to me."

"Yes, in order to confirm me still more in my error. Ah! Do you imagine that you can with impunity mock a Commissary of the Public Safety, conspire against the republic,"—

"Here I stop you!" Cried I. "I think that if ever a republic is possible in France,—and I confess I begin to doubt it—it will only exist on the condition of being eminently honest and virtuous. Those who conspire against it, are the men who make use of the name, in order to satisfy their base and vile passions ; who cover themselves with its mantle, in order to gratify their personal revenge ; who cry up liberty to day, whilst incarcerating their enemies. Equality, in exacting that every one shall bow before their power. Fraternity, in sending to the scaffold, those whose virtues or talents are a living satire on their immorality or incapacity."

" Hold your tongue, wretch," cried the Commissary, interrupting me angrily, " Hold your tongue, or I will have you gagged."

" Be it so," said I, " I will hold my tongue ; but at least do not arrest me on the pretence that I have conspired. Confess to me honestly as you can, the ridiculous part that I have involuntarily caused you to play, and that you thus revenge yourself."

My ex-colleague of St. Cunat did not think proper to answer me, and went away, after again recommending the vice-president to watch over my safety. In a short time, the same revolutionary troop who had arrested me, conducted me to the house of seclusion. At the door of that sad dwelling, stood three berlins, all horsed and ready to set out.

" For whom are those carriages intended," I asked of the turnkey who received me.

" What does it signify ?" he replied savagely. " Come, march !"

" Where are you taking me to ?' resumed I mildly. " I warn you that I have money, and that I prefer paying, rather than being consigned to the common hall."

The gaoler seemed to hesitate, then with a bad imitation of a smile :—

"Good," said he, "Give me a crown and you shall have a room."

One of the turnkeys who accompanied us, opened a low narrow door, and pushing me by the shoulders into a kind of unoccupied niche, turned the locks behind him, and left me to my sad reflections.

CHAPTER IX.

Bound for Paris.—Travelling accommodations, and travelling companions, —The Laughing Philosopher and the Weeping Willow.—The Anglo-Spaniard.—Brutality of our Conductors.—Arrival at Paris.—Prison accommodations at a premium.—The Conciergery.—The ruffian Pampin. —His practical sympathy.—The political section.—Mons. Riouffe.— Madame D———.—Citizen Bertrand.—Camille Desmoulins, Danton. Madame Roland.—I am sent to the Abbaye.—Infernal treatment.—I attack the turnkey.—Tête à tête with the governor.—A dinner and a bottle.—Am removed to the Evêche.—Examined by the Judge.—Am sent to St. Lazare.—Anselme again.—Fall of Robespierre.—Release, and parting with Anselme.—Nantes, Tours, and the Republican Camp. in La Vendee.—Captain Cherche-à-manger.—A terrible surprise.— Battle, and murder, and sudden death.—Again defeated by Charrier.— I am knocked on the head.

When that door closed upon me, it appeared as if I no longer belonged to the world, and had entered the anti-chamber of eternity. But my reflections were of short duration; scarcely had half an hour passed ere a key grated in the lock, and I saw the goaler appear.

"Come, get up and come along," said he, in a ferocious voice. "The convoy is ready."

"What convoy?" I asked, "Am I not to remain here? Have you not made me pay a crown for my chamber?"

"Who asked you for your crown? Nobody. You gave it, and I took it, that's all! Come, step along and hold your tongue."

Scarcely had I set foot in the street, when two gendarmes seized me, one by the collar and the other by the hind part of my uniform, and threw me into one of the berlins: at the same instant my rolling prison was hurled away by the horses.

The carriage contained three other prisoners. My neighbour on the left, was a large man with a round belly, florid complexion, red thick lips, and a vivid eye: he might be about forty-five years old. Seated in front of me, was a little old man, with a thin half starved body, and a melancholy countenance. At his side was a young fellow, whose swarthy complexion, and strongly marked features denoted a foreign origin. He smoked a cigar, without appearing to trouble himself about his neighbours. It was the large man who spoke first.

"It appears citizen," said he to me, "that the army pays its contingent to politics also, and that the uniform of the officer is not more respected by our legislators than the carmagnole of the artizan. May I be allowed to ask what has occasioned your arrest."

"I am accused of corresponding with aristocrats."

"And I have been arrested for the crime of cheerfulness; I assure you I am speaking quite seriously."

"Is it possible! I do not comprehend you."

"A shoemaker whom I had turned off because I was not satisfied with his work, denounced me for having laughed on the day when news came of a check received by our army. They apprehended and interrogated me. What would you have? The questions they put were so comical, and the judge so much given to pleasantry, that I could not resist the temptation of making him feel his impertinence. Consequently he saw that I was a federalist. The next day, they threw me into this carriage, in order to send me to Paris to give an account of myself. I now desire only one thing, that, when I appear before Fouquier Tinville, I may possess strength of mind enough to avoid laughing in his face."

"And I too, what shall I say then?" cried the little old man, who had not before taken any part in the conversation.

"Ah! Is that your voice, you unfortunate weeping willow?" exclaimed the other. "I thought you dumb; well, tell us what has been the cause of your arrest."

"Alas," replied the old man, "It is my sadness that has ruined me. Like the citizen, I have been denounced, and plunged into a dungeon, under the pretext that I appeared sad one day, when the news of a victory arrived. And they are sending me to offer my head to Fouquier Tinville, who will take good care not to refuse it."

"It is your turn now, citizen," said the fat man, addressing the stranger. "Inform us to what circumstance we owe the honor of your society."

The smoker withdrew his cigar from his mouth, and replied in the accents of a foreigner —"I have been arrested in my quality of foreigner, and in consequence an enemy of the republic."

"You are an Italian I think?"

"No, I am a Spaniard. The judge thought otherwise. They have sent me to Paris as an Englishman."

When once the conversation was opened, our jovial companion would not let it languish. At night-fall we stopped to dine; in vain I several times addressed the woman who attended us, she would not answer me. I remained therefore in complete ignorance of the place where we stopped.

At the conclusion of our repast, the Spaniard having drawn from his pocket a small knife, one of the gendarmes rushed furiously upon him, snatched the knife from his hand, and gave him a violent blow with his fist in the face. The Spaniard sprung over his chair with a bound, and seizing a large jug, full of water, dashed it at his cowardly aggressor. Then took place one of those scenes of savage brutality which the pen can hardly describe. The gendarmes, to the number of at least ten, hurled themselves upon us like wild beasts, and trampled us under their feet. Exasperated by this treatment I resisted energetically, and only succumbed when overpowered; but I paid very dear for my exploit. The Brigadier who commanded our escort, gave orders to rivet the leg of the Spaniard and my own, to a crossbar shot of forty-eight pounds. Our hands bound with a triple cord, were loaded with the weight of an enormous chain, which was also fastened round our bodies. These irons were so heavy, that if the carriage had overturned, our legs must have been broken in many places.

During the hundred and twenty hours that we remained shut up in our rolling tomb, our cruel gaolers did not allow us to set foot on the ground. From time to time our companions looked through the joints of the shutters of our berlin, upon the highway. Each time they saw carriages, berlins like ours, or closed cabriolets, surrounded with gendarmes, and conveying prisoners to Paris.

"But what is the good of sending these innocent persons whom they want to destroy, so far?" said I, "would it not be more simple to detain them in the provincial prisons."

"Don't you see," replied the gay criminal "that these convoys of pretended conspirators enable the agents of the Revolution, to make a parade of their zeal; we are playing at this moment the theatrical, and are serving to get up a scene."

At length, we arrived at the end of our journey; our berlin rolling over the pavement, informed us that we had entered Paris; a little after it stopped, and one of the gendarmes opened the door. Before us we perceived black walls, and a guard house filled with soldiers. We were preparing to descend, when one of the gendarmes of our escort came out of the guard house and addressing his companions.— " Come, get on the road," said he, " they cannot receive the rascals here; the Madelonettes overflow with prisoners."

Our berlin then went to another prison, where the same ceremony was repeated. They were full and could not receive us. For two hours we thus in vain went to all the houses of detention in the capital, the Madelonettes, the Lazare, the Luxemburgh, the house of arrest of Port Libre, and le Plessis; at each they refused to admit us.

"Postillions," cried the commander of the escort, "take us to the Conciergery." At this word of such bloody import we saw we were lost. All knew that the Conciergery was the ante-chamber of death. At the Conciergery, that vast tomb of the Danaides, they never refused prisoners, for each day, hour, and minute, the guillotine made voids in it, and left vacancies for others. It was not without trouble that they managed to get us out from the narrow stairs of the berlin. They threw the Spaniard and me, like a couple of bales of merchandise into the entrance in order to take off our irons. They laid us on our backs, and by means of a mallet, the turnkeys managed to detach the chain from the ball to which it was fixed.

"Come get up; do you not see we have done?" said at length one of the officers of the conciergery. I tried to obey, but my body was so exhausted and stiffened, that in the attempt I fell heavily on the ground. Two gaolers raising me brutally, placed me against a bench fastened to a wall and began the duty of searching me.

I was so broken down, both morally and physically, by the indignities I had endured, that I passively submitted to this last humiliation. Scarcely did the cries of joy uttered by the gaolers, on finding in my pockets, the ninety louis d'ors which remained of the heritage of the unfortunate Count de L———, awaken my attention. I had no longer strength to form an idea, and my sensations were so deadened that I comprehended but imperfectly what they were doing.

I have not the slightest recollection of being conducted to my cell. After being separated from my companions, I remember nothing, except it be the creaking of the keys in the locks, a confused noise of which produced a painful sensation at my heart.

How long I remained in this lethargic grief I am equally unable to say. All that I know is, that my stomach already felt the pains of hunger, when I recovered my recollection and opened my eyes. For some minutes I could see nothing in the gloom which surrounded me. By degrees, however, my sight became habituated to the obscurity, and I began to distinguish, close at my side, a large and dark body, but was not aware of its nature.

" Is there any one here?" I exclaimed.

" Certainly comrade, there is," replied a harsh voice ; " We are three of us. Don't you see us ?"

" Alas! I cannot raise my eyelids without an effort, they have tortured me most barbarously."

"Bah ! It is nothing, we are used to these matters. You are not used to them. But tell us, comrade, what has occasioned us the honour of your company ? Are you a politician or a workman?"

" I don't understand you citizen."

"And yet, the question is plain enough," interrupted a soft and clear voice which I had not heard before." You were asked whether you were arrested for a political offence, or some other thing."

"They arrested me on the charge of corresponding with aristocrats."

" Yes, you have been entered in the gaolers book as a federalist. They may either leave you to rot here for months, or take you in a few days before the Revolutionary Tribunal, and then—one,—two,—three,—judged, condemned, and executed; all over in four hours."

"You are doubtless a political victim also?" said I.

" I a political victim!" replied he, bursting into a roar of laughter; I am a club orator. I have harangued the people in the name of liberty, fraternity, and a crowd of things more than I can recollect, and they have carried me off in triumph. That was a good time, I did a capital business, realized considerable sums, and led the life of a satrap."

" But who are you then?" resumed I, interrupting my companion.

" Who am I? Parbleu, I am Pampin."

Ah, are you Pampin!" said I mechanically, and comprehending nothing of the import of the communication.

" The same, at your service, comrade," he continued. "You see the chance which has brought you here, has not used you so badly; if we remain together a fortnight, I will make you a remarkable man, a distinguished scholar."

" Citizen," said I, " I see that you are not an ordinary character; but forgive my ignorance, for, coming from the frontier, and being only a poor provincial, I confess in all humility, that until this day I have never heard your name spoken, consequently I have no idea what you may be."

" What, really, don't you know me?" exclaimed Pampin, with the greatest astonishment; " I am Pampin the terrible assassin; Pampin the celebrated robber; Pampin who has never trembled before a gendarme; Pampin who has thrice submitted to the torture; Pampin who will die, laughing in the face of the executioner! I hope you will not complain of the ambiguity of my discourse."

I confess that on hearing this reply, I felt a cold chill run through my frame.

"You won't converse any more now," resumed my terrible companion after a moments silence, "Your tongue is paralyzed by the horror I have inspired. But do you honestly think yourself in worse company with me, than if you had been shut up with political offenders? Frankly, such is not my opinion. When I murder, I spring like a wild beast upon my prey. The tiger loves blood; 1 love gold. I am no hypocrite, I am violent, and destitute of pity, that's all! I do not set up for a saint; what would be the use of it? I know myself to be, a scoundrel unworthy of pity! And yet, frankly, with my hand upon my conscience,—for I have a conscience like other men, only I do not listen to it,—I believe without vanity, that I am less guilty than certain persons, who, surely do not inspire you with so much aversion as myself. Does not that appear very odd to you?"

I was about to reply when I heard the locks of the cell door grate, and saw the turnkeys enter, bearing lighted torches, and each accompanied with an enormous bulldog. They came to bring us our pittance of food and make their inspection for the night.

By the glaring light of their torches, I perceived the interior of our cell, and the countenances of my companions in misfortune. The cell, which might be at most a dozen paces square, was hideously filthy. As to the physiognomies of my fellow prisoners, they differed greatly. Pampin exhibited one of those monstrous types of vice which are rarely met with once in a life. About fifty years of age, this celebrated assassin was blind of one eye, and crippled, and his face frightfully scarred and wrinkled. His powerful chest, broad and thick shoulders, unusually long arms, as thick as the thighs of an ordinary man, all indicated his extraordinary strength. The seal of the homicide was stamped upon his whole person; and one might have taken him for a ferocious monster of an unknown race.

Crouched at the feet of Pampin, was a young lad, scarcely more than a child, whose fine features seemed clouded by deep melancholy. Absorbed in his reflections, he scarcely raised his eyes when the turnkeys entered our cell.

Lastly, at a little distance, I perceived a third companion in captivity. Although his physiognomy was much less strongly marked that that of the terrible Pampin, it was still more repulsive, owing to the expression of base hypocrisy it reflected.

The turnkeys, after having finished their examination, deposited our repast, which consisted of a dish of questionable meat, and a salad, the leaves of which were dry and faded.

I had been fasting for forty hours and was famishing; but the sight of the wretched food disgusted me. My repugnance did not escape the notice of Pampin.

"It strikes me, comrade," said he, "you have no great inclination for the banquet before you; but don't distress yourself, we old prisoners possess certain little resources that the politicians are destitute of."

Scarcely had he spoken, when he struck a light, and soon after, a lamp, taken from some mysterious hole, which the gaolers failed to discover, was lighted and threw its rays upon us.

"Light! exclaimed I, with the joy of a child."

"And a ham too, and cold veal, and brandy," added Pampin,

placing them before him. "Comrade," continued the assassin professor, presenting me a knife, "cut yourself a slice of ham, and take a draught from this bottle, it will revive you."

I was too hungry to hesitate. I cut a piece of ham and bread, and drank from the bottle, which greatly refreshed me.

"Tell me," said Pampin, "How is it that you have no money about you; have you been visited?"

"I don't know what you mean by that. If being trodden under foot, searched and plundered, be what you call visited, I certainly have."

"That's the same; and have the turnkeys taken every thing?"

"All; about ninety louis d'ors that I possessed,"

"Ninety louis d'ors! And have the citizens left you nothing?"

"Absolutely nothing!"

"They have abused your ignorance. To-morrow I will make them return a part of your money to you; if you wish for forty louis, you have only to speak. Will you have them?'

"On what conditions?" I asked mistrustfully.

"On the simple condition that you give a receipt for the sum they have deprived you of. I confess that this sacrifice at first appears very great, but if you reflect that without my interference they would return nothing at all, you will find a great advantage in it. What will you do?"

"I accept with gratitude your offer of interference; you have only to name the sum you require for your assistance in this affair, and I will cheerfully pay it to you."

"Comrade," answered Pampin with dignity, "If you and I were free, and I knew that you had ninety louis d'ors, I would so manage as not to leave you a single one, for I am not partial to shares; but since we are both captives, occupying the same cell, your money is a sacred thing, and I would rather endure a thousand deaths, than rob you of a sous."

The next day, the gaoler with whom Pampin had negociated on the subject of my ninety louis, reported the answer. They consented to return me forty louis, if I gave them a receipt for the whole. I was obliged to submit: however Pampin stipulated that they should also allow me to write a letter, which they would put into the post. I therefore wrote an account of my arrest and misfortunes, and addressed it to my uncle the patriot, begging him to come to my assistance.

Twelve days had passed since my arrest, when one morning one of our gaolers opened the door of our tomb, and called my name; I started as if electrified, and in a bound, in spite of my weakness, I was on my feet.

"Where are you taking me to?" inquired I of the gaoler,

"To the political section," he replied. "Now as blessings never come singly, here are seventy-five livres, which I have orders to give you."

"Seventy five livres for me, and from whom?"

"It is all I have been able to save of the ninety louis they took from you on your arrival. My advice to you is, never to speak of that affair to any one, as it might comprise you as well as me, to whom you ought to be very grateful."

"Fear nothing," I replied, "I promise you that I will say nothing about it."

"Here's your room," said he, pointing to a door studded with iron, and at the top of which was traced in black, No 13.

"But the door appears half open," replied I, "Is that room inhabited then by no other person?"

"That chamber contains eighteen beds, the door is only shut at night, when the prisoners have retired."

"But can I mingle with those other prisoners?" I asked.

"What is to hinder you?" said the gaoler moving away.

My first care on finding myself at liberty, was to enter the chamber. The beds, which folded up, and were placed at a short distance alongside each other, were separated by high boards, so that each occupant resembled a statue in a niche. However, in comparison with the mouldy and infested straw, which since my arrival, had been my sole couch, they appeared to me luxurious.

I had got to the extremity of the chamber, when I saw a man asleep on the last bedstead of the range. Looking down I saw a quire of paper covered with fine and close writing, lying on the floor. I took the arm of the sleeper, and shook him briskly; he opened his eyes,

"What do you want? Why do you disturb me?" said he, in an angry tone.

"I beg pardon citizen," replied I, "But there [is at the foot of your bed, a quire of paper, written upon, which I think belongs to you."

"My history of the Prisons!" exclaimed he, springing up with a bound. "Faith citizen, the least I can do, is to make my humble excuses for my incivility. Your foresight has saved my life, this manuscript contains the impartial recital of my captivity in the conciergery. Now as I have been a prisoner fifteen months, I leave you to guess what frightful scenes I have witnessed and recorded. The service you have rendered me is therefore substantial. My name is Riouffe;* will you be my friend?" The reader may guess what was my reply.

Citizen Riouffe at this time, was about thirty years of age, of small stature but well proportioned. His voice was sonorous and pleasant, his language full of imagery and energy.

Honore Riouffe, a man of letters. He published, after the 10th Thermidor "*The memoirs of a Captive, to serve as a history of the Tyranny of Robespierre.* This work upon its appearance, produced a great sensa-sensation, and it is still held in repute.

He read with exquisite taste, and possessed a perfect knowledge of the Latin, Greek, and English languages.

"And you citizen," he asked " how long have you been in the conciergery?"

"About fifteen days."

"I cannot conceive then why I have not had the pleasure of seeing you before."

"There is nothing surprising in that. They had put me in the section of assassins, and I have scarcely been out of my cell an hour. May I ask you what was the cause of your arrest?"

"Your question is rather embarrassing; although I have been nearly two years in prison, I am still ignorant of the real cause of my arrest. So far as I can suppose it, it would appear that I am a conspirator. The fact is, it is not impossible that I may have evinced pity for the victims they sacrificed daily at Bordeaux, where I then lived. But I am a republican.

"Tell me, what is the general character of the prisoners in the conciergery?"

"With few exceptions, the conciergery, during the fifteen months I have been in it, has received only patriots. Its vaults are stunned with the noise of the Marseillaise, and for men of the opposite casts whom they massacre, I have seen them cut the throats of a thousand sans-culottes, whom they drag to the butcheries to the cries of 'Vive les Sans-Culottes! You will be convinced hereafter, if you are spared, of the truth of what I advance, by running over the list of the citizens judicially assassinated."

"But I am going now to pay a visit to a young lady, as interesting as she is virtuous, and whose fate distresses me greatly, for she is to appear this morning before the revolutionary tribunal. The prison of the women being separated from the men by a grating, we can communicate with our poor unfortunate companions, across the grating, or by the windows of two rooms on the ground floor, which overlook their court yard."

Riouffe then rose, and we went out of the cell together towards the lodgings of the women. "Do you know, my dear sir," said he, "that I have known Fonfrède, Duclos, Gensonné, Vergniaud, Valazè, and a host of other victims not less illustrious in this prison. I have seen them all file off before me, to the scaffold. More recently, I have heard the roarings of that tiger with a human face, Danton, whom the fear which his audacity inspired exalted beyond measure. I will tell you his last words, and paint him to you just as he was. But time passes, and Madame D—— will have returned from the tribunal. Let's hasten to the grating."

On arriving, we found many of our companions collected in the avenues. Each sought for the look or called for the voice of a loved friend; this, for his sister; that, for his daughter; some for their wives; others their betrothed. To my great astonishment, the prisoners of both sexes conversed with an entire freedom of mind, without betraying any signs of uneasiness or depression.

My companion approached close to the grating, and after respectfully saluting several ladies of his acquaintance, he inquired if Madame D—— had not yet returned from the revolutionary tribunal? and was answered, "No."

"May I ask you," said I, "who is this person, whose fate interests you so much."

"Certainly. Madame D—— is about seventeen years of age, and was sent some years ago to England to complete her education. Having been married last year, she was arrested about a month since, on making a journey to Paris with her father. They accuse her of having emigrated! And a hundred to one that she will be condemned to death."

At this instant, several persons called his name, to inform him of the arrival of Madame D———, in whose fate he was so interested. I do not recollect ever having seen a more charming woman, or one whose least movements were attended with more grace, distinction, and modesty.

"I thank you much, my good Mons. Riouffe," said she to my friend, "for the concern you have evinced this morning, in asking news of me. I have not appeared as I expected, before the revolutionary tribunal. They only took me before a Judge of Instruction, who has scarcely put any questions to me of importance. I don't know whether I amuse myself with a vain hope; but it appears to me by the polite and unusual manner in which he interrogated me, that I have been specially recommended to him."

Riouffe was about to reply, when a degree of agitation which took place amongst the prisoners, attracted our attention. It was one of the functionaries of the conciergery, citizen Bertrand, who had made his entry into the part of the prison occupied by the women. His appearance, it was well known, generally announced a bloody catastrophe; consequently his visit caused the agitation.

Citizen Bertrand, after a pause of a minute, which appeared a long one to us, and having fully enjoyed the terror his presence inspired, deigned to explain himself.

" I come to look for a citizen," said he slowly, casting round him a glance which rested a moment on the countenance of each of the victims; "I come to look for a citizen! But where is she? I do not perceive her. Ah, I see her, citizen D———, I did not see you on coming in."

"It is me then that you want, citizen Bertrand?" said Madame D———, in a voice stifled by emotion.

" Yes, it is you I came to look for," replied Bertrand harshly. ' Collect your effects and make haste, for I am in a hurry."

"Where are you going to take me, citizen Bertrand" demanded the poor woman, now pale as death.

"I shall answer you afterwards. Come, come, make haste the gendarmes have no time to wait."

"Oh, I am lost! Dear father, beloved husband, I shall never see you again, cried the poor creature.

Bertrand turned towards the prisoners who, sad and silent, waited the end of this scene. Raising his hand several times across his throat, and looking at the poor woman from the corner of his eye;—" The little mother is pretty," said he, accompanying the words with the look of a satyr.

"Adieu, companions of my sufferings! You also gentlemen, adieu," said Madame D———,turning towards our side. "Oh, do not fear that I shall disgrace you by my weakness; be assured that I shall know how to imitate the courage of the martyrs our companions, who have gone before us and await us in heaven. Once more, adieu."

Several of the prisoners then embraced Madame D——— affectionately, but without displaying in the last adieus a shade of weakness.

"A thousand pikes!" cried Bertrand in a sharp voice, "This comedy has lasted quite long enough. Come, let's be off, the gendarmes are impatient"

"Adieu Mons. Riouffe, said Madame D———, whilst Bertrand dragged her off: " If ever you recover your liberty, tell my father and husband that my last thoughts will be for them. Adieu once more."

"Farewell madame," replied my companion, "Pray for us who remain."

I expected that the departure of Madame D———, would have produced a deep impression on her companions, but I was mistaken. Scarcely had the unhappy young woman crossed the threshold of the door, than the conversation resumed its course, as if nothing had happened.

"Do not let this indifference either astonish or displease you," said Riouffe, guessing my thoughts, "It is natural, and you would be unjust towards us, if you accused us of insensibility. What would you have? If we were to give way to our feelings at the fate of every victim claimed by the scaffold, our days would be passed in despair and tears,"

"How is that? I dont' understand you!"

"Can't you understand that when Bertrand came to look for Madame D———, it was not to lead her to the tribunal, but to set her at liberty. The paper he carried in his hand was nothing less than the receipt of the jail book."

"Ah the wretch," exclaimed I, "And has he had the baseness, when he held the pardon of that woman, to make her believe that she was going to die."

"Bertrand amuses himself every day with such legerdemain, replied Riouffe. "It is his most agreeable pastime."

During our repast, I was struck with one thing, as a trait of character essentially French. It was the cheerfulness which all exhibited.

"After dinner I took Riouffe by the arm, and we walked together on the green.

"Let us resume our conversation," said I "You cannot imagine how much it has interested me. Have you known Camille Desmoulins?"

"Very little," he replied, "But still enough to form a decided opinion of him. Camille was never a true son of the revolution; his indecisive conduct occasioned a constant struggle between his levity and his virtue, and the latter unhappily has not always triumphed. Crushed by the irresistible domination of Robespierre, he suffered his dignity as representative and citizen to be disgraced by the cowardice with which he endured his outrages. He brought out his "Old Cordelier" too late. He was no longer able to raise his indignation, and confirmed that sad truth, that one may be the most pitiable of men, although a keen writer ; a pen in the hand of a pamphleteer is more frequently a tool he uses, than the echo of his soul. It is impossible to give an idea of the levity of judgment which characterized him, and which displayed itself in the most trivial actions. Such was his inconsequence that he could not see that his wife, who was denounced as a conspiratrice, was by that one fact irrevocably lost. On returning from the hearing at where he had been condemned, he said to one of his friends:—I am afraid they will arrest my wife. Happy want of foresight, which prevented him from carrying to the tomb, the painful conviction of having caused the ruin of her, who was most dear to him. On the whole, Camille died with courage, and I like to believe that posterity will give him credit for having, in the midst of a deluge of blood, been the first to give the signal of clemency, and to stigmatize the ferocity of the executioners.

"And Danton, that giant of the revolution, have you seen him, during his short stay in the Conciergery ?"

"Frequently. He was placed in a cell by the side of Westerman, and he never ceased talking, less to be heard by his companion in misfortune, than by us. This terrible Danton whose audacity knew no bounds, that insatiable cannibal, whose teeth have bitten deepest into the bowels of France, was, if I may be allowed the expression, quite out of countenance with his ridiculous fall. If he had been struck by a thunderbolt, his forehead would have preserved something of his self-conceited arrogance ; but the idea that he was overturned by Robespierre, lowered him in his own estimation, and constrained him before us. He could not comprehend how a giant such as he had been, could be outwitted by a pigmy."

During his imprisonment, Danton, like a captive tiger, had almost continually his face at the bars of his cage He attempted to sustain the semblance of a strong and indomitable mind. His phrases were interlarded with oaths or coarse expressions. Here are some of his sentences, which I have inserted in my manuscript.

"On such a day, I instituted the revolutionary tribunal; but I beg pardon for it of God and man It was not to be a scourge of humanity, but to prevent the renewal of the 2 September."

"I leave everything in a frightful pickle. There is not one who understands how to govern. In the midst of so many phrenzies, I do not regret having signed my name to some decrees that will prove I did not share in them."

"All my brother directors are Cains. Brissot would have guillotined me the same as Robespierre."

"I had a spy who never left me. I know that I should be arrested."

"What proves Robespierre to be a hero, is that he never spoke to Camille Desmoulins with so much friendship, as on the night before his arrest."

"In revolutions, the authority rests with the greatest rascals."

"The d——d brutes! They cried 'Vive la Republique!' on seeing me pass."

"Such," said Riouffe, "were some of the speeches of Danton, which I have written under what might be called his dictation. There is nothing particular in them, and I only offer them to you as an historical document. But let us pass to a less gloomy picture; and since you are so eager for these melancholy details, which passed yesterday, but which already belong to history, follow me to that same grating which separates the men's from the women's department. Do you see that still young woman of a majestic beauty! Her large black eye sparkles with intelligence; her gesture is stamped with a theatrical character. Attentive to her least words, the men stand motionless, and ranged in a circle before the grate. It is the citizeness Madame Roland. Her discourse,—for she does not converse,—commonly treats on politics."

"Madame Roland is partial to antithesis and effective words. She often wants simplicity, but never elevation and energy. I have always found that she reasoned too imaginatively, and that her imagination prevented her from reasoning. Common sense has a simplicity which displeases her. It may be seen that she has studied Roman History without understanding it."

"Her courage is genuine, but perhaps she is too fond of displaying it. I have never seen any other woman in the Conciergery who has so coquetted with the guillotine. One day, the femme-de-chambre who serves her, said to me in confidence, "Before you, madame collects all her powers, but in her room she remains sometimes three hours, leaning upon the window weeping."

I was going to make some observations to Riouffe, when a turnkey calling my name in the corridor, arrested the words on my lips. On answering the call, he remitted to me a letter from my uncle the patriot. My uncle informed me, that he was actively engaged in obtaining my liberation, and he hoped, knowing my ardent sans-culottism, that I should very soon return to my family. He concluded his letter by giving me to understand that he was using all his efforts to obtain my translation to another prison.

This letter produced an extraordinary excitement in my mind. I cannot express the joy I felt, on thinking that I was not abandoned by everybody, that I had friends who loved and interested themselves about me.

The fourteenth day after my entry into the Conciergery political section, I was engaged in making notes of my captivity, when they came to give me notice that I must prepare to set out. In vain I questioned the gaoler; he was inflexible and maintained an obstinate silence.

My bundle being put up, which was soon done, I went to take leave of Riouffe. " I guess the cause of our separation," said he, " It is your uncle, who has doubtless demanded and obtained your removal to another prison. May God protect you, we shall perhaps meet again in better times."

The carriage in which I was conveyed, stopped at the door of the Abbaye. I was horrified at the sight of those sombre walls, which were still stained with the blood of the victims of the second and third of September. My reception was no better than I expected. I passed an inspection as complete as it was humiliating, but they left me the small sum of money which remained.

Come, follow us, bandit !" said one of the gaolers, seizing me roughly by the collar; I shall know how to make you pay dear for your treason; you shall see."

The fellow was so intoxicated, that I judged it most prudent to put up with this insult without reply. The dungeon into which he thrust me, was little better than that I occupied at first in the Conciergery, except that it was lighter, and it was possible, by approaching the window, to read writing. The furniture consisted only of a worm-eaten table, disgustingly dirty, a heap of broken straw, and a miserable truckle bed· When at night I lay down, overcome by fatigue and distress of mind, my body was instantly attacked with myriads of vermin, which soon produced the effect of a single wound covering my whole frame. Never was a captive subjected to greater torment by the Inquisition, than I suffered on that dreadful night.

Four and twenty hours was I left in this horrible place, before any one approached. At last I heard the barking of dogs in the distance, then the march of a company of troops, and at length I saw a turnkey enter.

"Hold! traitor to your country!" said he, "Here's a pitcher of water to drink the health of the foreign satellites, and a piece of bread; it is much better than you deserve."

"Could you not procure me a chair," cried I eagerly, seeing the turnkey about to leave.

"A chair!" he exclaimed, bursting into a laugh, "Excuse me sir, you are an aristocrat! Why not ask, by the same rule, a fauteuil covered with velvet, and silk curtains."

With this polite reply, the gaoler shut the door violently and left me again alone. As soon as he was gone, having eaten nothing during the time I had been there, I examined the bread and water he had brought. Famishing as I was, I could not touch it; as to the water it stank, I took one draught, but so fetid and filthy was it, that I spit it out again, and in a fury threw the pitcher against the wall, and then attempted to sleep.

I was so exhausted and broken down, that in spite of the vermin which devoured me alive, I obtained some hours of repose; but, as soon as it was dark, the rats, which had found me out the evening before, returned in redoubled numbers, and kept me continually on my guard, and I walked about the cell the greater part of the night. The consequence of these annoyances was, that I was attacked with a violent fever accompanied by delirium, which for awhile rendered me insensible to my sufferings.

In this state I remained until the next day, when having recovered my reason, my first wish was for the presence of the turnkey; for even his brutality would have been a relief from the utter isolation in which I found myself. He however did not come, and the idea occurred to me, that they had resolved to let me die of hunger.

This thought so rapidly gained ground in my mind, that I was soon fully convinced that I was enclosed in an "In pace," or an "oubliette." Furious at this idea, I uttered piercing cries, calling for help. I hoped by this means to rouse my companions in misfortune, and induce them to attempt to relieve me. Alas! My cries, absorbed by the massy walls of the vault, soon ceased, and I fell insensible on the floor.

I was aroused the next day by a violent shake, and the first object I perceived on opening my eyes, was the ferocious countenance of my gaoler.

"Well," said he, "It appears the cookery of the Abbaye is not much to your taste. You have not touched your provisions."

"My friend," replied I, looking at the turnkey with earnestness, "If you were now to offer me a sumptuous dinner, I could not touch it; I ask only one thing, that you will bring me some water, and not leave me; I would not die alone and abandoned, oh remain I beg of you!"

My request seemed to make some impression on the iron heart of the turnkey. "Come comrade," replied he, "You must not let your spirits sink for so little a matter; as to keeping you company—"

"I don't ask you to keep me company," said I, interrupting him, "But I do ask at least that you will not again leave me two days and nights without coming to see me."

"Do you mean to say comrade, that you were not visited yesterday?"

"I have been alone for forty-eight hours."

"Ah, I see! We have every decade, a holiday, and my substitute must have forgotten that I was gone out. Well, I will make you amends for his negligence, by a double ration. I'll go and clean the pitcher, and fill it with fresh water."

In a few minutes he returned with the water; I eagerly

snatched the pitcher, and drank without taking breath. Having quenched my thirst, I felt a great relief and recovered a portion of my strength.

"To-morrow," said the gaoler going towards the door,— "Don't be impatient,—I will endeavour to be more punctual."

In a phrenzy, I rose and seizing the pitcher, flung myself between the turnkey and the door. "If you don't take me with you, I'll kill you," cried I, grinding my teeth.

In a fury he flung at my face the enormous bunch of keys which he carried in his hand. The mass of iron slightly grazed me in passing, and rebounded against the cell door.

In spite of my weakness, and with an energy superinduced by fever, I rushed upon the turnkey brandishing my pitcher. The wretch did not expect to find this energy in me; disconcerted and trembling, he had only time to throw himself upon his knees. At this cowardice my anger abated. "I will grant you your life," said I, "But on one condition, that you allow me to leave this dungeon, and take me to the common prison."

"I promise it," said he, "Walk on, and I'll follow you."

What was my delight when, after passing through a long corridor, I found myself in the midst of a crowd of prisoners. My appearance,—so unexpected,—produced the greatest astonishment; questions were rained upon me on all sides, but alas, my rage, and consequently the strength which had till sustained me then vanished; and unable to pronounce a word, I fell senseless at full length upon the floor.

When I recovered my senses and cast my eyes round, I saw that I was in a parlour fantastically furnished. Seated before a table was a large man, whose ruddy countenance and dull look did not indicate temperance. He held in his hand a glass of bohemian crystal, half filled with wine, in which he dipped a biscuit.

"Where am I?" exclaimed I, endeavouring to summon my recollection.

"With a good patriot," replied the stout man. "But tell me citizen, it appears that you wanted to assassinate one of my turnkeys? Hem! Hem! Do you really believe that the republic maintains turnkeys only to afford amusement to the prisoners?"

"Before answering your question," said I, "I beg to know who you are?"

"Who I am! repeated he laughing; "I am the Concierge, registrar, magistrate, everthing here."

"Then," replied I, "I give you notice that I will not return to my dungeon,"

"Ah bah! Do you believe so? And what will you do to avoid returning to your dungeon?"

"I will make them kill me by resisting."

'I like to hear you speak so," said the Concierge, filling his glass; "That shows me that you are a good fellow. What is it that you want?"

"I want bread that I can eat, and water that I can drink, and I will not allow myself to be thrown amongst vermin."

"You are very exacting, but all may be arranged. Listen, I have a good cook in my kitchen, and my house contains all you can wish for; have you any money? That's the question."

"I have got five or six crowns," replied I, hanging my head.

"And can you not procure any from your family?"

"My uncle, who is an intimate friend of Robespierre, is now in Paris. If you will allow me to write to him, it is possible that he will supply me with funds."

"So your uncle is the friend of the great Robespierre," repeated the Concierge, with a thoughtful look. But by the by, who do you call yourself?"

I told him my name and family.

"Stop there!" cried he interrupting me; "It appears to me that your name is familiar to me; yes, they have mentioned you quite recently. Now whether it was to recommend you to my severity or lenity, I cannot remember; I have so much to do."

He poured out a third glass of wine, then rang a small bell placed at his side on the table, and almost immediately a turnkey, whom I had not before seen, entered the parlour.

"Tell me Isidore," said the Concierge, "Have I not received a recommendation or a letter, for the prisoner in cell No. 17 here present?"

"A letter and a packet," replied Isidore.

"A packet exclaimed the Concierge, "And what did it contain?"

"Twenty-five louis in gold," replied Isidore laconically.

"So," said the Concierge, "Here you are with a capital of twenty-five louis; give me a receipt for that sum, which I will now pay you. If you agree to pay six livres a day, I engage to furnish you with wholesome food; will these terms suit you?"

"Certainly," I replied.

"Well then, sign this receipt.

"Here's the sum that belongs to you, less a hundred and eighty livres, which I keep back for your first month's board," said he counting the money. "Now, they are going to serve dinner; whilst you are at dinner, they shall clean out your cell. Citizen, Au revoir."

I wished to rise, but could not, the gaoler Isidore, seeing my embarrassment, took me upon his back without saying a word, and carried me to the refectory. I was here supplied with a bottle of excellent wine, a plate of meat, a herring, and white bread.

It may be supposed, that after fasting so long, I was quite ready for this excellent repast. The wine however, took effect upon my head, and by the time the bottle was empty, I had quite forgotten all my ills. The turnkey who attended me, was the most amiable of men, and Isidore, who never spoke a word, I declared to be an uncommonly clever fellow.

On returning to my cell, I found that the turnkey had certainly made a great improvement. I was so overcome with the wine and fatigue, that I threw myself on the truckle bed, and fell fast asleep; nor did I awake until the next afternoon, having slept twenty hours.

It would be tedious to the reader, to give a detail of all my sufferings and adventures during the months I remained at the Abbaye. Unfortunately, I fell sick, and was taken to the hospital, where the most frightful scenes were enacted. The brutal surgeon neglected the patients, and in fact, hastened their passage to the tomb. By accident I escaped the fate of many of my companions, and was removed to another department of the hospital, where, under the care of a humane surgeon, I grew better.

During my convalescence, I was removed to the prison of Avechè, where I was beginning to recover my strength, when one afternoon, they came to take me before the Judge.

After waiting an hour I was introduced to the cabinet of the Judge, who seated before a table covered with papers, and a bottle of brandy half empty before him; began my examination, without taking the trouble even of looking at me.

"You are accused," said he, "of having furnished to your son and grandson, money to enable them to emigrate. The proofs of your crime are in my hands. and it is useless for you to attempt to deny it."

So saying. the Judge took a draught of brandy, and nodding his head to a man seated at a small table near his desk:

"Registrar," said he, "write that the accused confesses his crime, and throws himself upon the mercy of the court."

"But I confess nothing at all," exclaimed I, seizing the arm of the Registrar, who was about to obey the order.

"Ah! you retract now," resumed the Judge; it is too late."

"Allow me," cried I, "I do not retract, on the contrary I ask to make a fresh confession."

"That's a different matter, speak."

"I have to confess," resumed I, first, that I am not married, and have never had any children. Secondly, that being only twenty-six years old,—

"What! "only twenty-six years old?" exclaimed the Judge, looking at me for the first time; "but your accusation says sixty-six. The fact is, "continued he, "you really don't look so old! Still, is not your name Mareil?"

"No, citizen Judge"

"May the devil confound the fools that brought you here, but it don't signify; tell me the cause of your arrest. We shall be so much forwarder, and I will send you afterwards to the tribunal."

The danger was imminent. A moment's hesitation, and I was lost. I took my resolution' instantly.

"Citizen Judge," said I, "I am an officer of the corps d'armie which is now acting in Piedmont. I was returning to pass some time with my family, in order to establish my health, when I was denounced by a rascal jealous of my happiness."

"Jealous of your happines? how is that?"

"Yes, I was the lover of a delightful creature as any in the world. But I dare not enter into the details of this love story, fearing to offend your dignity. Altogether it is a curious history."

"My duty is to hear everything," replied he. "Speak without fear, and don't omit a single detail."

The Judge then swallowed some fresh draughts of brandy, flung himself back in his arm chair, crossed his hands over his chest, and motioned me to speak.

I must confess to the reader, that, at the moment, the instinct of self-preservation predominated over my dignity, and I had recourse to a trick, not very noble or courageous. I related to the Judge a horribly scandalous history which I had heard from my ex-companion Pampin. I stopped two or three times, apologizing for my prolixity; but each time he ordered me with an imperious voice, to go on, and not omit a single particular. I found that I had gained my point and had managed to interest him. In fact, this man who had remained insensible to the most evident expression of the truth, to the supplications of a wife, the tears of a mother, yielded to the pleasure my recital produced. Several times he could not restrain a loud burst of laughter, accompanied with singular comments.

"Truly, citizen," said he, when I had finished speaking, "you seem to me a jolly fellow and an excellent patriot, and I hope your imprisonment will not be of long duration. Have you any friends who are interested in setting you at liberty?"

"I have an uncle, a friend of Robespierre, who has charged himself with raising the indictment."

"Then you may consider yourself clear of the business. Farewell, and a happy chance for you. I hope you will come and see me when you are once out of prison."

At my request, this Judge directed the Registrar to make out the order for my removal to St. Lazare, and I set off to my new destination. When I arrived, I went to the office to give in my name.

"Have you any money," asked the Concierge abruptly.

"A few crowns, which I had at the hospital, but I hope to receive more here in a few days."

"That's well! We will tax you afterwards."

What was my surprise and joy, to find my old friend Anselme in the Lazare. The pleasure was reciprocal, and was enhanced by his saving me from the brutal usage of one of the turnkeys, who certainly would have strangled me, but for my friend.

We lived several months in that prison, expecting daily to be called upon to appear before the Revolutionary tribunal, and afterwards guillotined. Anselme had concocted a plan of escape, which would probably have succeeded, had it not been discovered by two of the prisoners, known to be spies. One of these was an Italian named Manini, and the other a sub-agent of the name of Jobert.

We were denounced by these miscreants at the commencement of Thermidor, and momentarily looked for the order to appear before Fouquier Tinville, and Anselme had sworn that before he died, he would strangle Manini.

We passed an anxious time, for we hourly expected to be included amongst the number of those whom we daily saw carried off to the guillotine. Nearly every day, from fifteen to twenty of our unfortunate companions disappeared for ever from our eyes, but the new arrivals were so numerous, that the prison was constantly full.

On the 9th Thermidor, at the instant in which they were about to shut us up in our chambers, the turnkey Leduc came up to me with a mysterious air, and dropping his voice said:

"Be prudent, I have good news to tell you; Robespierre is not perhaps still alive."

Saying this Leduc left me hastily, and without giving me an opportunity of questioning him. I immediately communicated this incident to Anselme.

"Provided I can manage to wring Manini's neck, that's all I care about," he replied, with his usual stoicism. "The rest signifies little to me."

Presently we heard the drums beat the generale and the rappel; a little after, the turnkeys shut the intermediate wickets of the corridors. It was evident that an important event had occurred.

The anguish and uncertainty of our situation during that night, was beyond expression, and drove sleep from our eyes. Are they about to massacre, or to free us? We had no longer even the courage to communicate our conjectures to each other.

The next morning, some new prisoners informed us of the defeat of Robespierre and the Municipality. This was considered by us so happy an event, that we refused to believe it. At length, about noon, the fall of Robespierre was announced to us in a manner so positive and almost official, that we could no longer entertain a doubt of our happiness.

Then arose cries, tears, transports of inexpressible joy; we rushed into each others arms, and exchanged the endearing name of brothers; in short we were intoxicated with happiness.

One man alone perhaps, amongst us, preserved his presence of mind; it was Anselme, and the only reflection he permitted himself to make, was: —" That knave Massini has now a chance of his life."

I shall pass rapidly over the steps taken by Anselme, who was liberated before me, to obtain my departure from St. Lazare. I was ultimately allowed to leave the prison, but on condition that I would at once return to the army.

I was so happy to be able at last to live the life of everybody else, that I did not dream of complaining, at being again sent to serve under the flag of France. I passed my days with Anselme, and as I had received money from home, I made him dine twice a day.

" My friend," said he one night on leaving the table, " I lead a life worthy of a fat hog, and it cannot last; I am going to bid you farewell."

"Going? and where to?" I cried.

"I am going to Vendée," answered he; "you ought to remember, that that idea has haunted me for a long while. However, I will not say adieu, for I know we shall see each other again."

In spite of the regret which the departure of Anselme caused me, I still could not help laughing at his faith in our re-union in Vendée. Strange! fifteen days after, the battalion into which I had been incorporated in the grade of adjutant, was destined to set out for La Vendée, and the singular prediction of Anselme was realized.

I shall pass over my journey from Paris to Nantes with the remark, that the fall of Robespierre, although it was quite recent, had already produced an excellent effect in the provinces. The most timid people began to express their indignation,—too long withheld by fear,—and to curse the monsters, who for two years, had deluged France with blood.

It was not till I arrived at Tours, that I obtained details of the events which were then passing on the two sides of the Loire. The rapidity with which I had travelled since my departure from Paris, having placed me in advance in the stages marked out in my passport, I resolved to remain two or three days at Tours; I therefore engaged a room at the hotel of the "*Chariot d'Or.*"

The day after my arrival, I made the acquaintance, at the Table d' Hote, of a young officer, who, like myself, was on his route to the army of the west. This officer, however, had the advantage of me, in having a perfect knowledge of La Vendée, where he had already fought. From him I obtained some valuable information on the subject of the war, and a detailed account of the character and conduct of the rebel chiefs and their armies.

Four days afterwards, I arrived, towards the middle of the

day, at Nantes. My first care was to repair to the general officer of the place, to present my passport, and to ask a billet. The Commissary of war declared to me, that Nantes, a short time before, had ceased to form a rendezvous for part of the army of the west, and that he must sign my passport for the camp at Roullière.

The next morning at daybreak, I was on the march with a corps of the Nantese National Guards, for my new destination. The camp of Roullière was situated between Le Lognin and La Seine Nantaise, and crossed the road to Montaign. This camp, which occupies a space of about a league, was at nearly double that distance from Nantes. The spectacle, when I arrived was singular and picturesque. Barracks of all sizes, rose on every side without order or system. In the midst of these barracks, which reminded me of the trestle stalls of a fair, I perceived a ragged crowd of soldiers, of whom, some were walking with women, whilst others were occupied in cooking their repast. The first impression produced on me by this sight of my companions in arms, was not very favourable to them. They had more the appearance of bandits than soldiers.

"Captain," said I, saluting an officer, "will you be good enough to point out to me where I can find the colonel of the camp?"

"Do you belong to us?" he asked, twisting his moustache.

' Yes, captain, here is my passport,"

"Let's see," said he. "Hold, you form part of my company! Have you already been engaged?"

"Certainly, captain, I have made war on the frontier."

' Ah! so much the better! I shall have at least one man in my company on whom I can depend."

"How is that, captain? Are the republican troops then so unwarlike, that they dare not sustain the shock of peasants, ignorant of the art of war, and badly armed?"

"The republican troops are the best in the world," he replied, "but the forced volunteers whom I command, are not soldiers, the greater part being fathers of families, who have engaged themselves only for a limited time: if it had depended on me, I should long ago have got rid of all of them."

Whilst the captain was speaking, I examined him with a curiosity of which he certainly was worthy. Imagine a face slashed across by two enormous sabre-cuts, lean, yellow, bony, two-thirds covered with his moustaches, and sustained by a neck, long and fleshless beyond measure. The rest of his body, in perfect harmony with his head, presented a skeleton bareness. Still, one might see that he was endowed with extraordinary muscular force. As to his toilette, I give up making a description of it. Setting aside his epaulet, which proclaimed his rank, there was nothing else but rags.

"Adjutant," said he, "pointing to a barrack, "there's the colonel. When your passport is viséd, if you will come and drink a bottle of wine with me, you will do me a pleasure. If you don't find me,—for I have still a cruise to make,—you must tell my sentry to call me."

"I accept your invitation with gratitude, captain," may I ask your name?"

"They call me Cherche-à-Manger, and every body knows me," he replied, turning his back, and going off at a great rate.

I was proceeding towards the barrack of the colonel of the camp, when I came upon an old sergeant, who was cooking a magnificent leg of mutton, spitted with a sabre, and upheld by four sticks fixed crosswise in the ground.

"Serjeant," said I, "do you know Captain Cherche-à-Manger?"

"Parbleu! I believe so," answered he." Who is there that does not know Cherche-à-Manger?"

"But pray sergeant, inform me whether the words "Cherche-à-Manger," represent, as I suppose a soubriquet, or a proper name?"

" I believe it to be a nom-de-guerre, for the Captain is the roughest eater in the world. He would make only a mouthfull of this fine leg of mutton you see here. But he is a jolly fellow, and a famous officer. He has killed more brigands, than there are hairs on his head! He commands the volunteers of the camp of Roullière."

" Are these volunteers numerous?"

" About two hundred! If you form part of this corps, allow me to condole with you."

" Are they then bad soldiers?"

" They! they are not soldiers at all."

" What are they then?

" Inconsolable husbands who weep when they think of their better halfs; calico merchants or spicers, who sigh after their counters, raw boys, scarcely out of school, whatever you like in fact, except soldiers, I don't know what the representatives of the people can be thinking of in incumbering us with all these blockheads who consume a fourth of our provisions. If there were not in the camp six hundred and odd men of the line, it would be in the power of the brigands before eight and forty hours."

I left the sergeant-cook, (who be it said, *en passant*, did not appear to me to have much respect for the military hierarchy) and went to the colonel, by whom my passport was viséd and my arrival verified.

Free from all care, I then thought of rejoining captain Cherche-à-Manger who was upon the threshold of his cabin when I arrived, he hastened to meet me, and seizing my arm said,--"come my lambkin, make haste, I breakfasted more than two hours ago, and am dying of hunger."

Five minutes had hardly passed, when I was seated before

a table covered with enormous slices of cold meat, hams, and several bottles of wine.

The extraordinary facility with which the captain soon despatched a considerable part of the meats and drinks placed on the table, reminded me of my poor friend Anselme, and drew from me a sigh of regret.

" Well Adjutant," said Cherche-à-manger, when his voracity was a little subdued, " What do you think of the camp ordinary ?"

" If this profusion of dishes and bottles constitutes your ordinary, I must confess it is worthy of a Gargantia."

" The fact is, it would be unjust in us to complain. Thanks to the brigands, we swim in abundance."

" How is that, thanks to the brigands? Is it the Vendeans who provide with so much generosity, for your wants ?"

" Yes, adjutant, themselves, we take from them all that they possess. That's the reason abundance reigns here ; you cannot imagine what magnificent hits certain of our comrades have made in the farms. The brigands have a habit of hiding their money in the earth, and when we fall upon one of these nests, I promise you we lose no time. The camp of Roullière containing a great deal of money."

" Captain," said I, as I was about to go away. " I would fain know how you came by the name of Cherche-à-manger ?"

" Because whenever I am appointed to the command of an expedition, I say to the men in order to excite their enthusiasm ;—My friends, come, Cherche-à-manger, I am now so habituated to my soubriquet, that I have nearly forgotten my true name ; our generals always mention me in their reports, as captain Cherche-à-manger, and the pay master would refuse to remit me my salary, if I signed my receipt otherwise."

On leaving this singular personage, I learned that general Vinnieux, the Commander-in-chief, had been superseded by general Alexander Dumas. One officer who had served under the orders of this latter, and who knew him personally, delivered a pompous panegyric in his behalf.

It was on the 17th September, that general Dumas arrived in the west, to supersede, as the Commander-in-chief, his colleague Vimieux, deposed the 7th of August.

I must now go back some days in my narrative, for when I made the acquaintance of captain Cherche-à-Manger, it was the 2nd of September, and from that date to the 17th, I was compelled to be a witness of a serious affair, which certainly deserves to be related.

We had reached the 8th September, and during the week that I had been at the camp of Roullière, I had begun to get accustomed to my military life. With recruits to instruct, patrols to make in the interior of the camp, conversations arising from anecdotes of captain Cherche-à-Manger, and lastly, some mad pranks at Nantes, which I perpetrated incognito, I filled up my time in a very agreeable manner.

From time to time, there was a good deal of talk of Charette, but they represented him always either as on the eve of being taken prisoner, or as operating at a great distance from our camp. The name of the terrible general which, during the first nights of my arrival, had disturbed my sleep, after a week no longer caused me any emotion. I even began to be convinced that this Charette, so formidable and so much dreaded, owed his high reputation only to the intentional exaggeration of the generals sent in pursuit of him.

On the 8th September, towards four o'clock in the afternoon, I rose from table, and proposed to Cherche-à-Manger, a walk through the camp, which he agreed to.

" I will wager, my friend," said he, passing his dry and nervous arm through mine, "That if they were to ask you at this moment to make an expedition into the interior of this country; to go for instance, from hence to Fontenay, you would accept it without hesitation."

"The fact is," I replied,—"that my inaction begins to be disagreeable to me. I shall not be sorry to see these Vendéans who are represented to me in so terrible a light, but who never shew themselves."

Cherche-à-Manger shook his head.

"What!" I continued, nettled by this tacit expression of doubt, "Would you also insinuate that the brigands are equal to their reputation! I assure you that in proportion to my former credulity, I have now become sceptical."

"Wait at least till you find yourself face to face, and in line with the brigands; nobody detests these madmen more than myself, or experiences the pleasure that I feel, in hacking them with my sabre; but my hatred does not prevent me from acknowledging that they fight most admirably."

"Bah! These are your exaggerations captain," I cried, "It is plain that you would heighten your own glory by exalting the courage of your enemies."

Seeing that he did not reply, I turned towards him. With his neck and ears stretched out, and his eyes wide open, the captain seemed to be exploring the horison with perplexed attention. "Do you not perceive before us, at the extreme limits the eye can reach, something like a cloud of dust?" he asked hastily.

"Yes, you are right," I answered, after looking in the direction he pointed out. "Do the brigands then wish to give he lie to the bad opinion I have broached respecting them?"

"Come" said he, without answering my question, and redoubling his pace, "That dust which indicates the approach of a corps of cavalry, is so much the more perplexing, that we do not expect any reinforcements to-day."

"Bah! It is a detachment of the Nantois garrison, who are coming to look for wheat," I replied.

"This is possible! Never mind, let us advance."

On arriving ten minutes after, we found to the right of the camp, a detachment of a battalion of reserve. Cherche-à Manger ran towards a lieutenant, who with a pipe at his mouth, and his arms crossed behind his back, walked philosophically in front of his troops.

"Lieutenant," said he hastily, "Where is your commander."

"At Nantes captain, with the colonel."

"Are you the only officer here?"

"The only one captain, but I am not the more occupied for that. What is the use of these questions pray?"

"What's the number of men that can be disposed of at this moment," resumed Cherche à-manger with increasing eagerness, and without replying to the lieutenant.

"One hundred and twelve men, captain."

"Very good. Make haste and get them under arms."

From the manner in which Cherche-à-Manger spoke, the officer saw that he must at once obey, and he hastened to cause the movement to be executed. In less than five minutes the hundred and twelve men were formed in perfect order, presenting a line of bristling bayonets. The cloud of dust increased more and more in density.

Cherche-à-manger then began to explain to the lieutenant the subject of his fears, but at the first words he spoke, the lieutenant interrupted him smiling, and said, in a voice in which I perceived an involuntary shade of raillery;—" I am astonished captain, that you should allow yourself to be made thus uneasy. That is the expeditionary column which was expected to day from Montaign.'

"And why did you not say that at once? In fact I perceive the uniform of the Hussars." And, at about five hundred paces from the camp, we saw a detachment of Republican Hussars, advancing at a short trot.

"Let us continue our walk," said Cherche-à-manger abruptly, ashamed of his mistake.

"You see captain, that you do too much honour to the brigands, in imputing to them the boldness of attacking us in open day," I replied.

Cherche-à-manger made me no answer, but he quickened his pace towards the side opposite to that by which the hussars were advancing, probably to avoid coming further into contact with the republican detachment, which had so grossly misled him. Scarcely had we gone a hundred paces, when sharp cries of distress and grief made us turn our heads. We then perceived the pretended republican hussars sabering without mercy, the troops of the battalion of reserve, which was already in flight.

At this spectacle, as terrible as it was unexpected, I felt my blood freeze in my veins, and my legs tremble under me. "Well," said Cherche à-Manger with delight, "Was I deceived? Let us lose no time, run and collect the troops.

After the first moment of surprise, I took a desperate spring and darted off in the direction opposite to that taken by the enemy. But I could not avoid hearing behind me, the cries of the wounded who fell under the sabres of the Vendeans.

It is impossible adequately to describe the confusion which prevailed in the camp. Surprised and disarmed in the midst of their occupations or leisure, and utterly panic-struck, our men attacked each other without knowing what they did, and thus increased the danger of their position. It soon became a general 'sauve-qui-peut,' and those soldiers who, by chance happened to have their muskets, instead of using them against the enemy directed them against their own comrades, in order to clear themselves a passage.

One man alone, showed himself superior to the danger; it was Cherche-à-manger, who, throwing himself before the run aways and endeavouring to stop them, did all that was humanly possible to organize a resistance, but in vain. For myself, I do not hesitate to declare that I felt a lively sensation of pleasure, when after having crossed the ditch which surrounded the camp, I found myself in the open country. No obstacle opposing any longer my flight, I redoubled my speed. In less than ten minutes I cleared half a league of distance; then panting, my legs trembling, and my breathing oppressed, I stopped in order to recover myself.

"Allow me to congratulate you on the strength of your hams," said Cherche-à-Manger, who, on turning round at his voice, I perceived planted right before me, presenting arms. "Good heavens! that I should see the time when I could no longer keep up with you, although I ran nearly as quick as a hare!"

"Ah! what a frightful calamity, captain!"

"What calamity are you speaking of?"

"The attack on our camp."

"Bah! that event is not worth the trouble of thinking about. I have seen several such, since I have been making war in La Vendée. Well! my dear friend," said he, after a moment's silence, presenting arms again, anew in an ironical way; "Well! the Brigands always appeared to you insignificant enemies, only worthy of contempt? Does not this little brush make you change your opinion?

"Can you jest, captain, at such a moment? Do you see that smoke which rises in black whirlwinds in the direction of the camp?"

"Yes, the brigands are amusing themselves in burning our tents! I have burned more than forty of their farms, and I vow that the recollection of it just now is so precious, that it helps me to support philosophically, the loss of my baggage! But listen! Don't you hear a noise like that of a battalion on the march?"

"Yes, perfectly," I replied, lowering my voice, whilst Cherche-à Manger, with his ear placed upon the ground, tried to ascertain the direction of the noise.

Never shall I forget the extravagant delight I felt, when, a few minutes after, on reaching an eminence that we made for. I perceived the blue uniforms of the republican soldiers, "We are saved!" I cried, raising to heaven a look full of tears and gratitude

"Famous!" cried Cherche-à-Manger, rubbing his hands joyfully, "we are going to strike in our turn! let's run and warn our comrades."

In less than a quarter of an hour, streaming with perspiration, and exhausted with fatigue, we reached the republican column. Cherche-à-Manger, in a few words explained to the commander, the events that had taken place, and the latter immediately caused his troop to quicken their march.

"I think we are going to have our share of the fun," said Cherche-a Manger. "The brigands are engaged in burning our tents, and do not at all expect a retaliation on our part. They will be surprised, and we shall make a frightful slaughter, that will be delicious."

The republican column was little more than a quarter of a league from the camp, when a Vendean, emerging from a thin coppice where he had been squatted, darted off in the direction of Roullière. Fifty shots, were fired at him at once, but unfortunately, not one of them took effect.

"If that scamp reaches the camp he will give the alarm," said Cherche à Manger, furiously chewing his moustache; "cost what it may, he must be stopped in his route." Then suiting the action to the word, the captain darted in pursuit of the fugitive. Although the latter had considerably the start of him, it was soon evident that Cherche-à-Manger would reach the Vendean. The brigand finding that he must succumb in this struggle of speed, suddenly wheeled about, and putting his musket to his shoulder presented it at his pursuer. The instant that the Vendean fired at the captain, the latter threw himself on the ground, at the same time firing his pistol. The Vendean fell; his fall was however useless, for we then perceived, coming out of a bush at a hundred paces in advance of the scene of death, a second Vendean, who took his route in the direction of La Roullière.

"Soldiers," cried the commander of the column, "Quick march. Long live the republic!"

In another half hour we reached the camp, then in the hands of the incendaries; but we were too late. An admirable and well sustained fire, which proceeded from behind the intrenchments and threw down twenty of our men, proved that they were ready for us.

It is impossible to describe what then took place, for there are impressions which arise at such times, which cannot be depicted by the pen, recollections which float vivid and terrible in the mind, but which it is still impossible to bring into a tangible form.

Of all this scene of carnage in which I took a part as well as the rest,—for I had seized the musket of a soldier who was killed at my side, and amply discharged my duty,—I can recollect nothing but the cry '*Sauve qui peut,*' which finished it. That cry, which is still present to my memory, pierced me to the heart, and dispelled as by enchantment, the over-excitement produced, whether by the smell of powder, or the animation of the conflict, or the sight of blood which had till then sustained me.

Obeying the general impulse, and following the example of my comrades, I flung my musket away, and took flight. This flight of which I have retained only a confused recollection, cost us more people than had fallen in the battle. It was only on arriving under the walls of Nantes, that we began to recover ourselves; thanks to the cannon of that city, which arrested the furious pursuit of the enemy. I learned afterwards that the extent of our loss was four hundred men, and that we had had an affair with Charette himself.

The very next day after our deplorable defeat, I was ordered to accompany a reinforcement of troops, who were proceeding to the camp of Frèlignè, against which it was feared that the enemy, elevated by his recent success, would march in force.

I learned with great pleasure, that our detachment, whose march was attended with serious danger, was to be commanded by Cherche-à-manger, whom I had had opportunity of judging in action, and in whom I had every confidence.

On the morning of the 13th September we arrived at Fré lignè. This camp was admirably well fortified and defended; its shape presented a large square, bristling with formidable palisades, and surrounded with a deep fosse. General Guillaume commanded in it, assisted by the Chief of Brigade Prat, and lieutenant-colonel Mirnet.

"I ask only," said Cherche-à-manger to me, when I met him the evening of our arrival, "That Charette may come to attack us here! I consent to be shot for a traitor or a spy, if such an adventure does not procure us an ample revenge for our check at Roullière.

Alas! The captain's wishes were only too soon realized; the next day towards evening, a great tumult in the camp made me suspect the presence of Charette in the neighbourhood; nor was I deceived. We soon learned officially that the Vendêan general, seconded by his terrible lieutenant Couetin, was marching upon our camp, from which he was at that moment, at a very short distance. We passed the night under arms, and the next day saw the enemy appear.

As at this time, we were not only upon our guard, but had

completely taken our measures, and our camp was admirably fortified, the anxiety I felt was nothing like that caused by the surprise at Roullière. It was splendid weather when we perceived the first Vendean column; it was composed of about two thousand men, and advanced with so much audacity that its aspect was imposing. A little after, we perceived two new columns advancing upon two other opposite sides of our camp. A deep silence, only interrupted by the orders given by our chiefs, reigned in our ranks.

"Parbleu," said Cherche-à-manger in a low voice to me, " The brigands lead the way badly in their enterprize."

" How so, captain?" I replied in the same tone.

" Because their first division, which seems to me the most important of their army, manœuvres just in a manner to attack the camp on the side where it is best defended ; that division is going to be cut into mince meat in less time than it takes to make the prediction, you will soon see that this time we shall have some fun."

Cherche-à-manger was not deceived; the column which he pointed out as committing so terrible a mistake, arrived within forty paces of our intrenchments without a shot being fired on either side. It then began to attack the camp, not only at the point where it was best defended, but also on the only side perhaps where it was quite impregnable. Sheltered behind our intrenchments, we poured upon it a shower of balls, carrying, if not confusion, at least carnage into its ranks. A scene then passed which I shall never forget.

Two Vendèan standard bearers advancing calmly and smiling in the midst of the firing, came with a boldness, which I know not whether to call heroism or madness, and planted their standards upon our intrenchments. If Cherche-à-manger had not snatched a musket from the hand of a soldier, and fired upon one of the two rash standard-bearers who immediately fell dead, it is probable that the unfortunate youth would have retired safe and sound, as did his comrade.

At the moment in which we took possession of the enemy's flags, the news was spread in our camp, that the Vendean chief Delannay, the same who, with Charette, had so much contributed to our defeat at Roullière, had just been killed. Our shouts of long live the republic, and our discharges of musketry, increased in vivacity.

Our murderous defence, which at any moment might be changed into the offensive, appeared at last to terrify the brigands; their fire fell off by degrees, and a marked hesitation soon manifested itself in their ranks; soon in short, their column on the left withdrew in disorder :—we might consider ourselves as victors.

"Your predictions are realized to the letter, captain," said I to Cherche-à-manger; "But what's the matter now," I added, on observing his anxious countenance.

"The affair is in good train," he replied, "But I am far from considering it concluded. I am uneasy at the absence of Charette, for if this brigand is not found in the hottest of the battle, it necessarily follows that he is detained elewhere by some very important motive. I am afraid he has the intention of turning our camp by the wood of La Péarguière; if that's the case—Curse it!" cried Cherche-à-manger at that moment in a rage; "Do you hear? That's his voice, he has turned the camp! Look at him!"

In the midst of the waving smoke, between the space which separated us from the enemy, I then saw a lean nervous man of the middle statue, wearing a white scarf tied round his breast, and a plume of the same colour on his broad-brimmed hat:—I knew at once that it was Charette.

At the sight of their general exposing himself thus rashly to our balls, the Vendeans no longer hesitated, they threw themselves between him and us, in order to cover him with their bodies, and the battle began again with more fury than ever.

Infatuated by the presence of their chief, the brigands rushed like wild beasts up to our intrenchments, not with courage, but with delirium.

The flashes of their muskets approached us nearer and nearer, and almost burned our faces; it was clear that the enemy, having crossed our fosse filled with their dead, had finished by clearing the palisades, and penetrating into our camp.

General Guillaume, fully appreciating the imminence of his position, and feeling that a moment's indecision would ruin us, threw himself, sword in hand, in advance of us all, upon the Vendeans. The conduct of our brave general was equal to that of Charette; the chief royalist and the chief republican shewed themselves worthy of each other, but alas, a ball struck Guillaume in the midst of his progress, and threw him roughly on the ground.

"Long live the Republic, forward Prat!" cried he in falling.

Our chief of brigade, the worthy successor of our general, wanted not this appeal to shew himself equal to the task; he sprung forward sword in hand upon the brigands. Poor Prat! a few seconds after, he fell mortally struck, at the foot of the entrenchments.

The blood of these two martyrs demanded vengeance, and they were revenged. No further troubling ourselves to charge our muskets, we rushed with the bayonet upon the Vendeans, who after having cleared the palisades, had intruded themselves into our camp: our charge produced a frightful slaughter.

"My friends, my children," said the colonel to us, "It is useless any longer to defend our camp, we must march upon the enemy, and put him to flight. You are republicans, you have sworn to conquer or die, and I am at your head, success cannot be doubtful; Long live the Republic, and forward!"

The announcement of this sortie was received with enthusiastic shouts. In less time than it takes me to write it, a column formed itself as by enchantment, and rushed from the camp at the *pas de charge*.

At the sight of our bold movement, the Vendeans, surprised for an instant, seemed to hesitate as to the course they ought to take, and drew back.

By a chivalric imprudence which the critical position in which we found ourselves, could alone excuse, our commander marched twenty paces in advance of us.

There occurred then one of those heroic incidents, so common in the wars of La Vendée, and which a modern Homer might hand down to immortality. It was a scene which I shall never forget, and which is still vividly present before me.

The brigands, as I have before remarked, intimidated or surprised at our unexpected sortie, had retired before us, when Charette, advancing alone from the ranks of his soldiers, presented himself, sword in hand before our brave colonel. Planting in the ground a tri-coloured flag which he bore, Mermet rushed towards the formidable Vendean. The troops of our column, and those of the royalists were for a moment undecided, and as if struck with respect. Charette smiled.

In the meantime, this chivalric combat was not allowed to take place. On seeing the danger incurred by our chief, and recognizing the terrible Vendean chief, our muskets were pointed at the latter. The royalists on their part, knowing that Mermet was our last hope, shouldered their pieces and took aim. It was a thousand to one that both Mermet and Charette were about to pay for their boldness by their lives;

but fate was against us. A Vendean of colossal figure and herculean strength, carried of his general in his arms at the instant we fired, and running in the midst of a shower of balls, set him down unhurt in the midst of his own troops. Mermet for want of a similar act of devotedness on his behalf, fell dead.

The fall of our heroic colonel produced amongst us an indescribable sensation, and abated our ardour. We dared no longer continue the sortie, that alone could save us, and regained our intrenchments.

Our retreat, if it had its ignominy, was nobly redeemed by the conduct of an officer of the 39th regiment, who, planting himself sword in hand at the foot of the tri-coloured flag, placed there by Mermet, refused to follow us, and swore to defend the colours to the death. In five minutes he fell to rise no more; at the same moment, one of his comrades quitting the ranks, ran towards the flag, snatched it from the ground, and turning towards the Vendeans, waved it above his head, with an air of menace and defiance; a ball almost instantly reached the unfortunate man, who sunk down lifeless, near the corpse of his brother in arms.

In spite of my desire to hasten as quick as possible through this atmosphere of blood, I cannot pass over in silence, the touching and lofty grief of the son of Mermet, a lad of fourteen years of age, who, after having fought like a lion near his father, attached himself to his corpse. which he covered with kisses and tears, and refused to re-enter the camp.

Our chiefs dead, our standard taken, and the morale of our troops affected by so many rapid reverses, we were compelled ultimately to yield. The first royalist who, springing over our palisades, penetrated sword in hand into our intrenchments, was an old chevalier of St. Louis, with a head covered with white hair, and a sonorous and vibrating voice,

"Vive le Roi, my friends!" cried he, addressing the Vendeans, and plunging into the midst of us, "Forward!"

From this moment, I lost all consciousness of existence, and had no recollection of what was passing, beyond that of the cries of the dying imprecations, discharges of musketry, the smell of powder, which ascended to my brain, and so confused me, that it would be impossible for me to state precisely what occurred. As far as I am able to dive into this chaos, I believe that my comrades fought without either deigning to ask for, or obtaining mercy. The only impression which remains clear and distinct in this frightful scene of desolation and carnage, is that of a violent blow which fell on my head, and which deprived me of sensation,

CHAPTER X.

I escape the slaughter, and fall in with Cherche-à-manger.—We are captured by the Vendeans.—Death of Cherche-à-manger.—I am saved by Anselme.—Lucile.—A secret mission.—We are surprised by the Chouans; their matchless atrocities.—Bois Hardy and his troop.—Punishment of the false Chouans.—The villain Kernoc.—His mysterious escape.—We cross Bretagne.—I suspect Lucile.—Massacre of the inhabitants of Saint Laurent des Mortiers.—Coquerean.—The wood of La Henrcuscrie.—Francoeur—A proof of Lucile's treason.—Midnight attack.—The chateau of Jupellière.—Arrival of M. Jacques.—We defeat the Republicans.—Anselme and I overlooked.—My friend wounded by Kernoc.—M. Jacques' languishing death in a cave.—Anselme avenges himself on Kernoc.—Death of my friend.—Conclusion.

When I came to myself, I was sometime before I was able to connect the past and the present. By degrees however, I fully recovered my senses, and looked round me. I was lying in the midst of a heap of corpses, and the royalist troops, the masters of our camp, surrounded me on all sides.

It was midnight. I calculated, and my hopes were realized, that the royalists, fatigued by the battle of the past day, would not let the night pass without taking rest. Towards three o'clock in the morning, a deep silence reigned in the camp, only interrupted by the groans of the dying. I availed myself of this opportunity to rise and drag myself upon my hands and knees, and thus got away from the corpses, in the midst of which I had been lying during my unconsciousness. Being able only to crawl, I squatted in an excavation, which by good fortune I discovered near me, and easily escaped the search of the royalists.

The next morning I had a view in all its horrors of the field of battle; I was witness also of a fearful spectacle. The Vendeans, after having despoiled our dead of their clothing and arms, pitilessly put an end to the wounded, I lost not one of their cries, or their sufferings.

After the pillage of our camp, the Vendeans proceeded, as at Roulliére, to burn it. All that was not capable of being taken away, was destroyed by fire.

An hour after, the burning of the camp of Freligné was completed; half stifled by the smoke and heat, I quitted my hiding place. After a painful march, chance, or rather providence conducted me to the entrance of a forest, I hastened to the refuge it offered. The balmy freshness which prevailed in the forest effected such a change in my body and mind, that my courage revived, and I began to reflect upon the means I ought to take to avoid falling into the hands of my enemies.

I was not only a prey to fear, but also to hunger; since the night before, I had taken no nourishment. The day began to decline, when I discovered a nut bush, loaded with fruit; this good windfall quite re-animated me.

I was about to leave these benevolent nut bushes, when— " Who goes there ?" said a voice which appeared to me like the sound of a trumpet. " Who goes there ? Stir not or I will shoot you !"

This last recommendation was perfectly useless, for surprise nailed me to the ground.

However, on a second appeal, more threatening than the first, I recovered my presence of mind, and answered in a firm tone,—"A soldier of the Republic! Long live the country!"

The reader will easily comprehend the joy I experienced on hearing immediately—"Long live the Republic!" repeated with the exactness of an echo.

Almost at the instant, a man, clothed in a blue uniform, came from behind a bush and advanced towards me.

"Cherche-à-manger!" cried I, with as much delight as surprise, on recognizing my captain.

"Hold! Is it you my dear Adjutant?" answered he, clasping my hand like a vice. "I see that it is our destiny to meet on serious occasions, truly I am delighted with this adventure."

"You see me captain, at least as much delighted as yourself," I replied, "But how is it that I have the happiness of finding you again here?"

"Like you, I have endeavoured to save myself; only"—said Cherche-à manger, after a short silence, "I have kept my weapons."

"Whilst I have lost mine, I admit captain. Allow me however to remark. that before losing them, I made use of them in the best manner I could."

"I don't doubt it," replied the captain, in a milder tone, and I ask your pardon for addressing this reproach to you. Stop," he added, after reflecting a few moments, "I advise you Adjutant, not to attempt to share my lot, but to separate yourself from me."

"Why so, my dear captain?"

"Because in the state of exasperation to which I am reduced, if we should meet the enemy, I shall involve you in a deplorable manner; as therefore, you are only desirous of concealing yourself, it will be much better for you to continue your way alone."

"But without you, as I know nothing of the country, it will be impossible for me to find my route, and to reach a garrison town."

"You are right, let us remain together; if we meet no one we shall be to-morrow in safety at Mochecoul, if I happen to meet with Vendeans, you know what I have said, I shall engage with them."

"Agreed captain, and I shall pray fervently that we may not meet the Vendeans."

We had proceeded for about an hour in silence, when the discharge of a musket near us, made me start.

"Curse them," cried Cherche-à-manger, dropping his musket, "I am hit."

I was about to pick up my unfortunate companion's arms, when a dozen Vendeans sprung up as if by enchantment at my side, and threw themselves upon me. In less time than it takes me to write it, we were both securely pinioned.

"Shall we shoot them?" said one of the Vendeans, addressing his comrades, "Or won't it be better to lard them with a few bayonet thrusts."

"The bayonet is best," replied another brigand, "Don't waste the powder.

" Yes, bayonet them," cried several, advancing with their arms in a threatening manner,

"Before you die, would you wish to see a priest and confess yourselves?" inquired one of them in a calm but implacable voice.

"May the deuce twist the neck of all your scullcaps!" cried Cherche-à-manger. "If you send one to me, I warn you beforehand that I'll insult him.

" And you ?" said the Vendean to me.

" I shall be thankful if you procure me a priest."

My reply appeared to produce a good effect upon the Vendeans.

" Come, rise and follow me," said he who had proposed to procure a priest for me.

I obeyed, and began to march, guarded by two other royalists, after my conductor. We had scarcely proceeded twenty paces, when he stopped before a large hollow tree, into the cavity of which he threw a small stone; at the same instant a trap-door covered with turf rose before me, and displayed a flight of steps roughly cut in the earth.

" Come down," said my conductor, laughing at my astonishment; " Mons. Le Curé is in the hiding place."

After descending about a dozen steps, we reached the bottom of the cave. A party of royalist soldiers, lying on the ground with their firelocks near them, surrounded an ecclesiastic who, seated on a stool appeared to be delivering a sermon.

A man rose hastily on seeing me enter, and springing towards me took me in his arms, and embraced me with transport. " You here my friend !" cried he, " I knew that we should meet again !"

" Anselme ! Anselme!" exclaimed I, yielding to my feelings and bursting into tears. " Ah, do I find you again, at the moment when I am about to die ?"

" Die !" resumed Anselme, " are you wounded ?"

" No, but I am a prisoner and they will shoot me presently.

" Shoot you, a thousand million furies !" repeated my companion in arms, " Never !"

My recognition by Anselme had completely drawn off the attention of the Vendeans from the curé's sermon, and they drew round us.

" Sir," pursued Anselme, " I swear to you that my friend

here present, is an honest man in every acceptation of the word, and in setting him at liberty, you will not endanger our security; I will hold myself responsible for his word."

"My friend," replied the curé, after a moment's silent consideration, " I ask for nothing better than to save this brother in Christ; however, if he will not swear on the New Testament, that he will no more serve against us, I dare not interfere in his favour."

I took the oath: the curè smiled, and turning to the royalists, he spoke a few words to them in a low voice, and I found myself free.

I was considering in what way I ought to exert myself to obtain a pardon for Cherche-à manger, when a discharge of musketry reached my ears ;—It was too late.

"Follow me," said Anselme, ' I am going to present you to a person with whom, in all probability, you will form an intimate acquaintance."

Without giving me time to question him, Anselme dragged me to the furthest end of the cave. The reader will judge of my astonishment, on finding myself in the presence of a young woman handsomely dressed, and exceedingly beautiful. Her distinguished and rather haughty air, announced her to to be a person of condition or elevated rank.

"I congratulate you sir," said she, " For having been able to inspire such friendship in our brave Anselme; allow me however to express my surprise that you wear the republican uniform."

"Madam," I replied, "Consider me. I beg of you, only as a man who, if he had refused to march to glory, would infallibly have been shot. But," added I, " Will you allow me to ask in my turn, the explanation of what my friend has just announced to me?"

"Anselme probably thinks that in return for the service he

has rendered you, you will consent to share the danger of a perilous and delicate mission, which he is now discharging."

"Anselme has not deceived himself, madam ; May I ask what is this mission ?"

" I am charged," said Anselme, " With a mission extremely difficult to fulfil, namely, to conduct madam across the whole of La Vendèe to the court of Bretagne. Will you accompany us in the journey, and share our dangers?"

I accepted the offer.

"Well, good! I did not expect anything less from you,' exclaimed Anselme; " I knew well that you would not abandon me in danger."

As to the unknown, the smile with which she repaid me for my devotedness, was so enchanting, that dazzled and fascinated secretly rejoiced at my resolution.

Night had then set in, and we prepared ourselves to take some repose. I was so overcome with fatigue, that I soon fell into a deep sleep. The next morning Anselme woke me, and I instantly rose.

" My dear friend," said he, " The moment for entering upon our campaign is come ; if you repent of your resolution of yesterday, nothing hinders you from withdrawing from it."

"The fact is sir," said the unknown, with a most seductive smile, " I should be distressed if any misfortune befel you on my account, reflect therefore maturely, before you engage in our perilous enterprize."

" I have never had but one intention madam," replied I, " And I only regret at not being able to shew you by a great sacrifice, the admiration your courage excites in me ; Anselme, let us set out, I am ready."

I shall not detail all the incidents we met with in our journey across La Vendèe ; twenty times we were on the point of falling into the hands of the republican troops, but thanks to our caution. and to the excellent advice of Lucile we always escaped.

When we arrived in Bretagne, there was nothing talked of but general Hoche, who was then there. That officer was very superior to his predecessors, and saw at once, that there was no other means of reducing the rough Bretons, than those of mildness and clemency, he therefore deluged the country with proclamations containing promises and proposals of amnesty.

Unfortunately the Bretons had been so often deceived, that they put no faith in these promises. The principal chief of the Bretonne chouanery was Bois Hardy, who was located in the district of Brienne sur les Cotes de Nord. A man of remarkable activity and courage, he was unfortunately, implacable in his vengeance, and never shewed any mercy to the blue prisoners who were taken in battle.

During my journey, I questioned Anselme about the mission with which he was entrusted; he contented himself with saying that he had been sent by a personage of great importance to seek Lucile at Nantes, with orders to obey her in everything. "For the rest," said he, "I am completely ignorant of the object of our journey." He would not inform me who this 'personage of great importance' was.

We stopped one night at a farm house, composed of two rooms on the ground floor, the first being parted in the centre by a chimney, in which several persons might be seated; the second was used as a bed-room by the farmer and his wife. The first story, accessible by means of a ladder, had been converted into a granary, and here the farmer's son slept, when he was not with the royalist troops.

We were received by our hosts with perfect frankness and cordiality; our modest supper, which consisted of buck-wheat akes fried in fresh butter, and a jug of cider, being over. it was resolved that Lucile should sleep in the chamber of our hosts, and that Anselme and I should retire to the first story, or granary; here, crouched with my companion on a bundle of hay, I fell asleep. I was awoke by a noise of confused voices; —" Anselme," said I, arousing my companion, " Take your firelock, troops have arrived."

" So much the worse for them," he replied coolly.

We rose immediately, and seizing our arms, went on tiptoe to a kind of window which served as a door to the granary. Scarcely had Anselme set his foot on the first step, when we heard frightful oaths in the farm-yard. " It is too late," said he coolly, "Let us wait." Then he seized the ladder, and drew it up by main strength into the chamber.

At his suggestion, I had begun to work a hole in the floor in order to see what was going on below, when dreadful shrieks reached us, which froze the blood in my veins· " Death and furies!" said Anselme, " Tis hard work when we hear such music to remain with folded arms,"

I had soon accomplished my task; throwing myself flat on my face, I cast a look into the room beneath. Horrible! Never shall I forget the frightful spectacle that met my sight. The unfortunate farmer lay in the middle of the room, in a pool of blood; not far from him his wife, effectually garotted, was held by four Chouans, whilst a fifth twisted a knotted cord with his fingers, which cut into her flesh.

The other Chouans, to the number of about a score, amused themselves with breaking the furniture and utensils of the farm, with a pleasure worthy of true savages.

Such was my emotion caused by this spectacle, that I was unable to speak; I rose, and made a sign to Anselme to take my place.

Scarcely had my comrade applied his eye to the opening, than springing up with a bound :—" Death and furies!" said he, " Take your firelock, and at them!"

I seized my musket, and passing the barrel through the hole, fired, and a Chouan fell. " Parbleu ! That's good !" cried Anselme, " It's my turn now-"

A fresh discharge took place, and another Chouan fell. " Now you," said my companion, ' Whilst I reload my piece."

I fired again ; the Chouans surprised and frightened at this unexpected attack, hastily abandoned the scene of their abominations, and took to flight.

In a few moments we were in pursuit of them, with a warmth and impetuosity proportioned to our indignation. Unfortunately we did not know the country, and the assassins had the advance of us One only, who had dislocated his foot in running. fell into our hands, Anselme with a sabre, split his head in two.

" Ah! My God, and Lucile ?" exclaimed I, recollecting our unfortunate companion ; for this scene which had passed so quickly, had not left us presence of mind to reflect on what might be her fate.

At this exclamation, Anselme stopped short in the midst of his speed, and turning towards me said coolly :—

" I have promised him who entrusted her to me, to defend her to death ; if these brigands have killed her, I will blow my brains out. Let us return."

Scarcely had we taken a hundred paces, than we found ourselves in the presence of the charming young woman whose fate had disturbed us so greatly, and I leave you to imagine the joy this meeting caused us.

"Ah madam," said I, " We scarcely hoped ever to see you again, thank God who has preserved your days But pray inform us how it has happened that you have escaped from this fearful catastrophe ?"

" In a very simple manner," she replied, " The Chouans did not enter the room where I slept."

" But was not the farmer's wife sleeping with you?"

" No, the poor woman in order not to molest me, gave up her room to me. But," continued Lucile hastily, " We are talking whilst the unfortunate woman is dying, let us run, if it is yet in time, to save her." We ran towards the house, but were met by flames which burst from all parts of the building. The Chouans had fired it, and not a wreck was saved.

We had to resume our route in the middle of the night. During the first hour of our nocturnal march, we did not speak a single word ; we were still under the influence of the horrible events to which we had been witnesses. I looked for daybreak with impatience, but it was decreed that that night, already so fatal, should not pass without further adventure. We were coasting along the borders of a wood, when a ' *qui vive*'? stopped us in our march.

" God and the king!" replied Anselme, with his sonorous voice, and presenting his firelock.

Almost instantly we were surrounded by a numerous troop of Chouans.

" The first who takes a step in advance, is a dead man," said Anselme.

" Why are you afraid that we should come near you, if you are good royalists like ourselves?" said the man who carried the lantern.

" Because the Chouans are not royalists, but frightful and ignoble bandits, who only assassinate and plunder, replied my companion boldly.

" We! Are the soldiers of Bois Hardy, robbers and assassins? repeated the man with the lantern. " Pardieu ! You shall pay dear for those words."

Lucile, calm and smiling, advanced towards the Chouans, who had already presented their arms, and placing herself between them and us :—" Is your chief, Bois Hardy now here ?" said she in her enchanting voice.

At this apparition,—for Lucile was as handsome as an angel,—the Chouans manifested surprise and admiration which they did not care to conceal. " Yes he is," replied one of them, " If you wish to see him, I will conduct you to him."

Lucile ordered us to deliver up our arms to the Chouans ; when we had obeyed, she told us to accompany her. Marching behind the Chouan who carried the lantern, we entered the forest ; after a walk of about five minutes, our guide uttered a strange sound, which made me start ; almost at the same instant we heard in the distance the cry of a stag.

" M Bois Hardy is informed of your coming, and is waiting for you," said our conductor.

A few steps further, we perceived a light shining through the branches, and almost immediately we came to a hut constructed of boughs of trees.

I was surprised after having crossed the threshold of the door, at the picturesque scene which the interior of the cabin presented. All around the walls, constructed of branches of trees interlaced, and retaining still a part of their foliage, narrow couches were conveniently arranged, above each couch was hung a musket ; a dozen Chouans, clad in the Breton costume, and seated in a circle in the middle of the room, were employed in mentally repeating their prayers.

Our guide pointed with his finger to a man seated in the midst of the Chouans, and who was no other than Bois Hardy himself.

" Who have you brought us there, Le Bosec ?" said he to our guide.

To this question the peasant answered by a pretty long discourse pronounced in low Breton.

Bosec informs me," said the chief at last, when the Breton

had ceased to speak, "That you have treated my lads as assassins and thieves?"

"Bosec has only told you the truth," answered Anselme, "Only a few moments ago, I formally declared that the Chouans were all rogues, robbers, and assassins."

"Who are you?" asked the Breton chief, addressing my companion and myself.

"Royalists, who fight for God and their king, and not thieves and assassins like you!" cried Anselme.

"How has it happened that you are found at this hour of the night, upon the borders of the forest? Where do you come from, and where are you going?"

"We come from Nantes, and your bandits have met us in the forest, because the farm at which hospitality had been granted us to night, was burned two hours ago by Chouans, and we were compelled to fly in order to avoid falling into their hands."

"At what farm have you been received?"

"The poor farmer so brutally assassinated by your banditti is called Mathurin."

At these words, one of the Chouans rose, uttering a storm of rage and grief, and darting upon Anselme, and taking him by the throat, cried out:—"My father assassinated! Ah wretch, it is thou who hast murdered him; thou shalt die!"

On seeing their comrade throw himself upon Anselme, the Bretons rose and surrounded us, and Bois Hardy was obliged to use all his authority to restrain them. "My lads," said he, "I warn you that I will blow out the brains of the first of you who shall again threaten these people; if they are spies, there is no need of your aid to urge me to have them shot."

Lucile who up to this moment had not interfered in the discussion, now addressed herself to Bois Hardy. "Sir," said she, "I should have wished to maintain my incognito, but I am now compelled to declare myself; I am the good genius of Mons. Jacques in battle, and the companion of his leisure hours."

I confess that these words spoken by Lucile with emphasis and pride, produced in me extreme astonishment, from the prodigious effect they produced, both on the Chouans, and on Bois Hardy himself.

The Breton chief, bowing with a gallantry and respect that his bluntness rendered still more striking, took her hand, and carried it respectfully to his lips.

"Madam," said he, "I had already guessed you were a heroine, but I was far from expecting that my good star would conduct upon my route the good genius of the greatest warrior that the royalist cause has ever produced."

Lucile accepted this compliment as her due, although Bois Hardy was, at that period, reckoned amongst the most influential and renowned chiefs of the Breton insurrection.

As to the Chouans, since Lucile had spoken of M. Jacques, they evidently regarded her with an admiration and respect almost religious.

"Madam," said Bois Hardy, "Forgive me I conjure you, the request I am about to make ; as the companion of a warrior, you will understand better than anyone, what precautions and duties are incumbent upon the chiefs."

"I comprehend you sir," replied Lucile smiling, "You desire a proof of my identity : you are right sir, here is the last letter M. Jacques sent me at Nantes, and which has occasioned my departure, you may read the whole of it, as it contains no secrets."

Bois Hardy took the paper, but scarcely had he cast his eyes on it, than he instantly returned it to her, saying :—" I recognize the writing madam, it is quite sufficient." Then turning to Anselme, he demanded from him the particulars of the fire at the farm of M. Matharin, and the assassination of which that unfortunate man had been the victim."

Anselme related in a few words, but with scrupulous fidelity, the events which had happened to us. In many parts, his recital was interrupted by unequivocal exclamations of indignation and disgust from the Chouans present.

"My friend," said Bois Hardy, "Your recital most sadly confirms an intimation I have received, but which I could not believe, so monstrous did the thing appear to me, I need not now explain myself further on this subject. It is of the first importance that the wretches who have thus dishonoured our holy cause, should be punished for their misdeeds, that the honour of our Chouan name may be avenged."

Two hours later, as soon as day began to break, Bois Hardy took me and Anselme to accompany him in the pursuit after the incendiaries of the farm. He wished, he said, to have us for witnesses of the signal vengeance he intended to execute upon them.

It was about six o'clock in the morning when we left the forest, and we directed our steps at once towards the burned farm, in order to discover traces of the assassins. With a sagacity worthy of Mohicans, the Chouans soon discovered the road taken by the incendiaries.

Bois Hardy immediately dispatched several of his men, to take different orders for his moveable columns, and then without loss of time, proceeded to follow the fugitives. It was late in the evening, as we were passing through a village our attention was attracted by a great light which illuminated the horizon, at the distance of about a quarter of a league.

Half an hour later, we arrived at a burned cabin. Some hay stacks were still on fire around the humble dwelling.

"Forward!" cried Bois Hardy all at once, pointing with his

finger to a troop of men who fled. "Let us avenge the honour of Bretany."

In less than ten minutes after, the Chouans had reached the incendiaries. Not a shot had been fired.

Bois Hardy placed himself before the assassins and said, "I am Bois Hardy, and you are going to be shot."

The wretched men, to the number of twenty, did not attempt the least resistance; they threw down their arms and began to pray for mercy.

"Which is your commander?" said Bois Hardy.

A man, who might be about forty years of age, and whose appearance was not destitute of energy, immediately placed himself motionless before the Chouan chief.

"To what parish do you belong, and what is your name?" demanded the latter.

"My name is Kernoc, and I am from Plancoet."

"You lie! there is no Kernoc at Plancoet!" cried Bois-Hardy, "not only are you not from Plancoet, but thank God you are not even a Breton. See now, answer me the question I am about to put to you."

Looking the incendiary full in the face, Bois Hardy then addressed him in low-Breton. The rascal hung down his head, and remained silent.

"You see, boys," cried Bois-Hardy, joyfully, and casting a glance at Anselme and me, "You see plainly that this man is not of ours, he does not understand low-Breton!"

"Well I admit it; I am neither a royalist nor a Chouan," said the bandit, raising his head proudly; "But my secret shall die with me, and you shall remain ignorant of the advantage you might have derived from my capture, had you been generous towards me."

"The banditti who accompany you, are also not Bretons, is it not so?" resumed Bois Hardy.

"The men who accompany me," replied the pretended Kernoc, independently, "are honest galley slaves, escaped from the hulks."

These words raised a cry of rage and indignation amongst our Chouans, and the son of Mathurin, advancing towards Bois-Hardy, said to him, "Do you permit us sir, to shoot the assassins of my father?"

"Certainly, my lads! shoot, hang, burn these wretches; it signifies little what death you inflict upon them, provided you don't let one of them escape."

The Chouans immediately took from their false brethren their arms, and gagged them effectually. As to the son of the farmer Mathurin, he seized Kernoc by the throat saying, "It is upon thee that I shall avenge the death of my father."

The chief of the incendiaries turned pale, and hastily drawing back to the place where Bois Hardy stood:—"Sir," said he, "I do not fear death, but I wish to live a few days longer; if you consent to defer my execution for a week, I, will repay you for that favour by divulging a secret of immense utility to you."

Bois Hardy made a sign to Mathurin to remove farther off and casting a look of supreme contempt on the prostrate bandit before him:—"What is the nature of this revelation," said he, "And what benefit shall I draw from it for the king's cause, if I grant your prayer?"

"An immense benefit, that of unveiling to the whole of France, an abominable plot against the royalists, in order to dishonour them."

"Speak," said Bois Hardy, after having reflected a moment, "If your revelations appear to me useful, I will deign to grant you the the respi.e of forty-eight hours; if not, I give you up to Mathurin."

"Well know, Bois Hardy, that the republican mountaineers,

in order to destroy the Chouans in the estimation of the inhabitants of the country, have created amongst themselves false Chouans, whom they have commissioned to massacre, burn, and plunder; I am the chief of one of these bands, all the bandits who accompany me are men taken from the galleys to play the game of false Chouans."

The confession of Kernoc produced in the Chouans, as the reader may suppose, unspeakable surprise and indignation As to Bois Hardy, I saw by the smile which passed his lips, the value he attached to these revelations.

The astonishment of the Bretons at the monstrous inventions of the false Chouans, was not greater than the rage of the bandits of Kernoc on seeing themselves thus betrayed by their chief, forgetting for the moment the death which awaited them, they showered insults and imprecations on the revealer, but he remained perfectly insensible to their attacks.

I pass over in silence the bloody scene of the execution of the false Chouans.

As it is possible that I may be accused of having invented this tale for the purpose of getting up a dramatic episode, I beg to observe that my account, derived from experience, has been confirmed by a despatch of general Rossignol to the committee of Public Safety, and by a letter written by general Kreig to the representative Ballèt.

After the galley-slaves had been executed, Bois Hardy set out on his return with his lads, who, delighted with the success of their expedition, amused themselves during a part of the night in singing national songs..

Pleased with the opportunity that procured me the meeting with the famous Chouan chief, I ventured to address him. "My request sir, will probably appear very strange to you," said I, " But I much wish you would inform me who is this celebrated personage known by the name of M. Jacques."

2K

"Faith," replied Bois Hardy smiling, "I will tell you all I know :—After having fought in the Vendean army, M. Jacques having gone to Mans where no one knew him, signalized his presence in that country by such fortunate appearances in moments of danger, that the peasants, whose simple and naive imagination is admirably adapted to the mysterious, at once made of him a supernatural being. Comprehending the immense advantage that this reputation,—unsought for on his part,—would give him, M. Jacques has done everything in his power to preserve it, and has shrouded himself in a complete mystery. Rash to an extent, as it would appear, of which nothing can give an adequate idea, and which is only justified by the extraordinary good fortune in action which always accompanies him· M. Jacques is considered invulnerable, and besides, M. Jacques is a poet, and composes war-songs which his soldiers learn, and which lead them to victory. M. de la Puisaye, who alone knows the real name, antecedents, and vast projects of M. Jacques, will not entrust these details to any of us, for fear that an involuntary indiscretion on our part would deprive M. Jacques of the prestige which surrounds him. Now," added Bois Hardy, smiling, "You know as much on the subject as I do myself."

It was about three o'clock in the morning when we arrived in the forest in which Bois Hardy had for the time established his head quarters; we found Lucile on foot, and impatiently waiting our arrival. I related in a few words, the success of our expedition; the invention of the false Chouans provoked her greatly, and she thought the Bretons justified in having punished them with a severity that should serve as an example. "But my dear companion," said she, "Here's a day lost for our journey, if your strength is not too much exhausted, I would propose that we start without further delay."

Although Lucile accompanied these words with one of her

delightful smiles, I was so harrassed and weary that I refused, but Lucile insisted with so much tenacity, that I was compelled at last to yield.

Anselme, not less fatigued than myself, wished to expostulate, but Lucile imperiously cut him short. Bois Hardy, seeing the uselessness of our efforts, contented himself with expressing his regret at not retaining longer with him the companion of M. Jacques. " However, madam," said he, "As your departure is not urgent, you will grant me an hour to provide you with an escort."

This offer was too graceful and reasonable to be refused, however, I saw by the cold and almost harsh manner in which Lucile thanked Bois Hardy, that the delay annoyed her.

"Are you not at all curious madam, to see our prisoner Kernoc?" said he; " I have sent to fetch him."

"No sir, I thank you," answered Lucile drily, "I have no wish for the company of an assassin, your gallantry may be Bretonic, but certainly it is not good taste."

" Faith, madam," replied Bois Hardy, evidently vexed, "I did not think the companion of M. Jacques was so nervous and impressible as you are; shut your eyes then if the sight of a bandit makes you afraid, for here are my boys coming in with the prisoner."

He had scarcely spoken when Kernoc, with his hands bound and guarded by four Chouans, entered the cabin. The first person he saw was Lucile, who erect and motionless before him, resembled, by the paleness of her countenance, a statue of marble.

At the sight of the young woman, Kernoc uttered an exclamation of surprise; then in a stifled voice :—" What, unfortunate Justine, are you also a prisoner!" said he, looking at her with bewildered eyes.

"What do you want with me, miserable assassin?" exclaimed

she looking at Kernoc indignantly, " Have I then the misfortune to resemble a female of your acquaintance?"

" Ah, forgive me, madam ! Yes, I made a mistake," replied Kernoc, " But the resemblance is really so extraordinary, I beg your pardon for this error."

" There's enough said on that subject, I don't choose to be compared with creatures of your acquaintance," interrupted Lucile haughtily, then turning to Bois Hardy :—" Make them remove this man, whose conduct recalls such frightful scenes, his presence quite upsets me : I feel quite ill, and must give up my intention of setting off on my journey. Yes, if it will not inconvenience you M. Bois Hardy, I will ask you to grant me your hospitality for this night."

The response of Bois Hardy may be guessed ; to our great satisfaction, it was agreed that Lucile should not set out till the next day.

Within an hour we were all asleep, thanks to the fatigues of the day.

The next morning when I awoke, I found the lads of Bois Hardy in a violent rage, and overwhelmed with astonishment. The false Chouan had escaped during the night; this inexplicable disappearance produced an extraordinary impression on the Chouans. Bois Hardy himself was cast down by it; as to Lucile, she exhibited real despair at this mysterious event.

" What does it signify to you Madam," said I, in order to console her, " whether the rascal is at liberty or not? One would believe truly, to see and hear you, that his flight was an irreparable misfortune to you."

" You are right to scold me my friend," replied she, "But do not forget that with us women, the nerves and imagination play a great part, and that we ought to be forgiven for a want of reasoning. Yes, I confess how unfounded and ridiculous my fear is, but I feel an invincible presentiment that this Kernoc will press heavily upon my life and be fatal to me, and I feel alarmed. "I hope my friend, You do not think, said she in conclusion, "That I am cruel and sanguinary yet I would give ten years of my life if Bois Hardy had caused this Kernoc to be shot."

"Alas, madam, your regret ought to be much less respecting him than mine," exclaimed Bois Hardy, who, passing near us at the moment, had heard the observation of Lucile. "Not that the life or death of this wretch lies much at my heart, but his escape in so wonderful a manner, has produced a bad effect upon the mind of my men; I am come to tell you that I have received news that general Humbert who commands at Moncontour, will come alone and without an escort to me, to make proposals of peace.; I cannot express to you how much this homage rendered to our loyalty by a républican general, touches me. It gives the lie direct to the calumnies of the high mountaineers, who represent us as people destitute of faith, and as savage beasts always ready to bite both the innocent and the guilty. I ask your pardon for quitting you so abruptly, but Humbert is waiting for me on the lands of Gausson, and I must set out immediately ; however, before going, I will provide you a safe conduct, and give orders that you shall be escorted as far as the boundaries of Bretagne."

How far was Bois Hardy from suspecting at this moment, when he was so happy at the idea of a republican general trusting to his loyalty, that he would so soon fall a victim to his confidence in the word of the Blues, and be assassinated in a cowardly manner.

In our journey across Bretagne, but one single incident occurred worthy of being recorded. At a little village situated at a short distance from Mayence, a young herdsman put into the hand of Lucile a paper, and ran away without waiting for an answer. Our companion read this missive, which reached her in so singular a manner, without any emotion on her countenance, and continued to walk on without remark, and as Anselme and I knew that she was charged with a political mission, seeing that she did not speak to us about it, we considered it good taste not to question her.

The next day, having passed the night at a farm house, we were about to resume our journey, when a paper at my feet, attracted my attention. I picked it up, and read as follows : —" I arrived, my dear friend and coadjutor, at the same time as yourself, I am following on your track; trust to my prudence and manage not again to lose your presence of mind." A horrible thought crossed me, for I suspected that it was the same paper that had been given the evening before to Lucile.

" Madame," said I to her, putting the open letter into her hand, " See what I have found in the grass just now, walking behind you."

Lucile cast a look of indifference on the note which I presented to her :—" What is it ?" said she in an absent tone.

" A treasonable document."

' Read it !"

"I obeyed. Lucile listened attentively.

" I am of your opinion," said she, " There is treason under it, I should not be surprised if the author of this letter is known to me I received yesterday a caution which nearly explains your document.

If any suspicions had remained on my mind, the perfect calm of Lucile, when I shewed her the accusing paper, and the natural manner in which she answered me, would have sufficed to dissipate them.

Our entry into Mergenne caused us to be witnesses of a frightful scene, the recollection of which is still painful to me.

We had reached within about a league of Saint Laurent des Mortiers, when we saw a peasant, and by the white cockade placed in his hat, we recognized as a royalist. Coming from our hiding place, Anselme and I presented ourselves before him.

Although surprised, the peasant by no means lost his presence of mind; he poised his musket, and getting behind a tree, cried out :—" Don't stir, or I will shoot you."

" Please to observe, my friend," said Anselme, " That your threat is badly timed, because we are as good royalists as yourself.

" You royalists!" repeated the peasant distrustfully, " That's not very probable."

" And why so?"

" Because if you were royalists, you would not be found at such a distance from Saint Laurent des Mortiers, which this morning fell into their hands."

" We are going to Saint Laurent des Mortiers, will you serve us for a guide?"

" I don't wish to hinder you from going where you please, leave me quietly to do the same."

" Parbleu ! We are going to join M. Jacques," answered Anselme, " Do you know him ?"

" You going to join M. Jacques," repeated the peasant with visible emotion. " You know him then, do you ?"

" I am his friend," replied Anselme, " But since you refuse to be our guide, we will do our best to find the way alone, much pleasure to you in your suspicions, and farewell." With that, Lucile, Anselme, and I resumed our route.

We had not gone a hundred paces, when the peasant of the white cockade re-joined us, with his musket in his bandolin.

" What !" said I, smiling, " See how you deliver yourself up to your enemies."

" No, no," replied he, shaking his head, "I now know well that you are brave men on our side."

" And how do you know that ?"

"Because it is very certain, that if you were traitors or spies, you would not dare to pronounce the name of M. Jacques."

This answer, which disclosed on the part of the peasant more enthusiasm for his mysterious hero, than knowledge of the human heart, tended still more to shew to what an extent M. Jacques had gained the affections and good opinion of his adherents.

During our short journey to reach Saint Laurent des Mortiers, our new guide related to us in his way, the exploits of Lucile's friend. If we were to believe him, he turned aside, by a simple movement of his head the balls of the Blues aimed at him, and every enemy whom he touched with his sword, fell dead, as if struck with a thunderbolt.

These exaggerations, related with the most entire conviction and good faith, were approved by Lucile, whilst Anselme and I avoided throwing any doubt upon them; and when within a quarter of a league of Saint Laurent, I began to question our guide about the inhabitants of the place.

"Ah sir," said he, uttering a sigh, " You cannot imagine the bad treatment we have been compelled to submit to from them, their only occupation for a long time, has consisted in pursuing, pillaging, and shooting us. I can assure you that they have never shewn mercy to a single Chouan who has fallen into their hands. Availing themselves of the friendship they had contracted with some of our women, they kept up an espionage upon our movements, and fell upon us as soon as they knew us to be inferior in force, and not in a condition to resist them. They may boast themselves of having done us a great deal of mischief, but the hour of vengeance is arrived;

Coquereau has sworn to exterminate them, and he has never yet broken his word."

I could have wished to question the peasant about Coquereau, but the fear of awakening his suspicions by shewing him that I had never before heard of that chief who was so popular, prevented me.

" How has it happened," said I, " That Coquereau has been able to take Saint Laurent des Mortiers? The inhabitants must have been upon their guard.

" They did not suspect that we were coming to attack them to day, being Sunday; Coquereau has surprised them at the municipality, whilst they were engaged in reading the journals and the revolutionary decrees; he has now got the whole of them in his power."

"Were you present at this surprise ?"

" No, I only heard of it two hours ago, and I am hastening thither in the fear that all will be over when I reach it."

" What do you mean by these words,—' that all will be over'."

" Why, that they will have destroyed all those vipers then.'

" What! Do you think that Coquereau will cause all the inhabitants of Saint Laurent des Mortiers to be shot."

" You don't know Coquereau then ?" said the peasant distrustly.

" I know him well, but only from reputation.

" Then why do you put such a question to me ?"

" Because it appears to me that Coquereau himself would shrink from such a terrible art of justice."

"If he did we would at once withdraw from him," said the peasant, with a scowling air, and eyes sparkling with rage. "Do you know that I, who speak to you, had two of my brothers assassinated by the national guard of St. Laurent des Mortiers? Do you believe that we forget these things? I repeat that,—if not already done,—these cowards will also perish."

This answer produced a very disagreeable impression on me, for it forewarned me of a bloody drama. However, not wishing to draw back, I resigned myself to the spectacle that awaited me.

Alas! that spectacle soon presented itself to us. We had not gone far, when we saw before us a long and melancholy procession, composed of all the inhabitants of the surprised town, who bound two and two, advanced with slow steps between a double row of Chouans. At the head marched a peasant, of a savage appearance; it was Coquereau!

The melancholy cortege was followed by a weeping crowd of females who made the air resound with their cries and sobs. I looked at Lucile; but her impassible countenance betrayed no emotion. This insensibility greatly diminished the warmth of my friendship for her.

When the procession was within a few paces of us, Coquereau indicated to his Chouans by a motion of his head, a small meadow on the left of the road, and then cried with a thundering voice which sounded in my ears like the knell of death: "My friends, the hour of vengeance is arrived; exterminate the assassins of St. Laurent!"

Scarce were these words spoken, than the Chouans pushed their victims into the meadow, and the carnage commenced. What a harrowing spectacle! The wives and daughters of the unhappy condemned threw themselves between them and their executioners, and made a barrier of their bodies crying for mercy and pardon.

"Back, women!" repeated Coquereau, dragging them from before the prisoners; it is God's justice that is taking place; they have martyred us and ours for two years!"

A woman named Marie Chatelain,—so I was afterwards informed,—deaf to the voice of the implacable Coquereau, threw herself into the arms of her husband who had already received a bayonet-wound in his shoulder, and was herself grievously wounded. At this sight, her companions, renouncing all hope of obtaining mercy for their friends, shut their eyes and stopped their ears, or took flight.

In half an hour more, for to be still impartial, I must confess that in this abominable execution, extenuated by the excesses of the inhabitants of St. Laurent des Montiers, the Chouans of Coquereau displayed a cool ferocity,—in half an an hour, I say, there remained of all the men of the town only five, spared in consequence of their great age.

Two days after the bloody episode that I have related, we arrived, towards night-fall, at the entry of the wood of La Heureuserie.

"I think," said I to Lucile, "that we shall do wisely to seek a shelter for the night; otherwise we run the risk of sleeping in the open air,"

"We must on the contrary accelerate our steps," she replied; "we are expected in the wood. Proceed!"

It might have been about an hour after we had entered the wood, when the cry of a stag struck upon our ear.

"Answer, La Rochejaqueline and Mayenne," said Lucile to Anselme, and don't spare your lungs."

The stentorian voice of my companion immediately roared like the discharge of a cannon; and the echoes of the wood of La Heureuserie still vibrated, when we perceived at some paces from us a company of armed men. Lucile advanced at once to meet them, and we followed.

"Ah! you here, Francœur," said she, addressing herself to one of the new-comers; "I am very happy to see you. And *he*, why is he not come to meet me?"

"He has sent me in his place, madam, to inform you that an affair of the last importance keeps him absent for a day or two."

"And do you know what that affair is?"

"I regret not being able, madam, to answer your question. You are not ignorant, that nobody in the world ever knows what he does."

"You are right! I forgot. He cannot deceive himself, and what he does is always well done, is it not so Francoeur?"

"Yes madam, always, but what do you propose to do?"

"I shall wait here, have you a shelter to offer me?"

"Certainly madam, and a refuge where you will run no danger, the blues being ignorant of the presence of my band in the wood."

"So much the better, for I want repose; walk on, I will follow you."

"Who is this Francoeur, madam?" I asked.

"He is," said she, "The companion in arms of Michel Menaut, Gaultier, Tranche, Montague, Le Chandelier, Picot, Mousqueton, and many other chiefs, who fight under the orders of M. Jacques; you see I am now in a country where I am known."

"You are, madam, a queen in her states."

After half an hour's walk, we arrived at a very small cabin, roughly built of planks. "This has been constructed by my orders, in expectation of your arrival," said Francoeur, "I regret not having done better."

Why it is quite a palace," said Lucile, laughing.

"My band surrounds it," replied he; "Thus, if anything should happen, on whatever side you turn, you will find defenders and friends."

After this reply, the chief of the band took us with him to his encampment.

Francoeur's band was divided into posts, and the one to which he took us, was a large cart house, open on all sides to the wind; it contained thirty men. Our arrival awoke the curiosity of no one. Francoeur, whom his soldiers treated with affectionate familiarity, brought us himself a piece of bread, and some fruit for our supper.

"Faith," said Anselme, who at two mouths-full, had finished his own frugal repast, " I am not sorry at having arrived at the end of our journey ; I like M. Jacques with all my heart, because he has saved my life, but to speak frankly between ourselves, his madam Lucile begins with her imperious temper, to bear heavily upon my patience ; I am a soldier of the king, and not the garde-de-corps of a wandering princess· In short, thank God, I hope they will now set me at liberty."

" I confess Anselme, that Lucile, if she has for a moment dazzled my reason by her strange character and indomitable courage, has not awakened my sympathies. There is a presentiment which tells me that that woman is not worthy the love of M. Jacques."

" He will however, if I am not deceived, marry her shortly, replied Anselme. " After the manner in which he expressed himself about her before me, it was easy to see that he quite adores her."

Having shook hands with me in his customary manner, Anselme lay down on the floor, and was soon in a deep sleep, and I followed his example. I had slept for some time, when a violent shake awoke me in surprise ; on opening my eyes, I saw Anselme bending over me.—" What is it ?" said I, " Are the Blues come to attack us, what is the matter ? You seem quite excited."

" There's enough to excite me," he replied, in a tremulous voice, " Ah, if you knew—. But let us go out of this shed, what I have to tell you demands privacy."

I rose and followed him.—" Speak," said I, "And make haste, for I also have something to disclose."

Anselme leaned to my ear, and in a low voice said:—" Ah, my friend, what a frightful discovery! I am still asking myself if I am not under the influence of a horrible delusion or nightmare. About half an hour ago, I awoke with my mind uneasy and tormented; unable to sleep, I resolved to make a tour in the vicinity, in order to satisfy myself that all was quiet, and I at once started off. I was not more than thirty paces from Lucile's room, when suddenly the door opened, and I saw a man come out. My first thought was that it was M. Jacques, and I rushed towards him.

"And was it not M. Jacques?" said I, interrupting him; " Then who was it?"

"Guess; but no, you never could. The person who came out thus in the middle of the night from Lucile's room, was Kernoc the false Chouan! What do you think of that?"

"I am greatly astonished, but not so much perhaps, as you would imagine. I have suspected Lucile for a long time."

"Ah bah, and never said anything about it to me."

"I was afraid you would ridicule me, but finish your recital."

"You may conceive that my first thought was to run after the bandit, but the voice of Lucile who called me, stopped me in the midst of my career. "Anselme," said she, without giving me time to interrogate her, "I forbid you to reveal to any person whatever, the secret of which chance has made you the master. There is in it a serious political interest, which you will know at a future time but not now; you are not ignorant of the unfavourable impression produced upon me the first time I perceived that infamous bandit, Kernoc. You will believe then, that it has been necessary to appeal to all my love and devotedness to M. Jacques to obey him, when he sent me the order to receive this man."

"What! Lucile, is it by the order of M. Jacques?"

"Ask no questions, exclaimed she, interrupting me, "Soon M. Jacques will thank you for your discretion.. Hence, oblivion, and silence. After pronouncing this with the tone of a princess, Lucile re-entered her cabin and shut the door.

I was about to respond to the confidence of Anselme, by revealing to him my suspicions, when the discharge of firearms, followed by cries, arose not far from us in the wood. It was the Republicans who attacked us unexpectedly.

"Good heavens! said Anselme, " I'll wager my head against a dinner, that Lucile and Kernoc are not strangers to this surprise."

The Chouans, although taken unexpectedly, lost none of their coolness. Francoeur shewed himself quite equal to the responsibility which his command involved. He fought with the advantage of a perfect knowledge of the ground, which was not the case with the Blues. The Chouans, at first hard pressed, very soon took the offensive, and when after two hours fighting, the sun rose on the scene of carnage, the Blues fled in all directions.

When towards seven o'clock in the morning, I perceived Anselme coming towards me safe and sound, I uttered an exclamation of delight. As soon as he perceived me, he ran towards me.

"Ah, my dear friend," said he, " How much I regret that your republican principles prevented you from taking part in our diversion. I have been so amused that I have not once thought of my breakfast. But here comes Lucile, come, assume a smiling and amiable air, natural above all things, for that woman is sagacity personified."

As soon as Anselme had concluded speaking, Lucile accosted us.

" I am happy to see you again safe and sound, my good

friend," said she to Anselme, smiling in her charming manner. "The affair has been rough, but we could not be beaten, Francoeur was with us."

"Madam," said Francoeur, "I have only done my duty, and your presence amongst us rendered it easy. My lads knew whom they had to defend, and they would be all massacred rather than beaten."

"How has it happened sir," I asked, "That the Republican troops have attacked you? you told me yesterday, that they were ignorant of the position you occupy."

"Faith, I don't know how it has happened; there may have been treason.."

"I think not," said Lucile, "I see nothing but what is perfectly natural in what has happened. An expeditionary column, changing its route, would perfectly explain it."

"Yes, you are right." replied I, seeing her eyes fixed upon me. "The most essential point is, that victory is declared in our favour."

During the two days that I remained with Francoeur, I very rarely saw Lucile, who was almost always shut up in her cabin, and went out only once a day, in order to take an excursion in the wood. Francoeur came to us the evening of the second day, to give us notice to prepare for resuming our journey. These preparations were not great. We examined our arms, and made the best supper we could.

"Will you allow me to ask you, madam, where we are going?" said I to Lucile.

"We are going to the chateau of la Jupellière, where Mons. Jacques has provided a rendezvous for us."

The chateau of Jupellière, was, properly speaking, only a large farm house, which owed its title of chateau to the two towers with which it was flanked, and the ditch that surrounded it, outside of which was a stone wall. On our arrival we found a numerous company, or rather, a numerous assemblage, consisting of more than forty Chouans, who acted as scouts at the command of M. Jacques.

The proprietor of la Jupellière was an old lady of about sixty years of age. This lady, although entertaining a profound admiration for Mons. Jacques, received Lucile with the greatest coolness, her questionable position in connection with the mysterious hero not being at all consistent with her ideas of propriety.

The second day after our arrival, about one o'clock, a peasant came to warn us of the approach of the republican troops, who were scarcely a league distant from us.

The force that marched against us consisted of near twelve hundred men, and we were only forty in the chateau. The old lady proprietor, instead of uttering cries, and giving herself up to despair, began, with the help of her two servants, to make lint, and prepare beds for the wounded. At three o'clock, not seeing the troops appear, we sat down to table as usual to dine. We had scarcely half got through the repast, when one of the sentinels came to warn us of the approach of the enemy. Each then took his musket and rose in silence, and without disorder.

The immense disproportion between our force and that of the enemy, was to a certain extent compensated by our position. The wall was solid, and the ditch deep, which afforded us a great security, and offered serious obstacles to the blues.

Soon after, a loud report, followed by a shock which made the windows of the chateau shake, told us that the blues had not neglected to furnish themselves with artillery. From that moment I looked upon myself as a lost man.

I will not fatigue the reader with a detailed recital of this battle. It will suffice to state that at the approach of night, a breach large enough to admit two men was made in the wall that surrounded the chateau. The most important point for the Republicans, was to pass this breach and get at the door of the chateau; but this task, fortunately for us, was a very difficult one. In fact, the Chouans placed under cover in the apartments, within twenty paces of the breach, were sure to shoot down the Republicans who ventured into the passage.

It was clear to me that the besiegers waited for the shades of night, to mount to the assault, and I did not at all doubt that they would succeed in their attack. During a slight suspension of hostilities, employed by the Republicans in removing their wounded and dead men, Anselme came to look for me.

"Well, my poor friend," said he, "It is going on badly; I can't well see how we shall come out of this affair: can you?"

"Alas, I am equally at a loss."

He was about to reply, when cries of joy and enthusiasm resounded in the great hall of the chateau. We looked at each other with astonishment, amounting almost to stupefaction, and ran to ascertain the cause.

When we reached the great hall, we saw the Chouans waving their hats in the air in token of joy, and surrounding a young man who might be about twenty-five or twenty-six years of age, and eminently handsome. His large black eyes, full of expression and fire, his complexion rather pale, his white teeth, his fine moustache, and above all, the noble air which pervaded his whole person, formed a strange contrast with the energetic characters of the common and rude Chouans who surrounded him.

"Who is that stranger, and how has he been able to get in here?" said I to Anselme.

"Pardieu! It is Mons. Jacques," he replied. As to the means he has taken to cross the lines of the enemy, what does it signify to enquire? The essential point is to have him here."

When the enthusiasm produced by his presence had a little subsided, Mons. Jacques began to speak.

"My friends," said he in a clear and vibrating voice, "I have given you a rendezvous at la Jupelliére, in order to take you on an important expedition. I thank you for having been so punctual. To-morrow we shall enter on our campaign."

These words, spoken with perfect composure, and accompanied with a benevolent smile, seemed greatly to astonish those present.

"Mons. Jacques," said Mousqueton, "will you allow me to put a question to you?"

"Do my friend, I am ready to answer you."

"You speak of an expedition that you have projected, and you announce to us that to-morrow we are to enter upon the campaign. Be it so. But will it not be necessary for us first to get rid of the blues who have blockaded us? That appears to me the most pressing question."

"Ah! Mousqueton," cried Mons. Jacques, "have you imagined for a single instant, that the blues who besiege us will be able to resist our efforts, when we seriously set about putting them to flight? Don't you all know my friends," continued Jacques, raising his voice, and looking round him, "that we are going to beat the enemy?"

"Certainly! yes! yes!" responded these same men, who a few hours before, thought themselves lost, and who now, although the state of things was still the same, had no doubt of victory.

"And not to lose time," resumed Jacques, "let us at once commence our operations. In an hour from this time, the blues will be far from la Jupelliére!"

"Fresh acclamations succeeded these words. The Chouans fully believed that some miracle was going to be performed in their favour.

"The step which Mons. Jacques took to withdraw us from our critical position, was as simple as possible; and it succeeded to a wonder. Having remarked that the wind bore upon the enemy, he caused the Chouans to light in the court-yard before the breach, a hundred trusses of wet hay, which produced a thick smoke, and soon concealed us from the view of the blues. Ten Chouans placed before the breach, were ordered to keep up a continual fusillade, whilst Mons. Jacques, putting himself at the head of the thirty men remaining, went out at the back of the chateau; and dividing his little troop into two columns, fell at once on two opposite sides, upon the flank of the enemy.

The blues thought it was a surprise, and retreated in disorder, and believing that they had an affair with forces much superior to their own, took to flight, throwing away their arms in the passage, in order the better to save themselves. In half an hour, of the twelve hundred men who had just besieged la Jupellèire there remained a hundred dead ones.

Supper hour having arrived, we sat down to table as if nothing had occurred. This repast however differed entirely from our dinner of the same day. No more melancholy and careworn looks, no foreheads wrinkled with painful reflections, or ears listening to the least noise. Frank and noisy mirth almost approaching to a revel prevailed every where.

I remarked that during the whole time of the repast, Mons. Jacques, seated near Lucile, treated that young woman with the profoundest respect. Towards ten o'clock he rose from table,—Lucile and the old marchioness having previously left,—and stopping before Anselme and me:

"Gentlemen," said he, "if you do not feel too much fatigued, I shall be extremely grateful if you will consent to grant me an hour of your time. In that case, you will have the goodness to rejoin me in my room when you have done supper."

"We are at your orders, I replied, rising.

"Well then in half an hour," he replied, leaving the room.

After discoursing for some time, Anselme and I quitted the table to accept the invitation of M. Jacques. We found him on entering his chamber, walking up and down with a pensive air.

On seeing us enter, he came to meet us:—"I have to thank you, gentlemen," said he with warmth, "For all you have done for Lucile; believe me, the happiest day of my life will be that in which I shall be able to return the infinite obligations I owe you."

Anselme and I exclaimed against this, but M. Jacques stopped us.

"It is useless for you to attempt to deprecate your handsome conduct," said he, "Lucile has related to me your dangers, the delicate attentions you have paid her, and the deep respect you have always shown her; gentlemen, between you and me if you will allow it, our present connection is for life and death."

There was such an accent of frankness in the words of M. Jacques, that I felt myself drawn by a lively and deep sympathy for him. I now understood the ascendancy that such a character must exercise over those who act with him.

"He has the appearance of a haughty young man and a hard heart, this M. Jacques," said Anselme to me, when we had quitted the mysterious hero of the Chouanery, and found ourselves alone. "And to think of that base Lucile, a thousand thunders! Do you know that I was on the point of relating everything to him. Have you observed that since this history of Kernoc, the Republican troops have twice fallen upon us unawares, yet Francoeur, when they came to attack him, thought himself out of the reach of the blues. I do not pretend that these are proofs, I only say that it is strange, that's all."

The next day, after the raising of the seige of La Jupellière, M. Jacques took with him all the Chouans who were found at the chateau, except Anselme and me, whom he requested to remain, promising soon to send us some news.

" Why this exclusion?" asked my companion, "Am I then no longer able to fire a musket? mark already the malice of Lucile."

" You deceive yourself, Anselme, what you call an exclusion seems to me on the contrary, a proof of friendship and confidence, for it is probable that M. Jacques keeps you in reserve for some difficult and dangerous mission."

The next day, after a delicious night of repose, and with spirits exhilarated by pleasant dreams, I repaired to the dining hall, hoping to meet Anselme there, when one of the domestics of the chateau informed me that M. Jacques had, at daybreak sent for my friend.

After having breakfasted frugally, I prepared to take a tour in the environs, when on crossing the threshold of the door of the chateau, I saw Anselme returning. At this sight I ran and embraced him.

" My dear friend," said Anselme in a low voice, and gently pushing me from him, "you have made me suffer horribly in thus embracing me, for I am wounded."

" Wounded!" cried I, remarking then for the first time, the ghastly paleness of my friend's countenance.

" A scratch, my dear friend, but a deep one. A ball in the shoulder."

"Tell me, how did that happen?"

"That won't take long; some one fired a musket at me, he took good aim, and I was hit; that's the whole of it."

"But who fired the musket?" cried I, assisting Anselme to enter the chateau, for he had lost a great deal of blood, and was so weak that he supported himself with difficulty.

"Ah, here's the whole history of it," replied he, in the same calm voice, "But do you know that M. Jacques sent to seek me this morning?"

"Yes, they told me that."

"Well, they have deceived you; it was Lucile,—at least I have a strong conviction of it,—who made use of this pretext to draw me into a snare. As to the rascal whose bullet is still lodged in my shoulder, you have known him long enough:— it is Kernoc."

"Kernoc!" repeated I with horror, "In that case, Lucile must be guilty."

"There is no doubt of that."

"And this wretched Kernoc?"

"Kernoc still runs away. Ah, if he had not shot at such a distance, he would no longer be alive, but he had so much the advance upon me, that I gave up following him. If you find him by chance roving in the neighbourhood, do me the pleasure, as it does not touch upon politics, to lodge a ball in his head on my account, it would oblige me."

Anselme was of so robust and powerful a constitution, that he reached his room without fainting. I helped to get him into bed, and as no one yet, in the chateau knew of the accident, I went myself to look for assistance. His wound, although it presented no dangerous symptoms, was deep and serious. It kept him more than three weeks upon a bed of pain.

At last, thank heaven, he became convalescent, and the doctor permitted him to leave his room.

The third day of his return to convalescence, Anselme obtained from his doctor permission to take a walk. Happy to see him enjoy this indulgence, I offered him my arm, and placed myself at his command. We had scarcely crossed the threshold of the door of the chateau when we were accosted by a child about twelve years of age, who asked us if the chateau which he saw before him was not that of la Jupellière.

"Yes, my little friend," replied Anselme; "do you wish to see any one? I am myself from the chateau."

At the question the child seemed to hesitate, and stared with eyes wide open as if he did not comprehend what was said. Then, at last, appearing to make up his mind, replied "I want to see a young lady who lives at la Jupellière! do you know her?"

"Is it Lucile you wish to speak with?" said Anselme, pressing my arm under his own as he spoke; "If it is Lucile you wish to see, she is gone out this morning and will not return till night; you must wait.

This answer appeared greatly to disconcert the child, who repeated with ill humour, "Must wait! but my mother also waits for me. Tell me sir," continued he addressing himself to me after a short silence, "if I trust you with a paper that they have given me to bring to this lady, will you promise me to give it to her as soon as she returns?"

"I will," replied Anselme, taking the letter from him·

As soon as the little messenger was out of sight my companion unsealed the letter.

"Ah! my God!" cried he, turning pale, Mons. Jacques has been mortally wounded in the attack on the town of Daumiray, and he entreats this infamous Lucile to hasten to receive his last sigh."

This tragical intelligence produced a painful impression on

me I eagerly examined the letter, which was written with a trembling hand by M. Jacques himself; it described to Lucile the route she must take to arrive at the cave, situated near de Juvardeil, where he had taken refuge.

"There is no hesitating," said Anselme to me earnestly, "You must set out immediately, without losing an hour or even a minute."

"Yes Anselme, you are right."

"You may well conceive that it is necessary to take the advance of this frightful jade, Lucile ; who knows whether M. Jacque's wound is not the consequence of some new treason of this wretch?"

"You are right Anselme, moments are precious ; we cannot too soon warn M. Jacques of the danger he runs in placing confidence in the friendship of Kernoc."

"Ah, my dear friend, be careful of doing anything of the kind," cried Anselme eagerly, "Watch over M. Jacques with anxious solicitude, but do not poison his last hour by so fearful a revelation. Let him die at least,—if all hope for him is lost,—with the consoling conviction of having been loved ; yes, I see that it is revolting to you," said Anselme, observing a movement of indignation which I could not repress, "But remember that it signifies little here whether Lucile be or be not exposed ; the point in question is, to soothe the last moments of a gallant man, of a chivalrous and devoted heart, the deception under such circumstances becomes a duty."

"Alas, you are right my friend," I replied, "On cool reflection, it would be a real crime to increase, when on the contrary we can diminish, the agony of this noble young man. Fear nothing, I will manage to find a plausible pretext to account for the absence of Lucile, who must undoubtedly be gone to join Kernoc ; I will make him believe that he dies beloved by her."

2 M

In less than an hour, with my firelock on my shoulder and havre-sack furnished with provisions, I had taken the road.

The cavern in which M. Jacques had taken refuge was part of an old convent sacked in 1793. Thanks to the precise directions of the note written by the dying man, I was enabled to find him. He was laid upon straw, and suffering under delirium, and I saw at once that all hope was gone. Near him watched a peasant, whom my appearance surprised and frightened at first; but on learning my intentions he was glad of my assistance.

After a violent and protracted fit, M Jacques slept heavily for several hours. On awaking, my presence elicited a cry of surprise; but scarcely had I pronounced the name of Lucile, than he recollected me, and offering me his hand:—" Oh speak to me of her," Will she come soon ?

As I expected this question and was prepared for it, I was able to reply to him without hesitation, and in a manner to give him no suspicion, I arranged my reply so as to lead him to think that Lucile would arrive the second day at the latest.

" Oh my God ;" he exclaimed, with an expression so full of fervour and prayer, that I felt the tears spring in my eyes, " Oh my God, grant me four and twenty hours of existence."

I wished to console M. Jacques under his misfortune, but whether the falsehood threw a coldness and constraint into my words, or whether the dying man was conscious of his dangerous condition, he remained incredulous and would accept no hope.

" I know well," said he, " That my moments are counted; that every hour that flows, is carrying me rapidly to the tomb. Oh my mother ! Oh Lucile, Lucile !"

" Lucile will come to-morrow," replied I, in order to

calm him; as to madam your mother, she must have emigrated."

"My mother," said he interrupting me, "is scarcely a quarter of an hour's walk from this place."

"What! and you have not made her aware"—

"No," he answered without allowing me to proceed, "I wished to spare her the spectacle of my agony, and prevent her from compromising herself in the eyes of the republicans by the exhibition of her sorrow. It is the same consideration which has made me call myself, M. Jacques; my name,—and it is one without a stain,—is La Merozières. It does not matter! M. Jacques will live a long time yet in the memory of my brave Manceaux."

He remained silent a moment, and attempted to sleep, but I saw by the alteration of his features, although he uttered neither complaint nor sigh, that he was in dreadful agony and could only look forward to death to put an end to his sufferings.

"Do you know what distresses me most?" said he suddenly, whilst a slight blush animated his face for a moment, "It is the thought that I die by the hand of one of my own soldiers."

"What!" said I, shuddering, "have you been the victim of the treason of your Chouans."

"Oh no, not of their treason," he replied, "but of an accident undoubtedly. No matter, it is very hard, after having so often exposed my face to the shot, to die by a wound in the back."

It required great presence of mind to refrain from declaring the treason of Lucile, but I was silent Nothing however, will ever shake my conviction that the false Kernoc was the assassin of M. Jacques.

After a moment's pause, the unfortunate young man, fixing his tearful eyes upon me with a softened expression resumed:

—" May God forgive me, at the moment when I am about to appear before Him, my soul is still occupied with worldly passions! After the grief I feel at a separation from my mother and Lucile, the idea that torments me most is, that my name will soon be effaced from the memory of men. The dream of my youth has been to win a place in history: God has punished me for my pride, I die under a name which does not even belong to me, and without having been able to raise myself above the rank of a secondary partizan chief. Yet," added he, after a slight pause, "when I take a view of my past life, I do not see that I could have followed any other course; another year, and I should have reached the realization of the grand ideas that I had conceived. I rallied the Chouanery, and gave them a powerful organization, and from an obscure chief of a band, I have become generalissimo of the catholic army."

He remained for some minutes absorbed in reflections; then raising himself, he soon resumed, in a firm voice; "No one has yet comprehended, La Vendée! La Roche-Jacquelin my comrades, Lescure, Bonchamp, Cathelineau, have been great men in war, saints or heroes, but they wanted the political idea! They never saw, in that grand struggle of royalty with the republic, anything but marches, surprises, countermarches, nothing else! Military strategy was not sufficient to combat with a principle! I repeat, that it was necessary to know how to oppose principle to principle! After my death, what intelligent defenders will royalty still possess? Alas! none. There is certainly Charette, a character wonderfully endowed for civil war : but Charette, after all, is only a sublime and powerful machine, which, for want of a superior direction will not succeed in deeds of vengeance. De la Puisaye! yes, he looks higher, but he submits to English influence! Alas! I repeat that the hopes of royalty will die with me."

I will not repeat, sigh for sigh, suffering for suffering, the last agony of M. Jacques. Endowed with a powerful physical as well as mental nature, he struggled with unusual energy, with death; and it was not until the fourth day after my arrival that he succumbed to his wound.

Assisted by the peasant who had watched with me, I dug his grave in the cavern, and after having recited the prayers for the dead, I left the place with slow steps, my heart and my eyes swelling with tears. As to the absence of Lucile who had been the cause of his destruction, thanks to the delirium, which, from the first day had deprived him of his reason, he did not notice it, and thus escaped that sorrow.

Half blinded by the sun on coming from that dark retreat where I had passed four days, I was walking away, when the peasant, taking me by the arm and stifling as well as he could, the sobbing which broke his voice. "Sir," said he, saving your respect, you must not report that M. Jacques is dead! that would discourage our friends, and afford too much pleasure to the blues. You will not speak of it?" I promised I would not.

It was only just before arriving at la Jupellière that I thought of Anselme. I then felt astonished that my friend, so enthusiastic in his admiration of M. Jacques, to whom he owed his life, had not sent to learn news of him. Alas! how far was I from suspecting the motive which had hindered Anselme from proceeding, in spite of his weakness, to the cavern were his preserver was dying.

I had crossed the court-yard of the chateau, when a servant whom I met, uttered an exclamation of surprise on seeing me, and sprung to meet me, saying in a mournful voice, "Run sir, there is not a moment to lose; make haste, he is dying!"

"Who are you speaking of?" I demanded, my heart beating violently, for a dreadful thought crossed my mind.

"Of your friend," she replied, "of M. Anselme!"

Without waiting for any further explanation, I followed the servant, and entered the chamber of Anselme, whom I found engaged with his confessor. Our hostess, with tears in her eyes, stood at the other end of the room. On perceiving me, Anselme could not restrain a cry of joy, and stopped himself to say to me; "Wait a little my dear friend, I will finish my confession and then I am at your service."

A minute after the priest gave absolution to my poor comrade, who making a sign for me to draw near to him, took me affectionately by the hand, and asked me with eagerness, news of M. Jacques.

I held down my head and kept silence.

"I understand" said Anselme, "he is dead! Well my dear friend, I am going to rejoin him. If you have any commissions for him, make haste and charge me with them, time presses."

"In heaven's name," I exclaimed, do not speak thus! What has happened? You have been committing some imprudence, but, proper care and rest:—"

"Yes, eternal rest," said Anselme interrupting me in a feeble voice. "I have not time to explain the whole thing to you, two words must suffice; I have received from Kernoc, another ball in my chest. Oh don't be uneasy, although I am mortally wounded myself, I have not failed in my revenge, I killed him. Before he died he confessed every thing. That jade, Lucile is named Justine. She is a spy. It was she who caused the death of M. Jacques,—she was well paid for it. My friend, I no longer see you. Adieu! Think of me. I have always loved you. It is all over. Good night!"

I leaned over Anselme and raised him in my arms: he was dead. Here I finish my memoirs. What signifies my sorrow to the reader? I ought however, to add that the loss of

Anselme made me insensible to all that happened to myself, and rendered me a great service. Without leave, or troubling myself about the consequences, I returned home to my family, where, protected by my obscurity, I was suffered to enjoy in peace, a perfect immunity, and a tranquility which I had well earned.

www.ingramcontent.com/pod-product-compliance
Lightning Source LLC
Chambersburg PA
CBHW022116290426
44112CB00008B/697